Computer Storage Fundamentals

Storage system, storage networking, and host connectivity

2nd Edition

Susanta Dutta

bpb

www.bpbonline.com

Second Revised and Updated Edition 2025

First Edition 2018

Copyright © BPB Publications, India

ISBN: 978-93-65893-502

To View Complete
BPB Publications Catalogue
Scan the QR Code:

About the Author

Susanta Dutta is a senior storage R&D architect with more than two decades of industry working experience in *Hewlett-Packard Enterprise (HPE) Company*. He has been working with all types of storage product development and solution implementations with the latest storage technologies. He is an engineering graduate in electronics and communication from the *National Institute of Technology (NIT), Durgapur, India*.

Acknowledgement

The work presented in this book would not have been possible without a close association with my colleagues. Mentors, seniors and juniors, everyone contributed to this work directly or indirectly.

I express my deepest and sincere gratitude to my senior **Mr. Srikanth BK**, who introduced me to storage many years back and guided me to understand basic storage concepts.

I am also grateful to BPB Publications for their guidance and expertise in bringing this book to fruition. It was a long journey of revising this book, with valuable participation and collaboration of reviewers, technical experts, and editors.

I am also thankful to my organization, *Hewlett-Packard Enterprise (HPE)*, for the opportunities and exposure to work with different types of storage products and solutions.

Finally, I would like to thank my family for their love, support, and blessings.

Preface

In today's competitive markets, students and IT professionals are more aggressive to create a differentiating factor over and above regular courses, and they are more curious to learn about industry-specific technologies that can help in technical interviews and as well as performing job more efficiently.

On the other hand, the enormous growth of digital information has significantly increased the demand for the storage job market in recent years. Today, several universities, engineering colleges, and educational institutes are offering undergraduate/ postgraduate courses on storage technologies.

There are plenty of storage vendors who make storage products and implement solutions. Most vendors explain and advertise feature sets for their products using their terminologies through internet blogs, videos, etc. At times, it is hard to understand the context and underlying concept and larger objective of a feature and difficult to locate a document or write-up for conceptual understanding.

I wrote this book with the learnings captured from decades of working experience with storage technologies to fill the abovementioned gap and connect it with the need. This book explains the concept of storage features and functionalities without referring to or highlighting any vendor's product. It focuses on the fundamental and underlying concepts of storage technologies. Every Storage vendor builds their products using these technologies.

Therefore, the following readers would undoubtedly benefit from the content of this book:

- Engineering students
  - o Course/Syllabus that covers storage technologies
  - o Step-up skills for effective campus placement
- IT professionals
  - o The ramp-up of the newly hired workforce
  - o Upgrade the talent of existing employees to perform the job efficiently and effectively.
- Storage administrators:
  - o Administrators who manage and monitor their deployed storage systems and solutions.

Chapter 1: Storage Systems and Solutions - This chapter discusses the types of storage systems, the technologies to store data, and solutions that are deployed in small, medium, and large organizations. You will also learn about the pros and cons of all the storage systems with respect to their usage in the solutions.

Chapter 2: Storage Infrastructure - This chapter explains all the physical components of a storage system and their connectivity within it as well as storage networking and host server's storage components. In addition to it, the chapter also explains software defined storage concept.

Chapter 3: Storage Disk Array - In this chapter, you will learn about the design and implementation of various features and functionalities of a storage system, such as storage controller operation modes, different data caching techniques, and how user data is stored on to the physical disk using different RAID levels. This chapter also discussed the pros and cons of each RAID level.

Chapter 4: Storage Communication Protocols - A protocol is a set of rules and guidelines for communicating data between host servers and storage systems. In this chapter, you will learn about various standard storage protocols, such as SCSI, FC, iSCSI and FCoE, NFS, and CIFS/SMB. This includes how data gets transferred between the host server and storage system during read and write operations using each protocol.

Chapter 5: Storage Networking to Share Storage - In this chapter, you will learn different network topologies through which host servers and storage systems are connected. You will also learn about network configurations to control various access of the storage system by the host servers, such as zoning and LUN masking. Due to some specific network physical connectivity and access configuration, multiple paths get created between the host server and storage system. In this chapter, you will also learn about how virtual volumes are accessed over multiple paths along with load balance and failover.

Chapter 6: Storage Performance - In this chapter, you will learn about storage performance basics that include the definition of key factors to measure storage performance. This chapter explains how to determine whether storage is performing slowly or faster. You will also learn about the important features that are implemented within a storage system to enhance performance.

Chapter 7: Fault Tolerance and Data Protection - In this chapter, you will learn about various features that enable host applications to continue accessing the data in the event of failure within the storage solution or storage system. This chapter also explains storage technologies related to data protection, such as snapshot, clone, and replication, that allow data recovery in case of any corruption or accidental loss. Further, this chapter highlights the types of backup solutions that organizations implement to recover data in case of any loss.

Chapter 8: Space Efficiency - In this chapter, you will learn about the storage features that store data in the most efficient way. These features are thin provisioning, expand, shrink, space reclamation (UNMAP), deduplication, and compression. A detailed explanation of these features guides you in understanding how each feature works and efficiently stores the data in a storage system.

Chapter 9: Storage Management - Every storage vendor delivers some application software and a storage system to manage it. In this chapter, you will learn different types of management software and their purposes. This chapter explains the basic steps involved in implementing a storage solution, along with some examples. By the end of this chapter, you will have a clear idea of how storage solution is designed and implemented.

Coloured Images

Please follow the link to download the
Coloured Images of the book:

https://rebrand.ly/62e5bc

We have code bundles from our rich catalogue of books and videos available at https://github.com/bpbpublications. Check them out!

Errata

We take immense pride in our work at BPB Publications and follow best practices to ensure the accuracy of our content to provide with an indulging reading experience to our subscribers. Our readers are our mirrors, and we use their inputs to reflect and improve upon human errors, if any, that may have occurred during the publishing processes involved. To let us maintain the quality and help us reach out to any readers who might be having difficulties due to any unforeseen errors, please write to us at :

errata@bpbonline.com

Your support, suggestions and feedbacks are highly appreciated by the BPB Publications' Family.

Piracy

If you come across any illegal copies of our works in any form on the internet, we would be grateful if you would provide us with the location address or website name. Please contact us at business@bpbonline.com with a link to the material.

If you are interested in becoming an author

If there is a topic that you have expertise in, and you are interested in either writing or contributing to a book, please visit www.bpbonline.com. We have worked with thousands of developers and tech professionals, just like you, to help them share their insights with the global tech community. You can make a general application, apply for a specific hot topic that we are recruiting an author for, or submit your own idea.

Reviews

Please leave a review. Once you have read and used this book, why not leave a review on the site that you purchased it from? Potential readers can then see and use your unbiased opinion to make purchase decisions. We at BPB can understand what you think about our products, and our authors can see your feedback on their book. Thank you!

For more information about BPB, please visit www.bpbonline.com.

Join our Discord space

Join our Discord workspace for latest updates, offers, tech happenings around the world, new releases, and sessions with the authors:

https://discord.bpbonline.com

Table of Contents

Introduction

In today's modern world, almost all information is in the form of digital data, such as e-mails, documents, spreadsheets, presentations, databases, graphics, audio, and image files. The explosive growth in the volume of digital data in last few years caused demand for more computer storage systems. To access and process data, it has become more important to store data faster and efficiently. Therefore, computer storage skill has become the most important for all **Information Technology (IT)** professionals.

Almost all companies, small to large enterprises, deploy computers to meet their business objectives. These computers are primarily of three categories – servers, networking, and storages. All these three components are interconnected to run business applications. Applications, run on Servers, read and write data stored on to the storage systems.

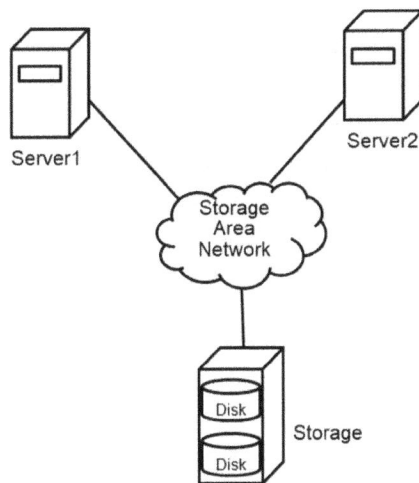

Figure 1: Servers, network and storage system

Hard disk drives were introduced in 1956 as data storage for an *IBM* system. Since then, storage evolved to meet requirements of today's world. With advancement of computer, mobile and popularity of internet, social media, digital data is growing exponentially. The current total global data is almost double than what was there two years back. Not only is the amount of data increasing, its criticality is also increasing significantly. This means that the impact due to the loss of digital data few years later, would be more severe than today. At the same time, the demand for rate of accessing data is also increasing significantly.

To optimize and improve efficient resource sharing, a storage system is typically shared by multiple servers to store their data, therefore it is important to have a modern storage system with higher space efficiency, performance and fault tolerance.

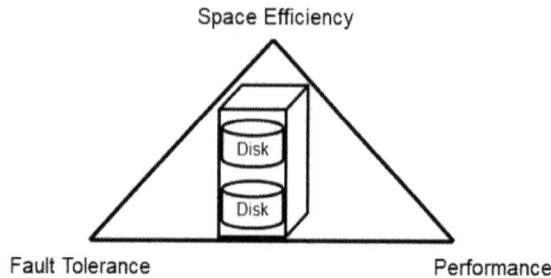

Figure 2: Three aspects of a storage system

A storage system is considered the best in the market, if it is capable of supporting higher degree of all three aspects.

An interesting part is that most features of a storage system that improves one of these aspects, impacts the reduction of other aspects. For example, RAID 0 improves storage performance, but reduces fault tolerance, deduplication improves storage efficiency, but impacts performance. It is a challenge for storage vendors to develop a storage that provides all the three aspects of storage systems.

Most storage vendors develop and sell multiple storage applications to manage other aspect of storage systems, such as performance, local and remote replication, backup and data recovery solutions.

CHAPTER 1
Storage Systems and Solutions

Introduction

Computer data storage has been evolving since 1950s. Initial storage systems were very simple and elementary. During those days, host servers were directly connected to its storage devices. The storage device was integral part within the computer system itself. There was no concept of a separate system for remotely storing data. Over the time for faster and efficient storing of data, storage system has become a separate entity, which can also be shared by multiple computers to store their data.

Structure

Upon successful completion of this chapter, you will be able to learn about the following:

- Types of storage systems
- Storage solutions
- Hyper-convergence

Objectives

This chapter discusses different types of storage systems, and the technologies to store data and solutions that are deployed in small, medium, and large organizations. You will also learn about the pros and cons of all the storage systems with respect to their usages in the solutions.

Types of storage systems

There are three most popular technologies available to store the data on to a storage system. Storage systems are categories based on how data is stored and accessed by the host servers.

Block storage

Block storage provides access to host server as raw block device. These blocks are controlled by server based operating systems and each block can be individually formatted with the required file system such as NTFS and VMFS. The application can then access the data on the file system for read and write operations. There are also intelligent applications available, which can access the raw volume directly without any file system.

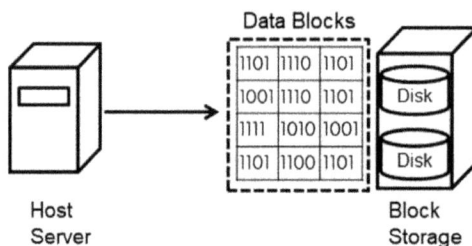

Figure 1.1: Block storage

Storage has no knowledge of the datastored in it, however operating system and application understands it. Here are some features of block storage:

- Block storage is primarily used for structured data, such as relational databases. Host server runs databases, supports random read/write operations. Many other client system access the application running on host server over the network.

- This level of storage can also offer boot-up of systems which are connected to them.

- Block level storage can be used to store files and can work as storage for special applications like databases, **virtual machine (VM)** file systems, and so on.

- The block level storage data transportation is much efficient and reliable.

- Each storage volume can be treated as an independent disk drive and it can be controlled by external server operating system. Block level storage uses Fibre Channel, iSCSI and FCoE Communication protocols for data transfer as SCSI commands act as communication interface in between the initiator and the target.

File storage

On a file, storage data is stored and accessed using filename and its directory location over **local area network (LAN)** or **wide area network (WAN)**. In file level storage, the storage space is configured to access files with a protocol such as **Network File System (NFS)** or **Server Message Block (SMB)** or **Common Internet File System (CIFS)**.

File storage system uses block storage internally with a local file system to store these files, and host server only has the access for reading and writing these files. File storage is deployed mainly in the environment where application requires to access data inside files or group of people require to store files such as documents, spreadsheets, presentations, audio, and image files in shared storage system.

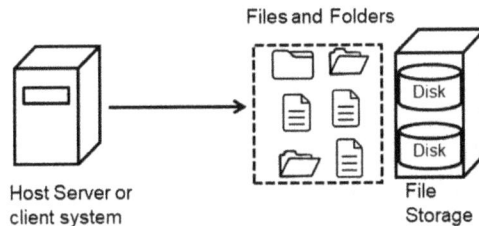

Figure 1.2: File storage

Computer systems that access the files and folder on the file storage are called **NAS clients**. They can run an application to read and write data on to those files and other clients access the application over network. For example, hypervisor enabled operating system can host VMs on **network attached storage (NAS)** shares, and the client can access those VMs.

Object storage

Object storage is a relatively new type of storage system that stores data as objects along with metadata and unique identifier. This storage has primarily evolved in recent years to support storing mass amounts of unstructured data in cloud, big data and mobility. Data that is often stored as objects includes songs, images, and video clips. Some examples of object storage in the cloud are Amazon **Simple Storage Service (S3)**, Azure Blob Storage, and Google Cloud Storage.

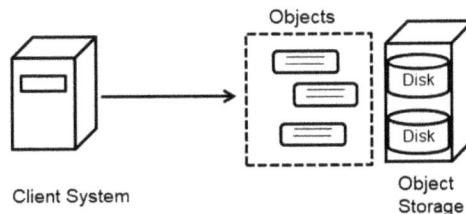

Figure 1.3: Object storage

Representational State Transfer (REST) API over HTTP is used to transfer objects to and from a client system.

Storage solutions

The hardware and software components that make a solution store and protect digital data is called a **storage solution**. A storage solution has the following two primary components:

- **Storage system**: The storage system is a hardware device connected to computers through a network for storing the data. Storage disk array is an example of a storage system.

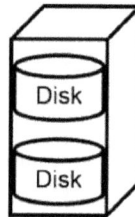

Figure 1.4: Storage System

- **Host server**: Applications that run on these computer servers, perform read and write datastored on to the storage systems. This is also called **application server, host computer** or simply a **host** or **server**.

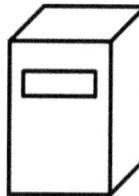

Figure 1.5: Host Server

A storage solution is formed by connecting one or more host servers to storage systems.

Types of storage solutions

Storage solutions are commonly categorized in two ways:

- Based on how storage systems are connected to host servers.
- Based on configuration and level of complexity of the deployed solution.

The type of storage solution chosen by the organization is primarily driven by requirement. The selection of type of storage system for the solution and connectivity with host servers also follows accordingly.

In the previous section, we learned that the three most popular storage system technologies are block storage, file storage, and object storage. Storage systems are also primarily identified based on these technologies.

Storage area network

Block storages are deployed in **storage area network** (**SAN**). Typically, SAN storage solutions are complex and expensive compared to other storage solutions. SAN is generally deployed in-house to host business critical applications that require high performance and data availability. Since block storages are generally connected in SAN, they are often referred as SAN storage. In SAN storage solution, file system is created within host server. Therefore different host servers with different operating system and file system can share the same storage system.

Network attached storage

File level storage deployed in Ethernet network environment. This solution is popularly called **network attached storage** (**NAS**) storage solution. Since files are stored on to the storage system, file system is created within it.

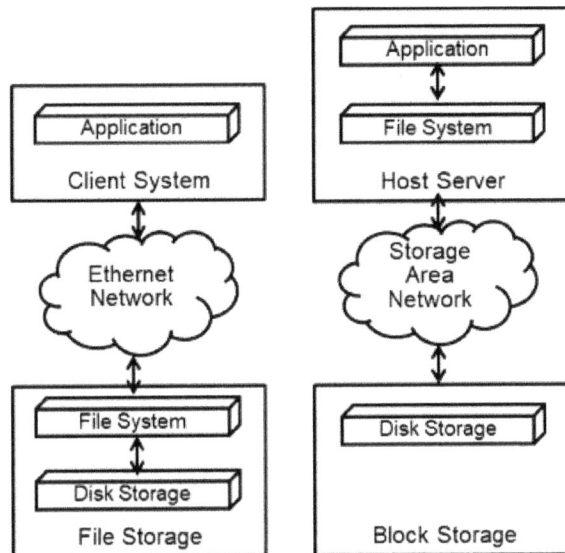

Figure 1.6: *NAS storage solution and SAN storage solution*

Direct attached storage

In **direct attached storage** (**DAS**), disk storage is directly connected to host server. A DAS supports block access to data just like SAN. This solution is simple to manage and less expensive. Due to multiple limitations, not many companies use this storage much today. These limitations are primarily inefficiency of utilization disk space utilization by not sharing across multiple servers, no storage virtualization, and so on.

Though this is a traditional storage solution, nowadays, this storage solution is becoming popular because of adoption of software defined storage, which is discussed in later chapters.

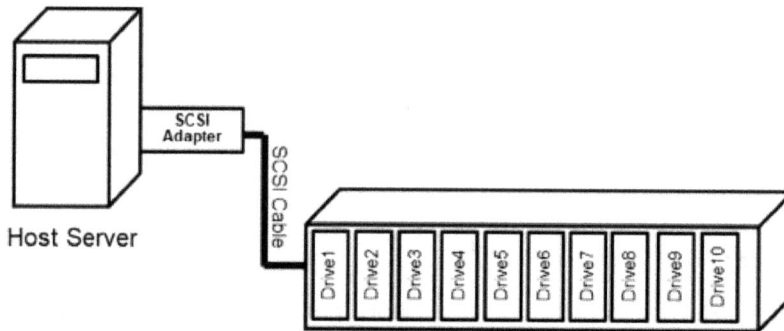

Figure 1.7: *DAS storage solution*

There are several models of DAS storage solution:

- Server with in-built internal disk enclosure.
- Server with external disk enclosure.
- Server with internal and external enclosures, both.

DAS storage with internal built-in disk enclosure saves rack space and power. However, for additional disk space, external disk enclosures are needed to be attached to it.

In DAS storage solution, disk storage, file system and application, all layers belong to the host server. For this reason, all resources are dedicated to single server, and sharing is not possible with other host servers.

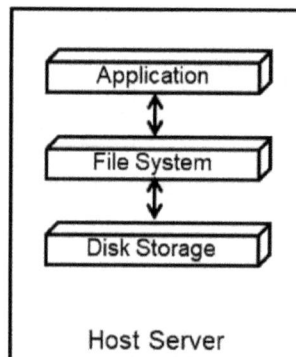

Figure 1.8: *DAS stacks*

All data finally stored as blocks

Host servers or client systems access storage system via different protocols and store data differently. For example, a client system accesses a file storage to store files. This is because file storage is designed to communicate via CIFS or NFS protocol via IP network interface. Here, according to the client system's perspective, data is stored as a file, but, within the file storage, files reside on the file system. File system within a file storage represents the set of data blocks on disk as the file to the client system, beneath the file system is storage blocks.

Although the type of storage is determined by the interfaces and communication protocol designed for client or host servers, fundamentally every storage is a block storage.

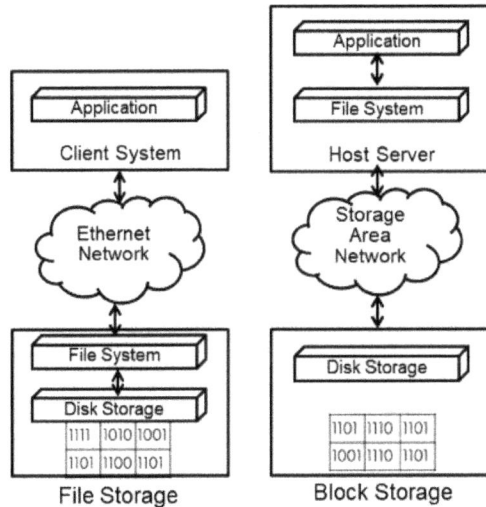

Figure 1.9: Data storing technologies

Cloud storage

Typically, large enterprise object storage systems are deployed in a data center and provided access to client computers and mobile devices stores their data on to it through the internet. This service model is called **cloud storage**.

It is a great advantage for a user to access the data from anywhere in the world. In general, personal files such as pictures, videos, and archival data are stored in cloud storage, but not business critical application data, as it requires faster response time.

Figure 1.10: Cloud storage

Cloud service provider ensures data availability to users by implementing various data protection solutions in the storage systems. Generally, service provider charges the user for this service.

- **Storage solutions based on deployment**:

  Storage solutions can also be classified based on configuration and level of complexity of the deployed solution:

  o **Entry level storage solution**:

    This storage solution is deployed when an organization has the requirement of storing less amount of data. Typically, this solution is implemented with either DAS or basic SAN or NAS storage. In DAS solution, storage devices can be internal to the host server or external. This is simple to manage and a low cost solution. It has several limitations, such as, failure of any component can cause loss of data, low performance and storage capacity can scale up to few **terabytes** (**TBs**).

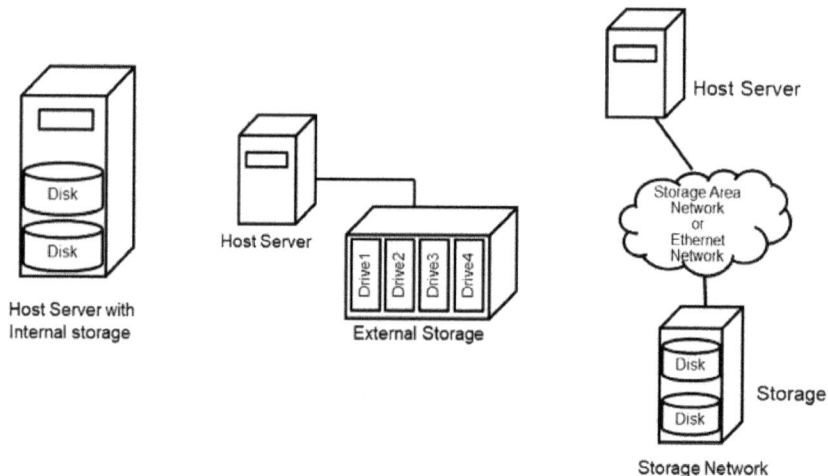

Figure 1.11: Entry level storage solutions

  o **Mid-range storage solution:**

    Mid-range storage solution is deployed when the organization has a requirement of storing about a few 100TBs. Typically, this solution is implemented using SAN or NAS storage with host servers in cluster for high availability. This is simple to manage and a low cost solution. It has several limitations, such as, failure of any component can cause loss of data, low performance, and the storage capacity can scale up to few TBs.

    If host servers in cluster configuration for high availability, each storage volume is provided access to all host servers in cluster, so that if any host server fails, other server can continue to access the data on the volume. Since the volume is shared across multiple servers, this volume access configuration is called **shared volume**.

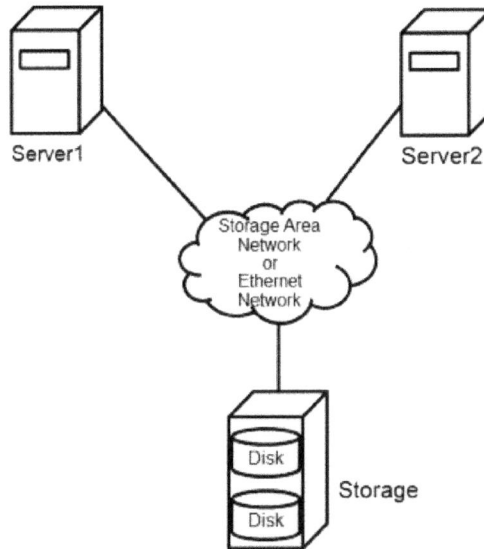

Figure 1.12: *Mid-range storage solution*

Some storage vendors assemble all the required hardware, pre-configure software and fine-tune in factory to consolidate all solutions for ready-made use and sell it as a single **stock-keeping unit** (**SKU**) product. This is called **converged infrastructure** or **converged system**.

o **Enterprise storage solution**:

A data center is a facility with adequate power, space and cooling to deploy computer servers, storage systems, and network switches to store and process massive amounts of data.

Large enterprise organizations run their business critical applications in a data center to store and process hundreds of petabytes of data. For high availability and disaster recovery, enterprise organizations also deploy a similar set of hardware at another data center located at different site, called **remote** or **secondary site**.

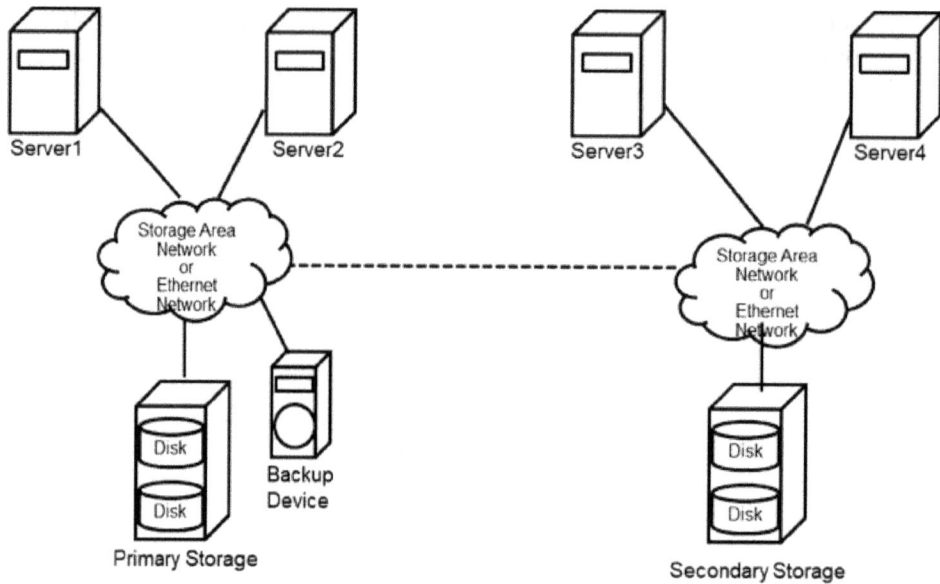

Figure 1.13: *Enterprise storage solution*

Though every storage solution requires backup solution in place to recover data, in case of any accidental loss, enterprise storage solution implements backup solution that make multiple copies of their critical data at different time interval in different systems.

Hyper-convergence

The **Information Technology** (**IT**) industry has been evolving since mid-20th century. The XT/AT PCs were in use during 1980s and 1990s, and computer networking came into picture during 1990s and 2000s. Further, SAN became popular during 2000s-2010s and finally VM came in use during 2010s. In this process of evolution, data centers started having multiple servers, storages, clusters, switches, and cables causing inefficiency in management, deployment and space, power consumption.

Hyper-converged infrastructure (**HCI**) is a type of infrastructure system with a software-centric architecture that tightly integrates compute, storage, networking, and virtualization resources. This has evolved from the concept of converged system discussed in previous section. Unlike converged system, technologies used in a HCI cannot be separated into components. For example, in converged system, storage, and servers are still separate piece of hardware, whereas in HCI, solutions are implemented within the software.

A hyper-converged system is typically sold as a software or software preinstalled on a hardware box. The software is installed on an existing hardware or any commodity hardware box.

All resources are consolidated within a single system to enhance efficiency of management, deployment and consumption of space, and power. For ease of management, HCI vendors provide single management application for the management of in-build technologies in a hyper-converged system, such as compute, storage networking, and virtualization.

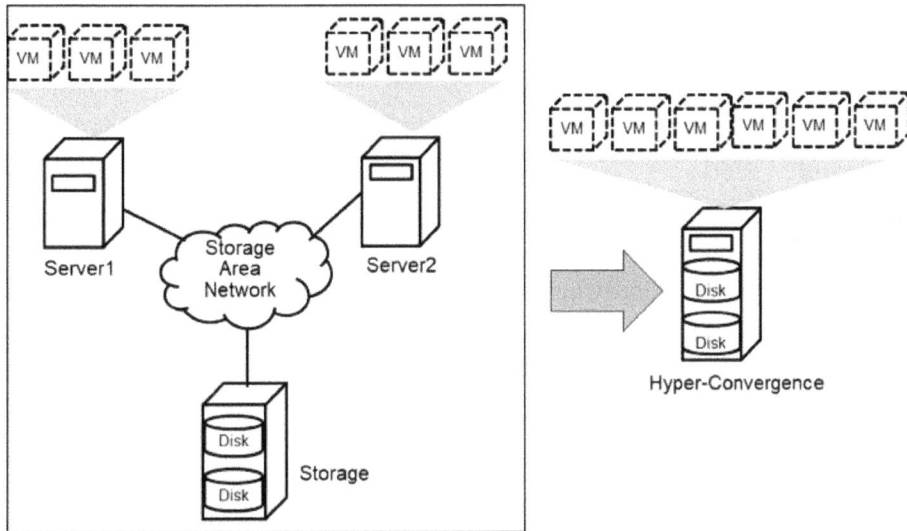

Figure 1.14: HCI

Hyper-convergence is designed to run VM, and the applications are installed inside VMs.

For high availability solution and more scale out resource requirement, multiple hyper-converged systems can be grouped together, which is known as the cluster of hyper-converged systems. Each system is referred as **node**. Once the number of VMs have reached the capacity, scaling out is easy, just by adding more nodes that includes more compute, storage, and networking resources.

Virtual desktop infrastructure (**VDI**) is an infrastructure deployment technology that hosts a desktop operating system on a centralized server and storage in a data center. Many storage vendors design, build, and sell hyper-convergence product to deploy and support VDI requirement.

Hyper-convergence products are not suitable for business critical applications that demands high performance and support thousands of users.

Conclusion

Storage system and storage solutions have evolved since many decades to meet different business objectives and use cases. Primary components of storage solutions are storage system, host server, switch, HBA, and management software. All these hardware components are connected and configured though the management software to deploy a storage solution.

Storage systems are classified based on the technologies used on how data is stored and accessed; these storage systems are block, file, and object storage.

The following table shows the comparison among all these types of storage systems:

	Block storage	**File storage**	**Object storage**
Storage solution	SAN	NAS	Cloud
Access data unit	Blocks	Files	Objects
Host server or client system	In-house or within data center	LAN or WAN	Internet
Communication protocol	SCSI on Fibre Channel, iSCSI	CIFS/SMB and NFS	REST over HTTP
Recommended for	Structured data (relational databases) and random and frequent read/write operations	Unstructured data and shared files and folders	Unstructured data with less updates
Advantages	High performance	Simplified access and management	Scalable and distributed access

Table 1.1: Block storage, file storage and object storage

Typically, host servers access block storage within data center. They are accessed via Fibre Channel or iSCSI protocol. Client systems access file storage via local or wide area network using SMB/CIFS or NFS protocol, and mobile devices access object storage over internet using Restful API.

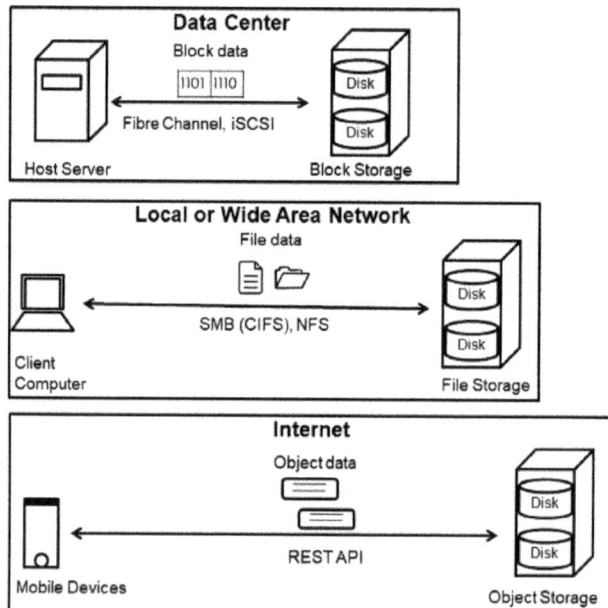

Figure 1.15: Block, file and object storage system

Based on the organization's requirement, storage solutions are built using the required type of storage systems; these solutions are SAN, NAS, DAS, and cloud storage. Each solution has its advantages and limitations over other solutions. For example, typically SAN solution provides high performance, but requires high cost, complex management, and on the other hand, DAS solutions are low cost and simple management, but performance may not be at the level of SAN solution.

Although there are different mechanisms to store and access data on different types of storage systems, design, and implementation of most of the parts of all these storage systems are common. Therefore, now-a-days most storage vendors make block, file, and object storages in the single storage system. The next chapter has detailed description about storage disk array.

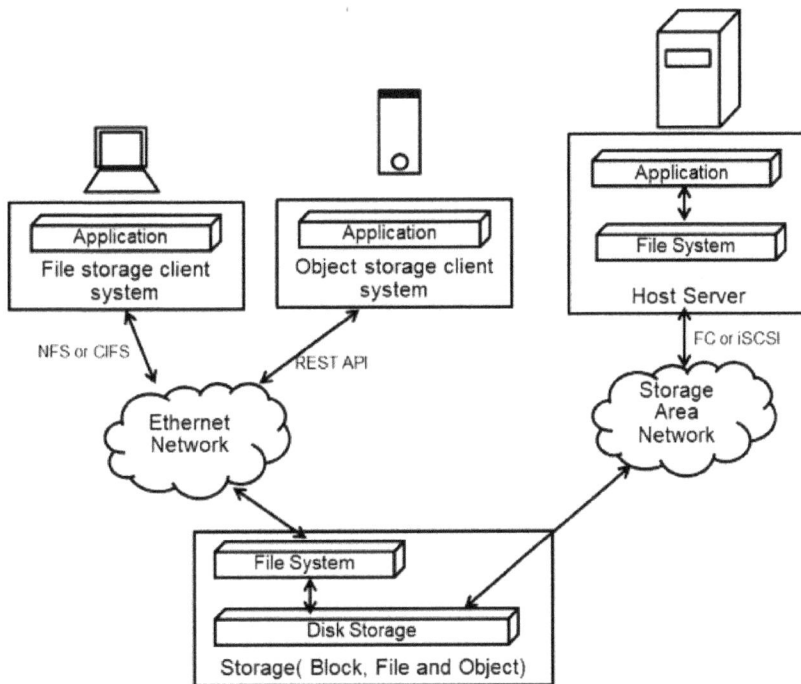

Figure 1.16: *Block, file and object on same storage system*

Case studies

Case study 1: Storage solution for user home directories

Let us look at the storage solution for user home directories:

Requirement

Your company has about 1,000 employees. Each employee has an average of 7 to 8GB of files, such as presentations, spreadsheet, word, and PDF documents on their laptop and desktop. The company is planning to deploy a storage solution to consolidate and centrally manage those files. Describe the storage solution that is suitable for this requirement.

Analysis

Since the requirement is to store only files, mid-range NAS solutions would be the most suitable solution. 10GB network speed to the storage system can be recommended for the fast and reliable access by multiple users. The current file storage requires approximately *1000 x 10GB =~ 10TB* of usable capacity. Considering future growth, at least twice the size of this storage may be recommended.

Solution

The file storage with about 20TB usable space is needed to be procured to deploy a NAS solution. All employees can access storage system via Ethernet network. The schematic diagram for the proposed storage solution is shown as follows:

Storage type: File storage

Storage solution: Mid-range NAS solution

Usable capacity: 20TB

Access bandwidth: 10GB/s

Space quota for each employee: 20GB

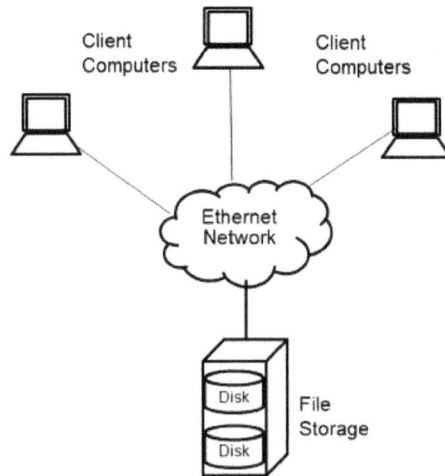

Figure 1.17: *Storage solution for user home director*

Case study 2: MSSQL Database application on cluster host server solution

Let us look at the MSSQL Database application on cluster host server solution:

Requirement

An organization wants to migrate from legacy database application on standalone DAS solution to MSSQL application in a highly available cluster host server environment. The database size is about 30TB, and describes the storage solution that is suitable for this requirement.

Analysis

To run database application, the host servers require faster access to storage system. Mid-range SAN solutions would be the most suitable solution from performance perspective. The host servers in cluster can also share the space of the storage system. Considering future growth, the storage with 50TB of capacity can be recommended.

Solution

The block storage with about 50TB usable space needed to be procured. To deploy SAN solution, FC HBAs for host servers, and a FC switch along with cables and connectors also needed to be procured. The schematic diagram for the proposed storage solution is as follows:

Storage type: Block storage

Storage solution: Mid-range SAN solution

Usable capacity: 50TB

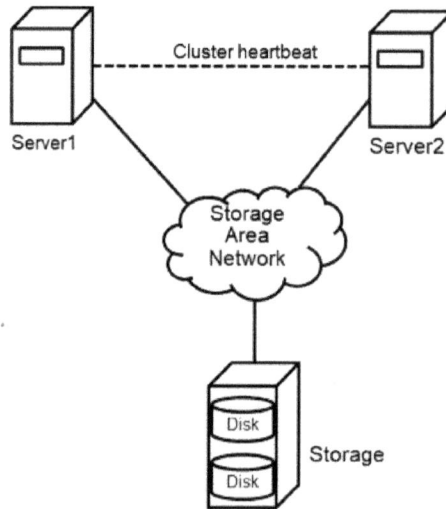

Figure 1.18: *Storage solution for host server cluster*

Case study 3: Virtual machines for test and development purpose

Let us look at virtual machines for test and development purpose:

Requirement

A software vendor wants to deploy virtual machines for their employees for their test and development activities. There are about 500 employees and the size of the workspace is approximately 100GB. Describe the storage solution that is suitable for this requirement.

Analysis

The best storage solution to deploy VMs is HCI. A hyper-converged system is preinstalled, configured and tuned for deploying VMs.

This system is also efficient in space and power consumption. The initial capacity requirement would be *500 x 100GB =~ 50TB*.

Solution

A high-end hyper-converged system with about 50TB space can be procured to deploy HCI environment. If the vendor does not support 500 VMs on single hyper-converged system, multiple hyper-converged systems can be purchased and cluster among them to load balance and failover VMs in the event of failure of any system.

Learning check

Objective questions

1. **A storage's capability is measured mainly on:**
   a. Fault tolerant
   b. Performance
   c. Space efficiency
   d. All of the above

2. **Which two sub-components are required in a specialized NAS operating system? (Choose two)**
   a. File system
   b. User interface
   c. Process scheduler
   d. Communication protocols

3. **Which type of storage provides great performance:**
   a. DAS
   b. NAS
   c. SAN
   d. All of the above

4. **Which is from the following list, the main disadvantages of DAS?**
   a. Scalability
   b. Cost
   c. Manageability
   d. All of the above

5. **Cloud Storage service is most suitable for:**
   a. Business critical application data
   b. Personal data–photos, videos
   c. OLTP workload
   d. All of the above

6. **Arrange these terms based on their association:**
   Block storage, Object storage, SAN, DAS, Cloud, Entry level storage solution, High performance, Low cost, Saleable.

a. Block storage – SAN - High performance; Object storage – DAS – High Performance; Block Storage – DAS – Cloud

b. Block storage – DAS - High performance; Object storage – Cloud - Scalable; Block Storage – DAS – Low cost

c. Block storage – Cloud - Scalable; Object storage – SAN – High Performance; Block Storage – DAS – Entry level storage solution

d. Block storage – SAN - High performance; Object storage – Cloud - Scalable; Block Storage – DAS – Entry level storage solution

7. **Hyper-convergence is a type of infrastructure system that tightly integrates:**

a. Compute

b. Storage

c. Network

d. All of the above

8. **Hyper-convergence product can be built on a:**

a. Special storage array

b. Vendor Specific hardware

c. Commodity server hardware

d. Hard drive

9. **Which storage has the file system layer in it:**

a. DAS

b. NAS

c. SAN

d. All of the above

Descriptive questions

1. Describe pros and cons of SAN, NAS and DAS storage solutions.
2. Explain the use cases of object storage and storage solutions in which this storage is deployed.
3. Describe the types of storage systems and their usages in related solutions.
4. Explain how all the data is finally stored as blocks in a storage system.

Quiz questions

1. Though there are different type of storage system, block, file and object storage, does data in a storage system always stored as blocks finally.

2. Where does file system reside in a NAS storage solution?

3. Is hyper-converge a consolidation of storage system or storage solution?

Glossary and key terms

- **Host**: The server that runs the application and accesses the storage volume to store data. Also a logical entity in the storage system that represents a host server. Virtual volumes are provided with access to it.

- **Host servers**: An application server that accesses the storage system to store and performs I/O operation on to a storage system.

- **Client systems**: Similar to host server, but accesses files or objects on storage system. It does not serve to other computers.

- **Storage system**: Pool of disk vers connected to storage controllers that stores and performs I/O requests from host servers.

- **Block storage**: Type of storage system on which host servers read and write data across blocks.

- **File storage**: Type of storage system on which client systems reads and writes data in to the shared files on it.

- **Object storage**: Type of storage system which allows client system store data as an object. Object include data along with a metadata and a unique identifier.

- **SAN**: SAN, a network of storage devices and the initiators that store and retrieve data.

- **NAS**: NAS, a storage system with file system in it. Client accesses files over network stored on this storage.

- **DAS**: DAS, a storage that is directly connected to host computer.

- **Storage solution**: Storage solution consists of host server, storage system, switch, HBA, cable and connector and storage management software that provides a solution to store application data for an organization.

- **Cloud storage**: Typically, multiple object storages are deployed and connected to internet. All client computers including mobile, tab, PC accesses the storage to store data as an object.

- **VDI**: VDI is an infrastructure deployment environment where users access multiple VMs with different operating systems and configurations.

- **HCI**: Consolidated and converged solution within a single system to host VMs for VDI environment.

- **Converged system**: Converged system refers to a ready-made assembled, pre-configured and tuned storage and host servers in single rack.

- **Data center**: A facility with adequate space, power, and cooling to deploy and install large storage and server solutions.

Join our Discord space

Join our Discord workspace for latest updates, offers, tech happenings around the world, new releases, and sessions with the authors:

https://discord.bpbonline.com

CHAPTER 2
Storage Infrastructure

Introduction

With advancement of storage virtualization, today's infrastructure is more software-driven than hardware-driven. However, both hardware and software components play an important role in a storage solution. Software is not only used to manage the hardware, but also every storage feature and functionalities are implemented through software. Therefore, both are tightly integrated to each other to provide desired solution. Firmware is a type of software, typically involved in basic low-level operations to make hardware device functional. In a storage solution almost all hardware components have firmware embedded into them.

Structure

Upon successful completion of this chapter, you will be able to learn the following key areas of storage infrastructure:

- Storage, network and host layer
- Physical layout and components of storage system
- Network hardware components
- Host server
- Host bus adapter

- Software defined storage
- Securing storage infrastructure
- Managing storage infrastructure

Objectives

In this chapter, you will learn about different hardware devices and software components that are deployed and configured in a data center to implement a storage solution.

This chapter explains all physical components of a storage system and their connectivity within it and also storage networking and host server's storage components.

In addition to it, this chapter also explains storage **software defined storage** (**SDS**) concept.

Building a storage solution

A storage solution is implemented by connecting one or more host servers with storage systems via a network. The network consists of either **Fibre Channel** (**FC**) or Ethernet switches.

Broadly the following five hardware and software are used to build a storage solution:

- **Storage system**: Storage system is a hardware device connected to computers through a network for storing data. Storage disk array is an example of a storage system. Storage disk array has a pool of disk drives to store large amount of data. Though a disk array is often referred as **storage system**, **backup** and **tape devices**, are also called **storage system**.

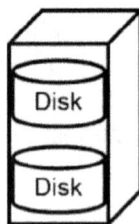

Figure 2.1: Storage System

Backup and tape devices are used to store a copy of the primary data, computer memory and other in-computer storage is not called storage system.

In a storage solution, storage systems are target devices.

- **Host server**: Applications that run on these computer servers, perform read and write datastored on to the storage systems. This is also called **application server**, **host computer** or simply **host**.

In a storage solution, host servers are initiator devices.

Figure 2.2: Host Server

In some storage solutions, where host servers do not host any application, but access the storage system directly, are called client systems. For example, mobile phone accesses object storage systems, for read write operations. Here, mobile is a client system.

- **Switch**: Host servers and storage systems are connected to the switches to form the network. Network allows host servers to communicate with storage systems. This network is not used to communicate one host server with another.

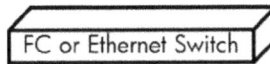

Figure 2.3: Switch

- **Host bus adapter (HBA)**: This is an adapter, installed inside the host server to connect to the switch. *Chapter 5, Storage Networking to Share Storage* discusses about this component in detail. The term HBA is primarily used for FC environment. In case of NAS solution, **Network Interface Card** (**NIC**) of host server itself can be used as HBA.

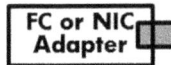

Figure 2.4: Host Bus Adapter(HBA)

- **Management software applications**: A suite of software products are required to manage and monitor the storage solution. A storage solution is incomplete without this set of software products. Using management software storage administrator creates storage volume and provides access to host servers. The application is then configured to store its data on to the volume.

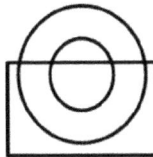

Figure 2.5: Management software

Hardware and software component stack

For better understanding of each component of storage solution in detail, let us divide the solution into three different layers–storage layer, network layer and host layer. The following table lists hardware, firmware, and software components for each layer:

	Hardware	Firmware and software
	Host server HBA **Small Form Factor Pluggable (SFP)**	HBA firmware and driver Adapter management software Multipath driver Storage utilities
	FC switch or LAN Switch SFP Cables and connectors	Switch firmware Switch management software
	Disk array controllers Physical disk drives Disk enclosure Backend switch and connectors	Disk array controller firmware Disk firmware Storage system management software Performance tuning and monitoring software Snapshot management software Replication management software Data protection and recovery software

Table 2.1: Storage hardware and software component stack

There are four major types of vendor involved in a storage solution–storage vendor, switch vendor, server vendor and HBA vendor. Firmware and software are developed by respective hardware vendor only.

Physical layout of a storage disk array

Typically any storage disk array has the following six hardware components:

- Rack
- Backend
- Switches
- Controllers
- Drive enclosures
- Disk drives

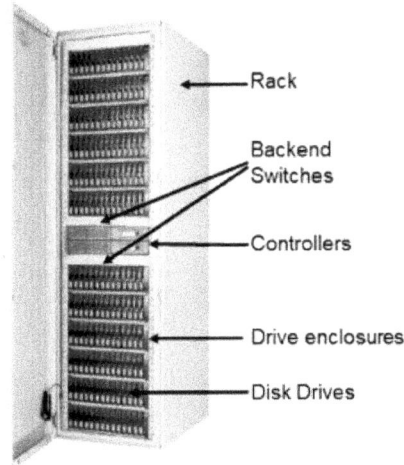

Figure 2.6: Storage system hardware components

Storage controllers

The primary hardware component that processes I/O request from host server and does the read and write operations on to the backend physical disk drives. Different vendors call this component different names–node,storage processor, and so on.

Controller itself is a computer and has:

- CPU
- Memory
- Cache memory for faster storing of user data.
- **Application-specific integrated circuit (ASIC).**
- Customized operating system, also known as **firmware.**
- Interfaces or ports–typically, a controller has:
  - o Frontend or host ports–for connecting to network or FC switches.
  - o Backend or device ports–for connecting to drive enclosures.
  - o Mirror or heart beat ports–interconnecting all controllers together.

Some vendors make the controller with designated ports, while others allow the user to configure port-based on requirement. The number of port in any controller depends on vendor product design and its model.

Most vendor's storage has two or more controllers in a storage system to have better fault tolerance and performance through load balance.

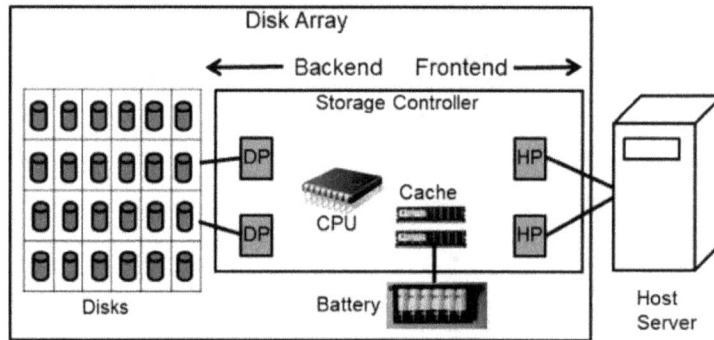

Figure 2.7: *Storage controller components*

In the preceding figure, HP is host port, and DP is device port.

Different storage vendor uses different name for these ports.

Physical disk drives

The most critical hardware component of a storage system is hard drive, which essentially stores the user data.

The disk has plates that rotate with speed expressed in **revolutions per minute** (**RPM**). This is the number of times the plates will do a full rotation in one minutes time. The head is fixed on arm to read and write data from the plates. Since the disk arm and the head are fixed in one position, it will often have to wait for the plate to spin to the right place. The common RPMs are 5400 or 7200 for consumer **Serial Advance Technology Attachment** (**SATA**) disks and 10000 or 15000 for high performance server/**storage area network** (**SAN**) disks.

There are mainly two types of hard drives available:

- **Small Form Factor** (**SFF**), 2.5 disks
- **Large Form Factor** (**LFF**), 3.5 disks

SFF disks consume less power and space compared to LFF. SFF disks are, generally, high cost, with **Serial Attached SCSI** (**SAS**) interface and used for high workloads environment and LFF disks are low cost, with SATA interface and used for high capacity storage.

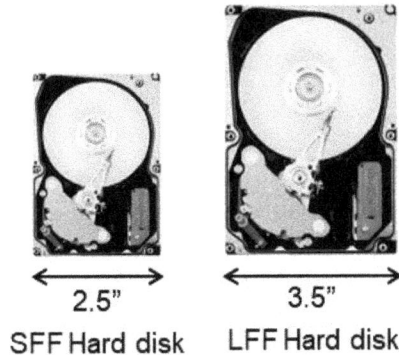

Figure 2.8: SFF and LFF hard drives

Each hard drive has **printed circuit board** (**PCB**) that runs firmware. When the hard drive is powered on, firmware checks the health of each part of the drive, sends the command to power on the motor, along with stabilizing and monitoring the speed. This is how the drives become ready to accept read/write commands from storage controllers.

Hard disk stores 0s and 1s in the form of magnetic fields. The circular part of hard disk is called **platter**, and a tiny magnetized region on the platter stores a bit. To write data on the hard disk, a magnetic field is applied on the tiny field in **North-South** (**N-S**) or **South-North** (**S-N**) polarities. The pattern of polarities represent 1 or 0.

For instance, reversals (N-S to S-N or S-N to N-S) represent 1 whereas same polarity (N-S to N-S or S-N to S-N) represents 0.

Solid state drive (**SSD**) has no moving mechanical part, like platter or motor in **hard disk drive** (**HDD**). SSD's performance is significantly higher than the traditional electromechanical disk drives.

Recently, SSD uses non-volatile NAND flash memory. A special type of **metal-oxide-semiconductor field-effect transistor** (**MOSFET**), called a **floating gate transistor**, isolated by a highly resistive layer, is used to permanently trap charged electrons. Each transistor can store a single bit. 1 is represented if the cell is not charged, and 0 if it is charged.

Figure 2.9: SSD

Storage systems which are designed and uses all SSD drives are also known as **all-flash array (AFA)**.

Storage Class Memory

In a computer system, storage device is the slowest component as compared to any other major components, such as CPU or DRAM memory. Typically, DRAM is known for high performance, high cost, but low capacity. On the other hand storage, such as SSD and HDD are known for high capacity, low cost, but lower performance than DRAM. **Storage Class Memory (SCM)** is a type of memory that has the capacity and price similar to storage but performance similar to memory.

Let us imagine, CPU operates in seconds, in that case, to get the data from DRAM takes about few minutes, whereas, to get data from HDD take a few months of time. Therefore, HDD is a significantly slower device compared to CPU and DRAM.

Though SSD has reduced this gap to less than a day now, there is still a huge difference between minutes and a day, as SSD is approximately 1000 times slower than DRAM. SCM brings that down to approximately 100 times, to just a few hours.

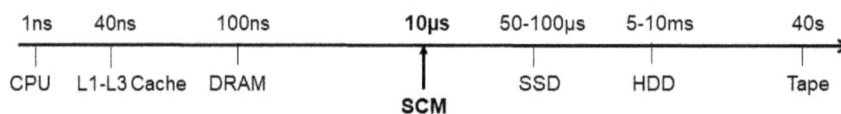

Figure 2.10: *Latency of memory and storage devices*

Recently, most storage vendors are planning to implement SCM in their storage systems. Based on evolution of storage devices so far, it is predicted that SCM may become the primary storage in future and SSD may be used as secondary storage for data archival.

Year	Compute	RAM	Primary storage	Secondary storage
1990s	CPU	DRAM	HDD	Tape
2010s	CPU	DRAM	SSD	HDD
2030s (Predicted)	CPU	DRAM	SCM	SSD

Table 2.2: *Evolution of storage devices*

Non-Volatile Memory Express

ATA and SCSI-based protocols support only single queue. Therefore, for accessing high-speed storage media, such as, NAND flash memory and SCM, these protocols have become bottleneck. **Non-Volatile Memory Express (NVMe)** is a storage protocol specifically designed for these storage devices.

While SATA and SAS protocols are best suitable for spinning HDDs, NVMe protocol suites NAND flash memory and SCM. NVMe protocol provides low-latency, high performance through large number of parallel operations over **PCI Express** (**PCIe**) bus. Due to the interface speed, performance of the new storage media, and proximity to the CPU, PCIe becomes a better choice of storage interface for NVMe protocol. NVMe is a NUMA-optimized protocol, which allows multiple CPU cores to share the ownership of queues, their priority, as well as arbitration mechanisms and atomicity of the commands.

As shown in following PCIe topology, NVMe disk subsystem is a PCIe endpoint which has primarily two components-NVMe controller and NVM.

Host interacts with NVMe controller to send read, write, system call requests and controller in turn accesses devices that are connected to it for performing **block I/O** (**BI/O**).

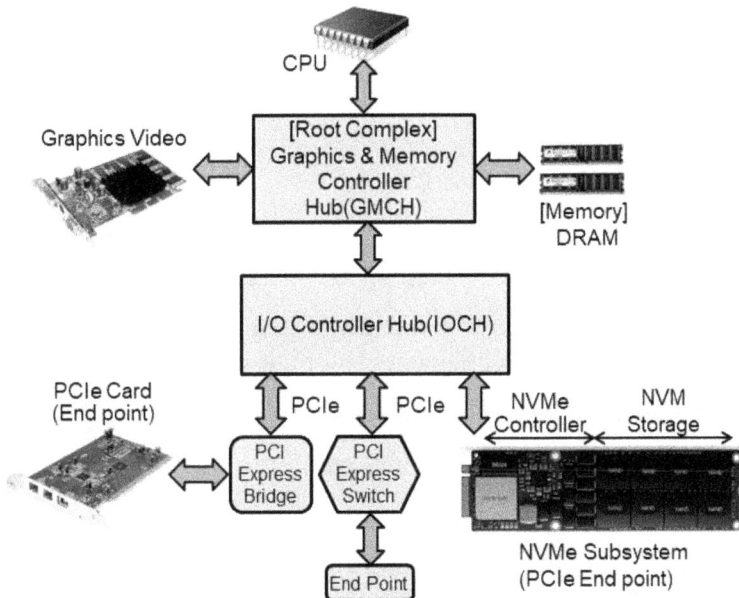

Figure 2.11: *NVMe topology*

Graphics and Memory Controller Hub (**GMCH**) is also referred as **Memory Bridge**, **Memory Hub** or **North Bridge**. **I/O Controller Hub** (**I/OCH**) is also referred as **I/O Bridge**, **I/O Hub** or **South Bridge**.

Though fundamentally data transfer on the PCIe bus is serial, with NVMe, every command and data transmission happens in massively parallel using multiple PCI lanes using multi-core CPUs and parallel access to the NAND devices. This is how NVMe achieves exceptionally high bandwidth.

```
# ls -l /dev/nvme*
crw------- 1 root root 245, 0 Mar 30 21:07 /dev/nvme0
brw-rw---- 1 root disk 259, 0 Mar 30 21:07 /dev/nvme0n1
brw-rw---- 1 root disk 259, 1 Mar 30 21:07 /dev/nvme0n2
#
```

/dev/nvme0 is character special file for NVMe controller, whereas /dev/nvme0n1 and /dev/nvme0n2 are two block special files for block devices attached to the controller.

Due to faster access of NVMe flash memory based disks, the following are the use cases and deployment models being adopted:

1. Boot disk of client computers
2. Server's internal storage disks
3. Server's cache memory of frequency used data
3. Storage system's backend disks

Recently, most storage vendors are designing their storage systems to support NVMe based disks to avoid any disk bottleneck at backend and improve overall storage performance.

Namespace

A namespace is collection of blocks of device connected to NVMe controller. This is similar to file system partition for better management storage space.

Here are some features of namespace:

- From kernel point of view a namespace is nothing but linear sequence of sectors.
- Each namespace has an ID.
- Namespace is created on flash memory and attached to the NVMe controller.
- NVMe can support up to 64K I/O queues, with each queue having 64K commands in it. Whereas SAS and SATA can only support single queue and each can have 254 and 32 commands respectively.
- One namespace can have a maximum of 64K queues ($2^{16} = 65535$) per controller. Total, ($2^{32} = 2^{16} \times 2^{16}$) commands are supported.
- There are two types of queues-admin queue to perform get and set for controller management and I/O queue (Read/write for NAND).

NVMe over Fabrics

NVMe is designed for local use over PCIe bus. Therefore, initial deployments of NVMe have been as local disk in a computer, **direct attached storage (DAS)** in servers and backend disks in storage systems.

Here are some features of **NVMe over Fabrics** (**NVMe-oF**):

- The NVMe-oF protocol is similar to NVMe protocol, designed to enable NVMe based commands to transfer data between a host computer and a target solid state storage device over a network. The network can be FC, Ethernet or InfiniBand.

- Local NVMe maps commands and responses to shared memory in the host over the PCIe bus. NVMe-oF uses a message-based model for communication between a host and a target storage device.

- NVMe-oF enables the use of alternate transports to PCIe that extends the distances across which an NVMe host device and NVMe storage drive. This includes enabling a frontend interface of SSD-based storage systems for communicating with NVMe host.

HDD capacity measurement

HDD manufacturers define: 1000 Bytes = 1 KB, 1000KB = 1MB, 1000MB = 1GB = 1 billion bytes

Whereas, the operating system (i.e. the computer) shows in powers of two value, therefore, a gigabyte (GB) is actually 1024 X 1024 X 1024 bytes.

- **Actual capacity**:

  = Advertised or manufacturer's capacity X (1000/1024) X (1000/1024) X (1000/1024)

  = Advertised or manufacturer's capacity X 0.93

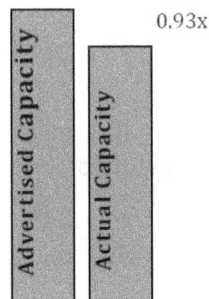

Figure 2.12: Advertised Vs Actual Capacity

- **Example**:
  - o Formatted Capacity of 300GB is equal to *300GB X 0.93 = 279GB*
  - o Formatted Capacity of 1TB or 1000GB is equal to *1000GB X 0.93 = 931GB*

  The greater the capacity, the higher is the difference between advertised value and actual capacity.

In some way, older storage systems incorrectly used GB, but they meant 1024 X 1024 X 1024 bytes. As per *National Institute of Standard and Technology (NIST)*, 1024 X 1024 X 1024 is basically GiB, not GB. All modern storage systems use following units as defined at **http://physics.nist.gov/cuu/Units/binary.html**

Unit	Abbreviation	Number of Bytes
kibibyte	KiB	1024
Mebibyte	MiB	1024 X 1024
Gibibyte	GiB	1024 X 1024 X 1024
Tebibyte	TiB	1024 X 1024 X 1024 X 1024

Table 2.3: Storage capacity units

Drive enclosures

It is an enclosure that contains pool or array of physical disk drives. Drive enclosure is also called **Just a Bunch of Disk (JBOD)**. Typically, all storage arrays support multiple enclosures.

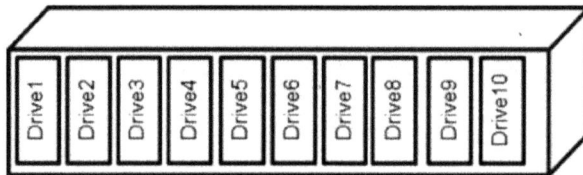

Figure 2.13: Disk enclosure (JBOD)

The number of drives that can go in and the orientation of drives are depended on vendors that the JBODs designed. All the drives are connected to two I/O modules at rear via a backplane. Firmware runs inside I/O module. Usage of two I/O module is to provide fault tolerance and load balance capability.

JBOD makes storage system modular, as it allows organizations to buy the amount of storage they need initially. Later, they can buy disks along with the enclosure as and when they need more storage space.

Due to the array of physical disks in enclosure, the whole storage system commonly referred as a **storage array** or an **array**.

Backend switches or backplane interconnects

Different vendor's storage systems are designed to use different technology to connect physical drives to the controller. Some vendors connect physical drives via cascade cabling or switches, while others connect via backplane circuit board. The storage controller's device ports are connected to these switches or the backplane. Again, disk drives are connected to these switches or the backplane.

The data received by the controllers from the host server at the frontend are processed and passed to the backend for storing them on to respective disk drives.

Cables and connectors

Cable and connectors are mainly used to connect drive enclosures, power, and so on. Typically two or more cables are used to connect a disk enclosure to increase bandwidth and load balance and fault tolerance due to any cable fault.

Large or high-end storage disk array may have long and complex cabling, whereas smaller disk array may have short and less complex cabling.

Rack

This is a refrigerator like box in which all hardware components are mounted, including storage controllers and disk enclosures. This ensures that cabling of all the components are secure and intact. Smaller disk array may not need an entire rack.

Storage network components

The components that form a network between the host server and storage system and help host servers to communicate with the storage system are called **storage network components**. These components vary from type of solution implemented. For example, FC SAN network requires one or more FC switches, and IP network for NAS solution requires Ethernet switch. The major component in the storage network is the switch. DAS solution does not use any switch, instead, it just uses a direct cable between host and storage system for communication purpose.

Multiple switches are installed and connected to each other to form a vast network.

Components that comprises a storage network are: HBA, switches, cables, and connectors. Though HBA is installed inside the host server, and is a part of the host server layer, it can also be considered as one of the networking components.

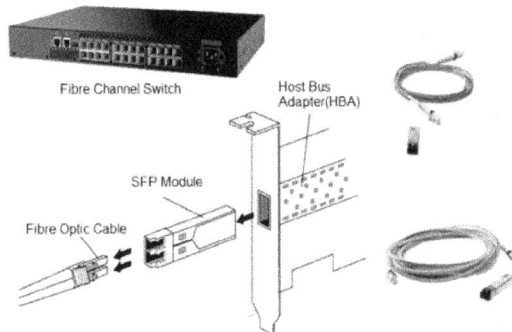

Figure 2.14: Switch, fibre optic cables and SFP

HBA and switch, both run firmware to activate their functionalities.

In FC based network, FC supports both media options and can run on copper cables or optical cables.

Optical fibre supports:

- Long distance up to 10Km.
- High-speed up to 64Gbps.
- Immunity to induced electromagnetic signals.
- Requires an SFP at both ends of the cable to convert light signal to electric signal. SFP is also referred as **gigabit interface converter** (**GBIC**).

A fibre optic transceiver or SFP transceiver usually consists of a transmitter and a receiver in a single module.

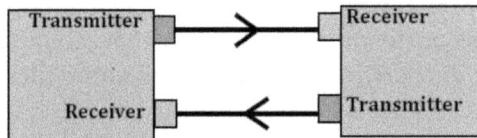

Figure 2.15: *Fibre optic transceiver and receiver*

In fibre optic data links, the transmitter converts the electrical signal into an optical signal from a laser diode or LED. The light from the transmitter is coupled into the fibre with a connector and is transmitted through the fibre optic cable. The light from the end of the fibre is coupled to a receiver where a detector converts the light back into an electrical signal.

SFP is hot-pluggable component.

When devices of different speed are connected, speed negotiation takes place from higher speed, then steps down to lower.

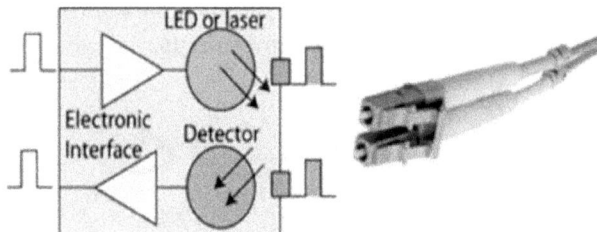

Figure 2.16: *Block diagram of an SFP*

1. Light transmission in an optical fibre by total internal reflection.
2. Core.
3. Cladding material.

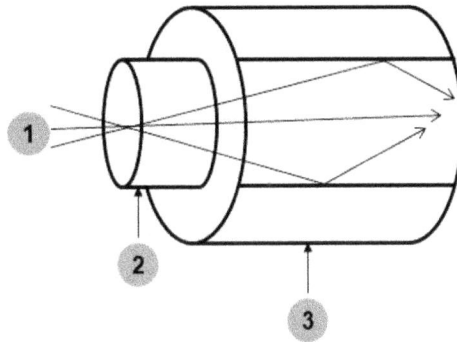

Figure 2.17: Light transmission through an optical fibre

There are two type of fibre cables, multimode and single-mode:

- **Multimode fibre** has a relatively large light carrying core, usually 62.5 microns or larger in diameter. It is usually used for short distance transmissions with LED based fibre optic equipment. In multimode, beams of different photons reaches at different time, it makes it difficult to know, 1 or 0. Therefore, supported distance becomes shorter with speed.

- **Single-mode fibre** has a small light carrying core of 8 to 10 microns in diameter. It is normally used for long distance transmissions with laser diode based fibre optic transmission equipment. Single-mode fibre has a recommended maximum length of 10km.

Electrical cables are low cost alternative to short distance–30meters.

Figure 2.18: FC electrical copper cable

Software defined storage

Generally, a storage system comprises specially designed hardware and firmware. Primary hardware components are controllers and physical disks. Firmware is designed to run on the controller as an operating system. All storage features such as RAID, local and remote replication, thin provisioning, de-duplication are implemented within the firmware. Management software is the upper layer component that is designed to manage the storage system.

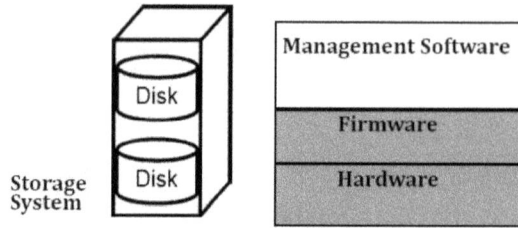

Figure 2.19: *Storage system with hardware, firmware and management stack*

SDS is a solution implemented inside a customized operating system that can run on any commodity hardware, thus, decoupling storage firmware and management software from the physical storage hardware. With SDS, end user can buy any commodity hardware with required disk space and deploy a **virtual machine** (**VM**) in which the customized operation system is deployment.

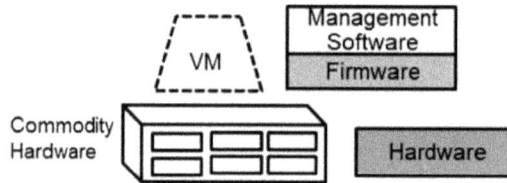

Figure 2.20: *SDS: Firmware and management stack decouple from hardware*

Primary advance of SDS is cost effectiveness, as it does not require any special hardware. However, for enterprise workload regular storage system is best suitable.

Due to the popularity of SDS, DAS has recently caught attention. Many companies buy commodity hardware and configure DAS and deploy SDS on it to have an intelligent storage system.

Securing storage infrastructure

Today almost all organizations store their business critical information as digital data on to storage systems. Security of this critical data is a big concern in today's world. Therefore, the computer information data security is a wide subject by itself. The primary objective of data security is prevention of unauthorized disclosure, data tampering, accidental corruption or deletion.

As per *Storage Networking Industry Association* (*SNIA*) storage security is technical controls, which may include data integrity, confidentially and availability controls that protect storage resources and data from unauthorized users and uses.

Confidentiality is disclosure of information only to authorized persons. Integrity ensures that information remains in its original form without altering it. And availability indicates information is ready to access within stated operational parameters. Availability also ensures in case of data corruption of deletion, how fast data can be restored to get back business operational.

Storage infrastructure security is related with the physical, technical, and administrative controls as well as the preventive, detective, and corrective controls. That applies to the following infrastructure components:

- Host server with **host bus adapter** (**HBA**)
- Storage arrays
- Storage network switches
- Cable for storage networks
- Storage management
- Backup systems
- Virtualization
- Cloud storage
- Specialized services such as encryption, compression, and deduplication

There are several methods and strategies that can be implemented to secure storage infrastructure from attackers. SNIA recommends, instead of focusing on abstract concepts of **confidentiality, integrity, and availability** (**CIA**) the following four technology components can be considered to secure storage infrastructure:

- **Storage system security (SSS)**: Securing storage controller firmware, the embedded operating system and applications that integrates external authentication services, centralized logging, and firewalls.
- **Storage resource management (SRM)**: Securely provisioning, monitoring, tuning, re-allocating, and controlling the storage resources so that data may be stored and retrieved.
- **Data in-flight (DIF)**: Protecting the confidentiality, integrity and/or availability of data as they are transferred across the storage network, the LAN, and the WAN.
- **Data at-rest (DAR)**: Protecting the confidentiality, integrity and/or availability of data residing on storage arrays.

Managing storage infrastructure

Managing storage infrastructure is an integral part of storage solution that assists the deployment, provision and monitors health of the solution.

The primary management software is to manage the storage system itself. Every storage vendor supplies management software along with the storage array, which helps administrator to configure provision and monitor the storage system. Other management software allows protecting data by creating copy of data or creating backup copy.

The management software for other hardware components, such as switch, HBA is also a part of storage solution. Hardware vendor of HBA and switch supplies management software along the hardware to configure and monitor these hardware components.

Chapter 9, Storage Management, explains more about storage management and all related software suite.

Conclusion

Storage infrastructure is collection of hardware, firmware and software components that comprises to form a storage solution. Components can be divided into three different layers storage, network, and host layers.

Storage system or the storage disk array is the primary device or component in a storage solution. It stores application data and performance host server's read/write requests.

Storage disk array has six hardware components—storage controller, physical disk drives, disk enclosures, backend switches or backplane interconnects, cables and connectors and a rack.

Hardware components of storage network are HBA, switch, cables and connectors. HBAs are installed in host servers to connect to the network. Switch is the primary complement in a network. Storage network is formed using one or more switches.

Information data security is big concern in today's world. Technical controls on CIA help protect storage resources and data from unauthorized users and uses.

Managing storage solution includes initial deployment, providing and monitoring all the hardware components. The software suite that enables to manage the infrastructure is also part of storage infrastructure.

Case studies

Case study 1: Assembling hardware devices to build a storage solution

Let us look at assembling hardware devices to build a storage solution:

Requirement

Your company has received the following hardware devices from a supplier. You are asked to connect the devices and implement the storage solution.

1. Host server
2. FC HBA

3. FC switch

4. FC cables

5. SFPs

6. Storage controllers

7. JBOD

8. Disk drives

9. Storage system management software

Analysis

First, identify the hardware components of different layers discussed earlier in the chapter. Disk drives, JBOD, and storage controller belong to the storage system layer, SFPs, cable, switch in network layer and host server and FC HBA in host layer.

Solution

- First, install the disk drives into JBOD. Connect JBOD to device port of storage controller.

- Connect host port of storage controller using FC cables. Install SFPs in switches and connect other end of the FC cable to the switch.

- Install HBA in host server connect to switch.

- Install management software to configure and deploy the solution.

Case study 2: Converting legacy DAS solution to latest storage technology

Let us look at converting legacy DAS solution to latest storage technology:

Requirement

Your company has quite a few unused legacy servers, which are attached with direct attached JBODs. Company is looking for an option to utilize these hardwires to convert to a high performance and availability storage solution.

Analysis

Legacy DAS solutions do not provide much storage features for better performance and availability. However SDS component can be deployed on top of it can make it more intelligent. Using SDS, virtual volume can be carved out with different RAID levels from the legacy disks. Other storage services, such as snapshot, deduplication and compression are also available with latest SDS solution.

Solution

SDS solution is recommended for this requirement. This is a software component of a VM that can be procured and deployed on to the legacy hardware to implement high performance and availability storage solution.

Learning check

Objective questions

1. **If you create a 1TB storage LUN give access to a host, what would be the capacity shown in the operating system.**

   a. 1024GB

   b. 931GB

   c. 1000GB

   d. 831GB

2. **If you buy a 1TB disk from a shop and install and format it in your laptop, what would be the usable capacity.**

   a. 1024GB

   b. 931GB

   c. 1000GB

   d. 831GB

3. **Type of HDD and their physical size:**

   a. SFF, 3.5

   b. LFF, 2.5

   c. LFF, 3.5

   d. SFF, 2.5

4. **Which component of a storage system is connected at backend of any storage controller:**

   a. Virtual volume

   b. Physical disk

   c. Host

   d. Cache memory

5. **What is a disk array?**

   a. JBOD that consists of enclosure where set of hard drives are hosted in many combinations such SCSI drives, SAS, FC and SATA.

   b. Independent physical disks behind one or more controllers and allows configuring virtual volumes or RAID volumes.

   c. A high-end server consists of large number of hard drives in it.

6. **What is the purpose of disk array?**

   a. Performance

   b. Fault tolerant

   c. Scalable

   d. All of the above

7. **Device port of a Storage controller is a:**

   a. Initiator

   b. Target

   c. Both

   d. None

8. **Host port of a storage controller is a:**

   a. Initiator

   b. Target

   c. Both

   d. None

9. **Which is not a primary component of a disk array?**

   a. Network Interface Card

   b. Storage controllers

   c. Physical disk drives

   d. Disk shelves

10. **Which interface of a storage controller not used for I/O traffic?**

    a. Frontend or host port

    b. Backend or device ports

    c. Network interface port

    d. Controller interconnect ports

11. **Which of the following interfaces are used for storage management and monitoring purpose. Select all choices that apply:**

    a. Frontend or host port

    b. Backend or device ports

    c. Network interface port

    d. Serial port

12. **Which hardware component is not part of a storage controller?**

    a. Fan

    b. Power supply unit

    c. Power distribution unit

    d. Battery

13. **Which is not a SAN component?**

    a. Storage device

    b. FC switch

    c. HBA

    d. DIMM

14. **Which of the following is correct order of storage devices according to their performance?**

    i.   HDD > SSD > SCM > Tape

    ii. Tape > HDD > SSD > SCM

    iii. SCM > SSD > HDD > Tape

    iv. SSD > HDD > SCM > Tape

    a. (i)

    b. (ii)

    c. (iii)

    d. (iv)

15. **Which of the following statements related to single-mode and multimode is incorrect**

    a. In multimode, beams of different photons reaches at different time, it makes it difficult to know, 1 or 0.

    b. Optical core for single-mode fibre is 62.5 microns.

    c. Single-mode supports up to 10KM distance.

    d. In multimode, supported distance becomes shorter with speed.

16. **Which type of cable supports the longest distances between devices?**

    a. Single-mode fibre optic

    b. Multimode fibre optic

    c. Copper

    d. SCSI cable

17. **Can you change or replace GBICs when the Switch is up and running.**

    a. True

    b. False

18. **Which of the following comparisons is not meaningful**

    a. NVMe vs SSD

    b. NVMe vs SAS

    c. SATA vs SAS

    d. SSD vs spinning disk

19. **Match the followings**

    i. NVMe   1. Supports one queue with maximum of 32 commands in it

    ii. SAS   2. Supports maximum of 65535 queues with maximum of 65535 commands in each queue

    iii. SATA   3. Supports one queue with maximum of 254 commands in it

    a. (i) - (1), (iii) - (2) and (ii) - (3)

    b. (i) - (1), (ii) - (2) and (iii) - (3)

    c. (ii) - (1), (i) - (2) and (iii) - (3)

    d. (iii) - (1), (i) - (2) and (ii) - (3)

20. **Which of the following disks is not made by any disk vendor:**

    a. SAS spinning disk

    b. NVMe spinning disk

    c. NVMe solid state disk

    d. SATA solid state disk

Descriptive questions

1. Describe different components within a storage controller.

2. Define storage security and why it is needed. Also describe technology-oriented components that can be considered to secure storage infrastructure?

Quiz questions

1. What does SCM stand for? Why it is important for next generation storage systems.
2. Does DAS solution uses any switch for network between host and storage device. Justify your answer.
3. Explain benefits of NVMe.

Glossary and key terms

- **Storage disk array:** A storage system with independent physical disks behind one or more controllers and allows configuring virtual volumes or RAID volumes.
- **JBOD:** Just a Bunch of Disks. A disk enclosure that holds number of physical disk connected to one or more controllers.
- **SFF:** Small Form Factor, 2.5 hard drive.
- **LFF:** Large Form Factor, 3.5 hard drive.
- **SSD:** Solid state drive, high performance disk drive with no mechanical moving component.
- **SCM:** Storage Class Memory, high performance storage device.
- **HDD:** Hard disk drive, stores data on magnetic media.
- **AFA:** All-flash array, storage disk array with SSDs.
- **SDS:** software defined storage that decouples storage services from underlying hardware.
- **NVMe:** Non-Volatile Memory Express.

Join our Discord space

Join our Discord workspace for latest updates, offers, tech happenings around the world, new releases, and sessions with the authors:

https://discord.bpbonline.com

CHAPTER 3
Storage Disk Array

Introduction

A storage disk array is a storage system that consists of a pool of physical disk drives and one or more storage controllers, which stores terabytes of data and performs multiple host server's **input/output (I/O)** operations. Storage vendors design and implement several features in storage system to improve read/write performance and data fault tolerance. Some of those features are controller operations, data caching technics, RAID concepts, and so on. RAID implementation in storage system has greatly influenced both performance and fault tolerance aspects of a storage system. For this reason, in the last three decades all storage vendors have been implementing it in their storage systems. Modern storage disk array implements Virtual RAID, which enhances performance and fault tolerant factors at greater extend.

Apart from RAID, disk array also has several intelligence features implemented to provide highly optimized I/O processing, fault tolerant and efficient storage capabilities. Some of those features are storage tiering, **quality of service (QoS)**, replication, thin provisioning, deduplication and compression and many more. These features discussed in details in following chapters.

Therefore, storage arrays are referred as **intelligent storage arrays (ISA)** or **intelligent storage systems (ISS)**.

Structure

This chapter primarily focuses on storage system and you will learn about following aspects of a storage system:

- Physical layout and components of storage system
- Storage controller operation modes
- Caching techniques
- RAID concept
- Virtual RAID
- Storage virtualization

Objectives

By end of this chapter you will learn about design and implementation of various features and functionalities of a storage system, such as storage controller operation modes, different data caching techniques and how user data is stored on to the physical disk using different RAID levels. This chapter will also discuss the pros and cons of each RAID levels.

Controller operation modes

To provide fault tolerance and load balance storage controller level, most of the storage systems are configured with minimum of two storage controllers.

There are multiple controller operation modes available. Storage vendors design their controller based on their targeted model and pricing of the storage system.

Active/standby

One of the two controllers is always in idle state and wakes up when other controller dies.

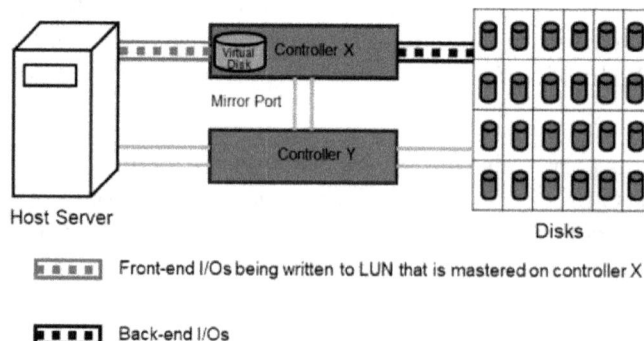

Front-end I/Os being written to LUN that is mastered on controller X

Back-end I/Os

Figure 3.1: Active/standby controller operations

Since only controller is active at a time, there is no load balance; this configuration is not seen in modern storage system.

Active/passive

Both controllers serve I/O, but only for the **logical unit numbers (LUNs)** that they own.

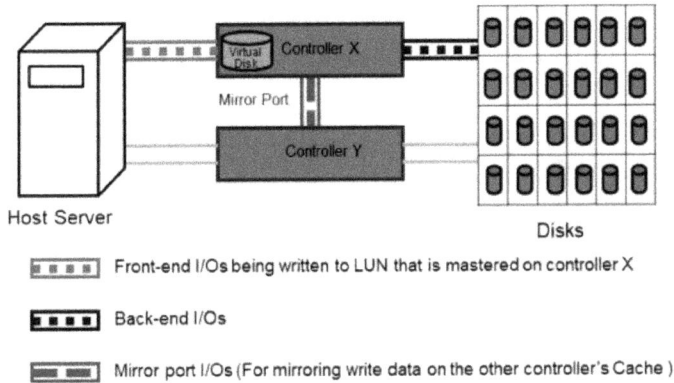

Figure 3.2: *Active/passive controller operations*

- Only owned controller accepts host requests.
- LUNs are statically distributed among controllers by setting preferred to certain controller. In the figure, for illustration purpose, only one LUN is shown on Controller X. There can be many LUNs owned by either of the controllers.
- Data is written to the primary controller's cache, then to the secondary controller's cache, complete status is sent to the host and then data is written to the disk.

Asymmetrical Active-Active

Both controllers accept host requests, but only owned controllers interacts with backend disks. In the following figure, for illustration purpose, only one LUN is shown on Controller X. There can be many LUNs owned by either of the controllers.

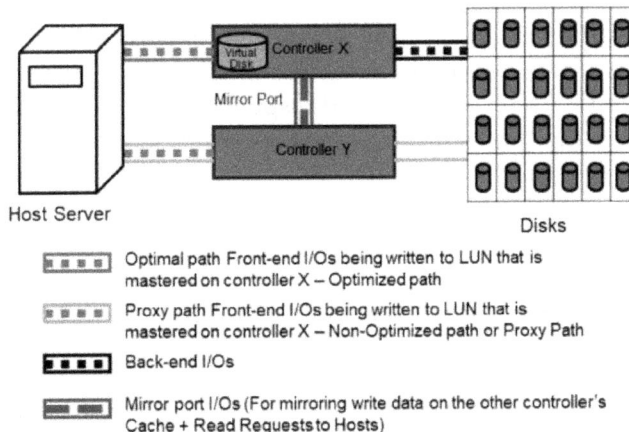

Figure 3.3: *Asymmetrical Active-Active controller operations*

- Data is written to the primary controller's cache, then to the secondary controller's cache, complete status is sent to the host and then data is written to the disk.
- For read through non-optimized paths involves extra path, that is mirror path. No impact on write, as both controllers always has the data.
- LUNs are statically distributed among controllers by setting preferred to certain controller.
- **Asymmetric Logical Unit Access (ALUA)** enabled OS can determine optimized and non-optimized paths.

True Active-Active

Both controllers accept host requests, and also interacts with backend disks for a given LUN. Most modern storage systems have this controller operations implemented.

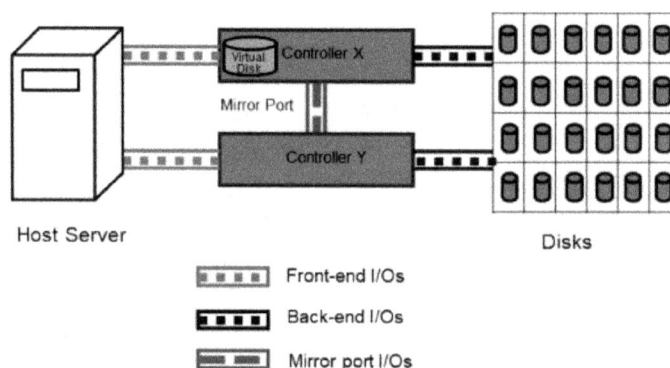

Figure 3.4: *True Active-Active controller operations*

Caching techniques

A cache is a temporary storage area that keeps data available for fast and easy access. Almost all storage systems have caching mechanism implemented, in which frequently accessed data is stored in faster memory and respond back to hosts without delay. Cache memory is installed in the storage controller, hence, there are various caching techniques available for storage system.

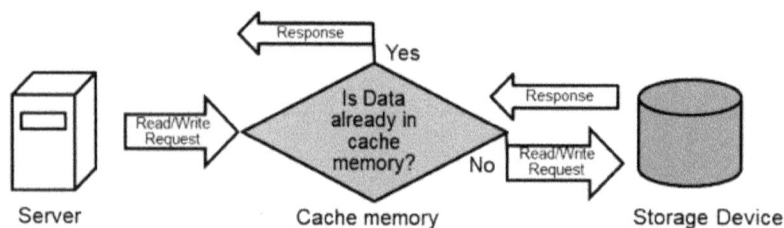

Figure 3.5: *Caching techniques*

Some of the commonly used caching techniques are as follows:

- **Write-back**: A cache management method that increases the performance of host write requests by decreasing the storage system's response time. When the host requests a write operation, the storage system controller writes the host's data first to the cache memory, completing the host's request quickly. It performs the slower operation of flushing the data to the disk at a later time. The host sees the write operation as complete when the data has reached the cache.

- **Mirrored write-back**: In this policy mode, mirrored write-back provides the high performance of write-back under normal operation, but reverts to the safety of write-through in case of failure. In mirrored, half of each controller's write contains a copy of the companion controller's write, providing a high level of data protection.

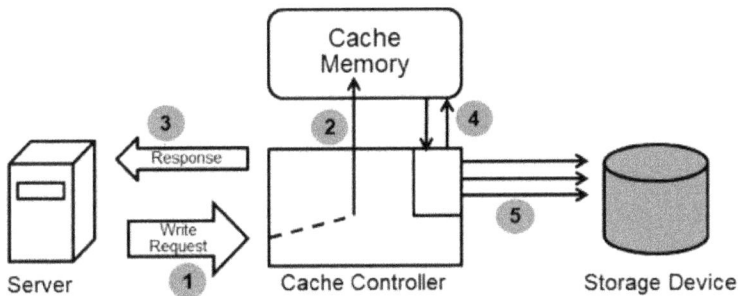

Figure 3.6: Write-back caching technique

- **Write-through**: A cache management technique for holding the write data in cache memory as well as writing the data to the disk. The write request operation is complete only after the data to be written is received by the disk. This technique allows the controller to complete some host read requests for this same data from the cache memory rather than from the disk, greatly improving the response time to retrieve data.

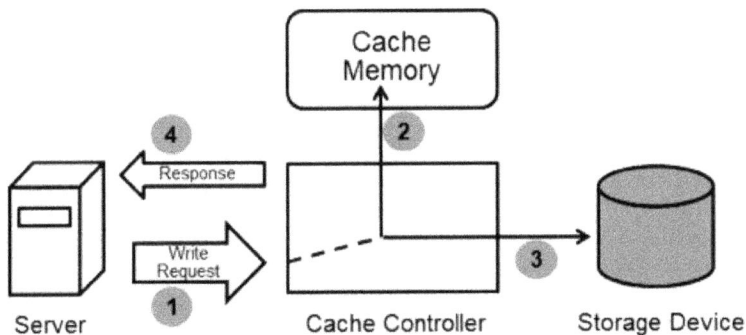

Figure 3.7: Write-through caching technique

- **Read**: A block of high-speed memory used by a controller to buffer data being read from storage devices by a host. A read cache increases the controller's effective device access speed by satisfying host read requests from its local cache memory when possible instead of external storage devices.

- **Read-ahead**: Cache management technique for improving performance of synchronous sequential reads by pre-fetching data from disk and placing it into cache. The controller maintains, in the cache, copies of data recently requested by the host, and may fetch blocks of data ahead in anticipation that the controller will access the next sequential blocks. In normal read cache, host write requests are done as usual, without the caching mechanism.

- **Adaptive**: More advanced technique than read-ahead caching. The adaptive cache algorithms anticipate host requests based on previous patterns. The blocks of data most likely to be requested are cached for quicker transmission to the host.

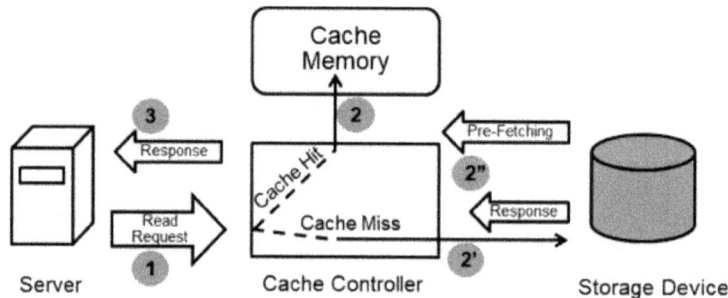

Figure 3.8: Read caching technique

Purpose of cache battery:

- Unwritten cache data or unflushed data resides in cache, battery provides power to protect it, in case of any power failure.
- Usually write cache is battery backed up, read cache is not.
- But if single DIMM is in use, both read and write are battery backed up.
- Newer storages are being designed with flash-backed cache, hence does not require any battery.

RAID concept

In 1988, RAID levels 1 through 5 were formally defined by *David A. Patterson, Garth A. Gibson* and *Randy H. Katz* in the paper, *A Case for Redundant Arrays of Inexpensive Disks (RAID)*. The term RAID was first introduced in this paper; it spawned the entirestorage industry.

RAID is an example of storage virtualization, which is discussed in the later of part of this book.

What is RAID?

- RAID - Redundant Array of Inexpensive/Independent Disks.
- Conceptualized by a paper presented in 1987 at *University of California, Berkeley*.
- Fundamentally, RAID is the use of multiple HDDs in an array that behaves in most respects like a single large, fast one.
- Improve availability of data.
- An attempt to bridge the widening gap between performance of processor vs. performance of disks.
- To support faster data access required by video and multi-media applications warranted new storage architecture.

Purpose of RAID

Due to mechanical and magnetic parts, disk in any storage system has higher failure rate than any other component in it. RAID concept brings mainly two advantages:

- **Performance**: Combine multiple small, inexpensive disk drives into a group to yield performance exceeding that of one large, more expensive drive.
- **Availability**: Support fault tolerance by redundantly storing information in various ways. Increase capacity.

A virtual volume is a logical reference to a portion of a storage subsystem. Virtual volume is means of provisioning space to host server.

Storage systems generally have large storage capacity, many host servers share this space. So the space is sliced into smaller volumes, and then resented or exported it to the host servers. In host, this appears as if it is a disk connected locally to it. In Windows host, after partitioning, formatting a disk drive, drive letter, such as D:, E: are assigned to it. Data can be stored on to it. In Linux host disk appears as/dev/sdb or /dev/sdc or something similar. This can also be partitioned and formatted and mounted to a folder, e.g./data. Data can be stored on to this folder.

Virtual volume also simplifies the management of storage resources because they serve as logical identifiers through which you can assign access and control privileges.

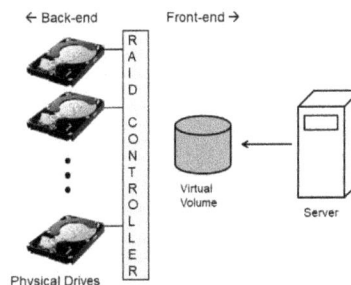

Figure 3.9: *Virtual volume concept*

Virtual volume appears as a single disk to the computer (server).

RAID controller is itself is a computer, physical drives are connected to its backend and it all drives behind the RAID controller is invisible or unknown to the computer.

There are significant benefits of performance and fault tolerance, but there is no benefit of space efficiency from RAID technology.

Virtual volume is also referred by different vendors in their product as storage volume, RAID volume, virtual disk, logical disk, logical volume, LUN, but fundamentally they all are same.

In most implementation:

- BUS value is assigned from HBA location in PCI slot of the server
- Target corresponds to host port of storage controller
- LUN value is nothing but LUN number assigned to each logical disk while presenting to server

Concepts and terminologies

- **Mirroring**:
  - o For an example, when you copy a file of size 10MB to a storage system, both drives get 10MB each. Same data gets stored in both the drives.
  - o Each block of data from server gets copied in both drives in parallel.
  - o If any drive fails, 10MB is still available.

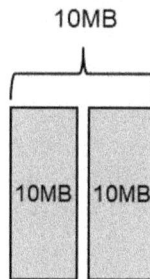

Figure 3.10: *Mirroring : How it works*

  - o Minimum of two drives required to implement, maximum depends on vendor's implementation, some vendor supports a mirror set of 6 drives.

- **Striping**:
  - o For an example, if you copy a file of size 10MB, to a storage system, each drive gets 5MB each.
  - o Each block of data from server gets divided into two and then gets written to both the drives in parallel. In case of striping across more number of drives, data gets written faster.

 o If any drive fails, only 5MB left, half of each data block is available–application cannot read it!

10MB

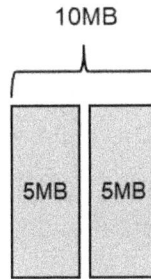

Figure 3.11: *Striping: How it works*

 o Minimum of one drive is required to implement, maximum depends on vendor's implementation.

Parity–how it works

For an example, if you copy a file of size 10MB, to a storage system, each drive gets 5MB each and third drive will get parity of first two data.

- Each block of data from server gets divided into two and then gets written to two the drives and also a parity data is calculated and stored on third drive.
- If any drive fails, there must be some way to retrieve the data on failed drive.
- Minimum of three drives required to implement, maximum depends on the vendor's implementation.
- Data: Parity ratio can also be decided by the vendor. Tradeoff between space efficiency and availability.

A	B	$P = A \oplus B$
0	0	0
0	1	1
1	0	1
1	1	0

Table 3.1: *Data and parity*

To improve the performance, block of data is considered instead of each bit; therefore parity calculation is just not XOR. Its bit complex than this, but concept remains the same.

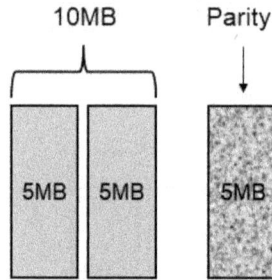

Figure 3.12: Parity: How it works

I/O size, block, chunk or stripe size

Different vendors use different terms for size of data for reading and writing purposes in different scenarios.

- **Host I/O size**: Amount of data host sends for writing or ask for reading through one request.

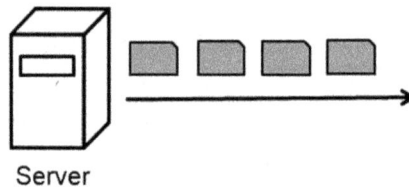

Figure 3.13: Host I/O size

- **Stripe size**: Amount of data gets written on to the member drives of a RAID unit at a time. Some vendor refer this as block size or chunk size.

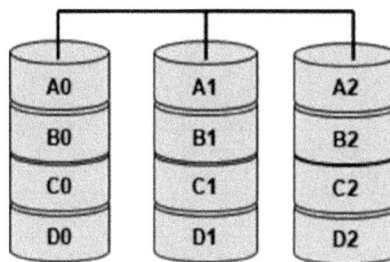

Figure 3.14: Stripe size

Spare drive

In the event of any drive failure the RAID volume goes into degraded state. When RAID volume is in degraded state, another drive failure may result in data loss situation. Therefore it is important to bring the RAID volume as soon as possible in healthy state by replacing the faulty drive. To avoid manual intervention of replacement, most vendors implement spare drive. A spare drive is an idle drive during normal operation. Upon failure of a drive from a RAID volume, data start rebuilding on to the spare drive automatically. At the end of the rebuilding process, data on failed drive gets regenerated on to the spare driver and the spare drive become part of the RAID volume. Later, the administrator can replace the failed drive with a new drive and configure it as spare.

Advantages:

- RAID volume is in a degraded state for the minimum time.
- RAID volume becomes healthy without any human attention.
- Failed drive can be replaced later part of the time hot-sparing is a spare device that is available in the subsystem, upon failure of any operating disk, system automatically uses the spare disk. All modern storage allows the failed drive to be hot-swapped, meaning drive can be removed and inserted keeping the system running.

RAID types

The following are various types of RAID:

- RAID 0 to RAID 7
- RAID 0, 1, 3, 5 and 6 are commonly used
- RAID 2 and 4 do not offer any significant advantages over other types
- Hybrid RAID levels (Combinations of RAIDs)
  - o RAID 10 or RAID 1+0 = RAID 1 + RAID 0
  - o RAID 50 or RAID 5+0 = RAID 5 + RAID 0

RAID 0–striping

The data is broken down into blocks and each block is written to a separate disk drive.

- **Advantages**:
  - o I/O performance is greatly improved by spreading the I/O load across many drives
  - o Easy to implement
  - o 100% space efficiency
  - o Requires minimum of one drive to implement

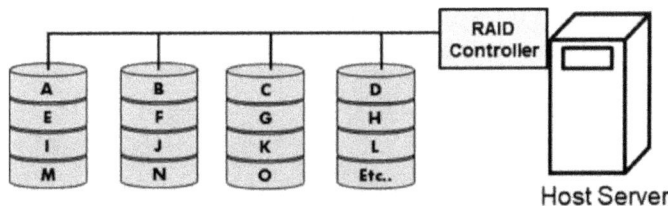

Figure 3.15: *RAID Level 0: Striped disk array without fault tolerance*

- **Disadvantages**:
  - o Not a true RAID because it is not fault tolerant
  - o The failure of just one drive will result in all data in an array being lost

RAID 1–mirroring

It is the copy of each data block on two different disks.

- **Advantages**:
  - o Twice the read transaction rate of single disks, same write transaction rate as single disks
  - o Simple to implement
  - o Highest level of fault tolerant
  - o Requires a minimum of 2 drives to implement

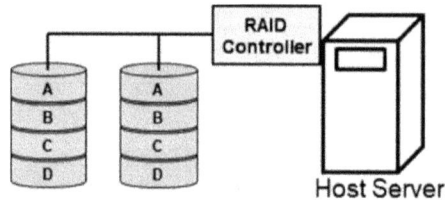

Figure 3.16: RAID level 1: Mirroring and duplexing

- **Disadvantages**:
  - o Requires twice the disk capacity of required space
  - o Increase in cost per bit storage only 50% of available space is utilized

RAID 2–bit level striping with ECC parity

RAID 2 is implemented by splitting data at the bit level and spreading it over a number of data disks and a number of redundancy disks. The redundant bits are calculated using Hamming codes, a form of error correcting code (ECC).

- **Advantages**:
  - o Each time something is to be written to the array these codes are calculated and written alongside the data to dedicated ECC disks; when the data is read back these ECC codes are read as well to confirm that no errors have occurred since the data was written.

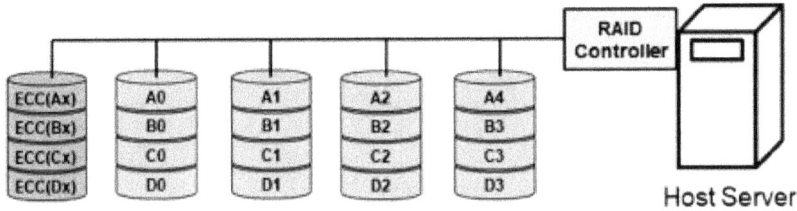

Figure 3.17: *RAID level 2 : Bit level striping*

- **Disadvantage**:
  - o No practical use; same performance can be achieved by RAID 3 at lower cost.

RAID 3–byte level striping with dedicated parity

Each data block is subdivided (striped) and written on the data disks. Stripe parity is generated on writes, recorded on the parity disk.

- **Advantages**:
  - o The performance of the array is identical to the performance of one disk in the array except for the transfer rate, which is multiplied by the number of data drives (i.e., less parity drives).
  - o Excellent performance for large, sequential data requests.
  - o RAID level 3 requires a minimum of 3 drives to implement.

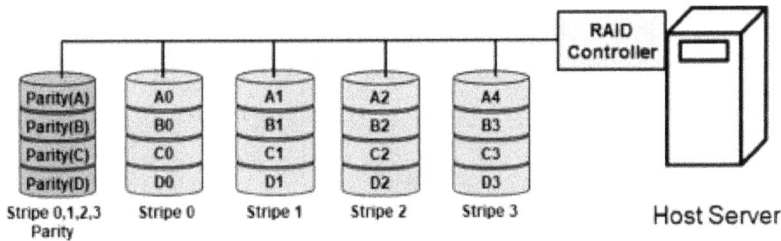

Figure 3.18: *RAID level 3: Byte level striping*

- **Disadvantages**:
  - o This technology is fairly complex.
  - o Performance is slower for random, small I/O operations.
  - o Speed is limited by the slowest disk.

RAID 4–block level striping with dedicated parity

Each block is written onto a data disk.

- **Advantages**:
  - o Parity is generated on writes, recorded on the parity disk.

o Very high read data transaction rate.

o RAID level 4 requires a minimum of 3 drives to implement.

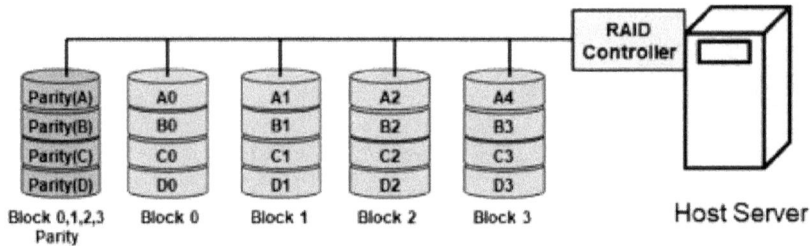

Figure 3.19: RAID level 4: Block level striping

- **Disadvantages**:
  o Single parity drive is involved in every write and becomes the bottleneck as RAID 3
  o Worst write transaction rate and write aggregate transfer rate

RAID 5–block level striping with distributed parity

Each data block is written on a data disk.

- **Advantages**:
  o Parity for blocks in the same rank is generated on writes.
  o Recorded in a distributed location.
  o RAID level 5 requires a minimum of 3 drives to implement.

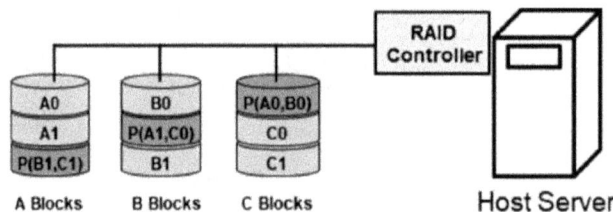

Figure 3.20: RAID level 5: Block level striping with distributed parity

- **Disadvantages**:
  o Disk failure has a medium impact on throughput
  o Most complex controller and its firmware design–difficult to rebuild in the event of a disk failure
  o Medium write data transaction rate
  o Data on virtual volume becomes inaccessible if two disks failed together or second disk fails when volume is in degraded state due to previous disk failure

Recovering from a disk failure

RAID 5 can tolerate the failure of one of the disks. In the case of failure of a drive, data on the failed drive is calculated by RAID controller with parity and data on other surviving drives. During this ,the system runs slow, as it has to calculate user data from parity. The following table shows a simple example on how data(Ax or By) is derived when any disk fails. In reality, parity is a complex function of user data (Ax and By)

Ax	By	$P = Ax \oplus By$
0	0	0
0	1	1
1	0	1
1	1	0

$Ax = By \oplus P$	$By = Ax \oplus P$
0	0
0	1
1	0
1	1

Table 3.2: Recovering data on failed disk from parity

Rebuild process

When a failed drive is replaced with a new one, data of the failed drive get generated from existing data and parity and then written to the new drive.

$D1= D2 \oplus P$
0
0
1
1

New Disk	D2	P
	0	0
	1	1
	0	1
	1	0

Table 3.3: Rebuilding data on to a new disk

RAID level comparisons

RAID 2	RAID 3	RAID 4	RAID 5
Bit level striping with ECC parity	Byte level striping with dedicated parity	Block level striping with dedicated parity	Block level striping with distributed parity
All disks write and read as one. This lowers the tolerance for non-identical drives		Disks write and read independent of on another	
Good performance for large amounts of data or the applications that process large blocks of data		Applications that manipulate small amounts of data, such as transaction processing applications and fewer writes than reads	
Not used	Widely used	Rarely used	Widely used

Table 3.4: Raid 2 vs. 3 vs. 4 vs. 5

RAID levels 4 and 5

Single parity drive in RAID 4 is involved in every write, thus limits parallelism, whereas RAID 5 distributes the parity blocks among all the *N+1* drives and enables parallelism.

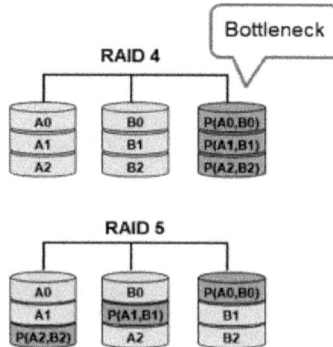

Figure 3.21: RAID level 4 vs. RAID level 5

Why RAID 3 provides better large block sequential read/write performance than RAID 4 and 5?

- Each block of data is spread across all the drives in the array. All disks serve requests together, but only one host I/O request at a time. Hence sequential request and large block perform better on RAID 3. RAID 3 cannot service multiple requests simultaneously.

- In case of RAID 4 and 5, different block of data resides on different drives, hence simultaneously random requests performs better on them.

- For an example, a read request for block A consisting of some bytes (A0, A1) would require all data disks to seek to the beginning first byte and reply with their contents. A simultaneous request for block B would have to wait.

- In case of RAID 4 and 5, a read request for block A would be serviced by first disk. A simultaneous read request for block C would have to wait, but a read request for B could be serviced concurrently by second disk.

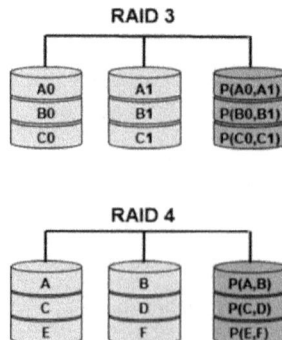

Figure 3.22: RAID Level 3 vs. RAID Level 4

- If the size of a stripe is reduced below the OS block size a RAID 5 array then has the same performance pattern as a RAID 3.

Why does one disk become bottleneck in Raid 4, but not in Raid 3?

- Referring to the *Figure 3.22*, in addition to the simultaneous writes of block (A and B) to their respective drives, both need also to be written to the parity drive. In this way RAID places a very high load on the parity drive in an array.
- In case of RAID 3, all drives synchronously–all serve same requests.

RAID 6–bock level striping with dual parity

- Two independent parity computations are used in order to provide protection against double disk failure. Two different algorithms are employed to achieve this purpose.
- Essentially an extension of RAID level 5.
- RAID level 6 requires a minimum of 4 drives to implement.

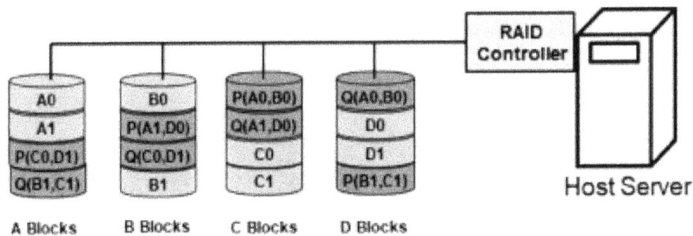

Figure 3.23: RAID level 6: Block level striping with dual parity

Disadvantages:

- More complex controller and its firmware design
- Slow write performance because of controller overhead to compute parities
- Requires $N+2$ drives to implement because of dual parity scheme

Hardware versus software RAID

- **Software RAID**:
  o A software solution implements the RAID
  o Software RAID: run on the server's CPU
  o Directly dependent on server CPU performance and load
  o Occupies host system memory and CPU operation, degrading server performance
- **Hardware RAID**:
  o A piece of hardware or hardware controller.

o   Hardware RAID: run on the RAID controller's CPU.

o   It does not occupy any host system memory, alsoIt is not operating system dependent.

o   Host CPU can execute applications while the array adapter's processor simultaneously executes array functions: True hardware multi-tasking.

Hybrid RAID levels–RAID X+Y

Hybrid RAID levels are implemented by combining virtual volumes which already formed from physical drives. Following example shows, RAID X is formed from physical drives, now again one more time virtual volume is formed using RAID Y of those virtual volumes.

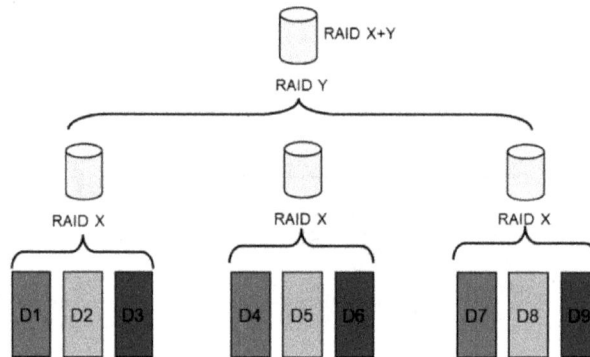

Figure 3.24: Hybrid RAID

Some examples:

If X=5, Y=0, If you copy 30MB Data to D1, D2, D4, D5, D7, D8 will get 5MB each and D3, D6, D9 will have the parities.

If X=1, Y=0, If you copy 30MB Data to, each drive will get 10MB RAID 0+1,RAID 01,RAID 0&1 (Mirror of stripes)

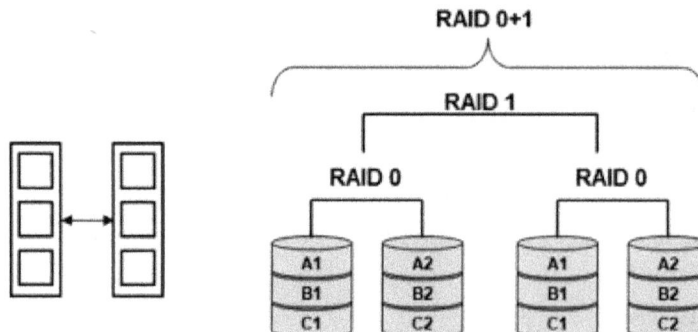

Figure 3.25: RAID 0+1: Mirror of stripes

- RAID 0+1 configuration where multiple disks are striped together into sets and then sets are mirrored together.
- Minimum number of disks required to implement RAID 0+1 is 3, where the data is striped across two disks in RAID 0 and then all the data is mirrored on a third disk. But it is more common to use a minimum of 4 disks.

RAID 1+0, RAID 10, RAID 1 and 0 (Stripe of mirrors)

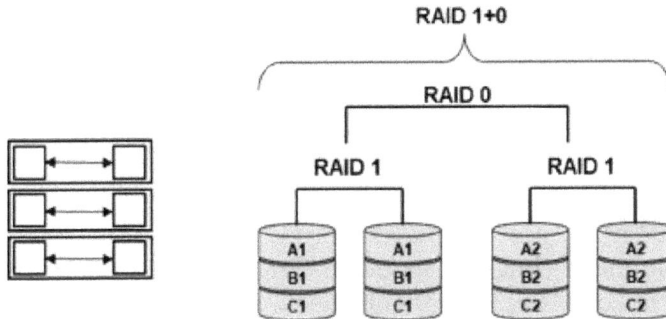

Figure 3.26: RAID 1+0: Stripe of mirrors

- RAID 1+0 configuration where data is mirrored in sets and then multiple disks are striped together
- RAID 0 array of mirrors require a minimum of 4 drives

RAID 1+0 vs. RAID 0+1

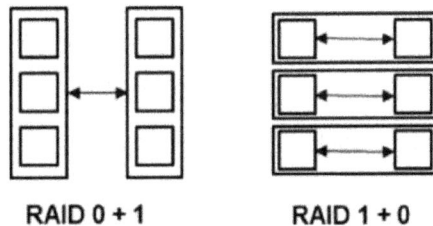

Figure 3.27: RAID 1+0 vs. RAID 0+1

- RAID 10 provides better throughput, speed, performance, and latency than all other RAID levels (except RAID 0).
- Any drive failure will cause the RAID unit to go into degraded state, now the chance of second drive failure from another set in RAID 0+1 is more than RAID 1+0.
- In a degraded state, performance, especially read performance does not get reduced in RAID 1+0 compared with Raid 0+1.
- The rebuild will complete faster after replacing a failed disk.

- Generally, all vendors prefer to implement RAID 1+0 in their products.

RAID level use scenarios

- Selecting the proper RAID level for a specific data storage application requires consideration be given to the benefits of each

RAID	Use
• RAID 0 (1 disk)	• Video/audio streaming
• RAID 1 (2 disks)	• OS boot
• RAID 5 (3 disks)	• Transaction/webserver
• RAID 10 (4 disks)	• Database
• RAID 50 (6 disks)	• Data warehousing
• RAID 6 (4 disks)	• Large capacity disk arrays

RAID metadata

- Metadata is nothing but data about data, in other word, information about another information. For example, index of a book.
- In RAID, technology metadata is a mapping table between logical disk to physical disk.
- For example, metadata table looks something similar to the following table. If the host server wants to write data on block X of logical disk 1 (RAID 1), data essentially gets written to block A of physical disk 1 and block 2 of physical disk 2.

Metadata	Metadata
Logical disk 1, block X	Physical disk 1, block A Physical disk 2, block B
Logical disk 2, block Y	Physical disk 1, block C Physical disk 2, block D

Table 3.5: Simple example of a metadata table

- In reality, metadata is extremely complex, dynamic and critical part of a storage system.

Host-based RAID controller

External storage system has two or more storage controllers. Storage controller also alternatively called as **RAID controller**. RAID controller can be installed within the host server itself and connect to internal or external disk enclosures. This DAS configuration is commonly used for entry level cost effective storage solutions. This RAID controller is called **host-based RAID controller**. All modern RAID controller supports SAS protocol.

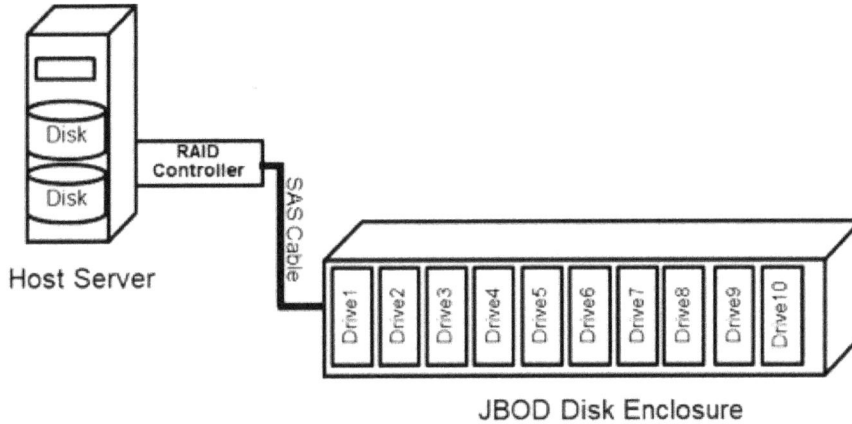

Figure 3.28: *Host-based RAID controller*

Virtual RAID

Most modern virtualized storage system has Virtual RAID implemented–each disk is logically divided into smaller chunks.

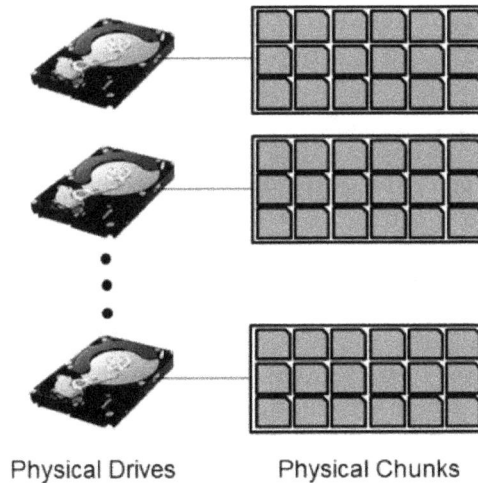

Figure 3.29: *Physical chunks*

For simplicity of implementation, generally the size of physical chunk is fixed in a storage system. Larger virtual volume uses more number of logical chunks.

Logical disks that we discussed above are formed based on those chunks and then concatenated them to form a virtual volume for host server to access. Something similar to hybrid RAID level discussed in previous section. For instance, Virtual RAID 1 is internally RAID 1+0.

To ensure fault tolerance, each logical volume chunk is formed from physical chunk resides on different physical drives, so that failure of any drives should not impact virtual chunks, depending on RAID levels.

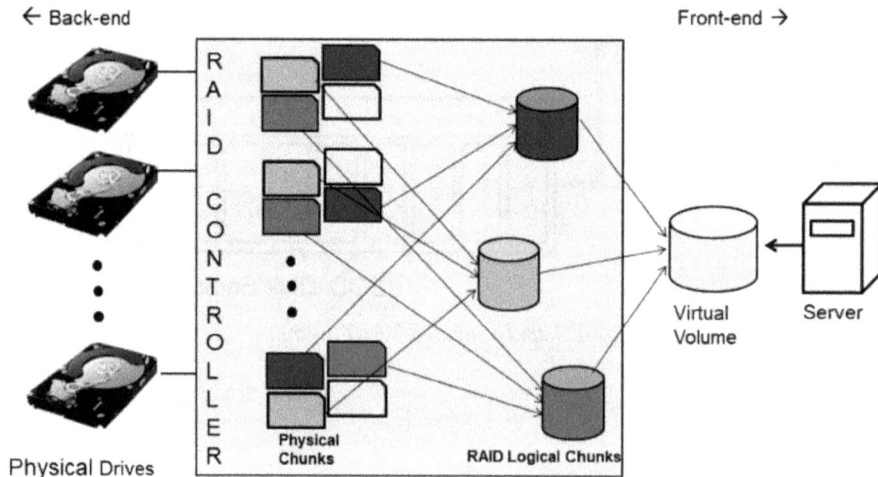

Figure 3.30: Virtual RAID concept

For example, if you have 20 numbers of 10GB disks and physical chunk size is 1GB, when you create a 10GB RAID 1 virtual volume, it actually creates 10 number of 1GB RAID 1 logical volume chunks underlying to it. Each logical volume chunk again has two physical chunks reside on two different physical drives, thus involving all 20 physical drives.

In this case, even if maximum of 10 drives, one from each pair, can fail, still data on virtual volume would be intact.

If you create a 10GB RAID 1 virtual volume on a storage without Virtual RAID implemented, it only involves two drives, in which, performance may not be as much as the Virtual RAID implemented storage.

In reality, this design is much more complex. Above example is just to illustrate a simple example to describe the concept. In some cases, data recovery also becomes complex in the event of multiple drive failure.

To understand fault tolerance in Virtual RAID, let us consider a user created a RAID 6 virtual volume with data and party ratio 4:2 on a storage system with 18 drives. There would be total three logical volume chunks, each of them formed from physical chunk from individual physical disk. Now let us assume that 6 drives failed together in such a way that two physical chunks from each logical chunk impacted. Since each logical chunks are in RAID 6, none of the logical chunks are impacted. Data on virtual volume would also be intact.

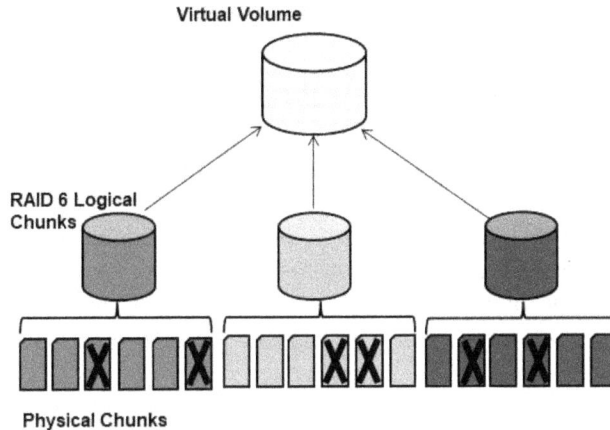

Figure 3.31: *Disk failure situation in Virtual RAID*

But if 3 drives fails together in such a way that one logical volume chunk is impacted, in that case data on virtual volume may not be accessible.

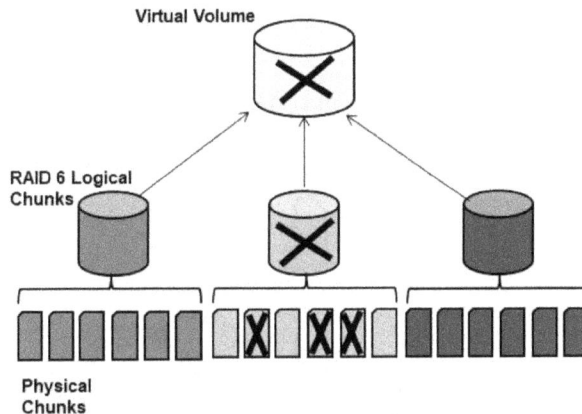

Figure 3.32: *Logical volume chunk failure situation in Virtual RAID*

In summary, with the Virtual RAID, there can be multiple drive failure may not impact data in a virtual volume as long as each logical chunk is healthy, as opposed to a storage system with the traditional RAID, where any three disk failure together would make data inaccessible.

Some physical chunks from each drive are kept aside for spare purpose. This is called **distributed spare**. In case of any drive failure, these spare physical chunks are used to rebuild each logical chunk. The number of physical chunks allocated for spare is typically based on the storage system's internal design or user-defined policy.

Primary advantages in this design, every virtual volume that user creates are resided on all the drives in the storage systems to boost read/write performance and degree of fault tolerance.

Most vendors use different names for physical and RAID volume chunks and keep this internal to product design.

Distributed Sparing: Within the Virtual RAID implementation, physical chunks are designated as spare chunks. Storage system internally or allows administrator to reserve some space for physical chunks. For example, if each physical chunk size is 1GB, disk size is 10GB and administrator reserves two disks capacity, then total 20 physical chunks are designated as spare chunks. In case of any disk failure, rebuild process generates data on all the chunks on the failed disk and stores on to the reserved spare chunks on other working disks. After completion of rebuild process logical chunks become healthy and number of spare chunks reduces until administrate replaces the failed disk with a working one.

Storage virtualization

Following is an example of a traditional non-virtualized storage environment, where a single disk attached to an application host via a SCSI adapter. There Following are the disadvantages:

- Entire disk is mapped to a host. This may be larger than the requirement, thus wasting space.
- Unused space cannot be used by another host.
- If the disk fails, data is lost.

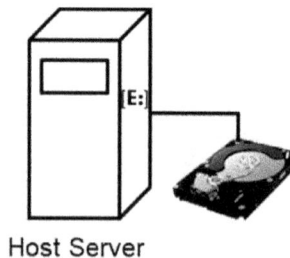

Host Server

Figure 3.33: Non-virtualized environment

The virtualization software or device uses the metadata to re-direct I/O requests. It will receive an incoming I/O request containing information about the location of the data in terms of the logical disk (virtual disk) and translates this into a new I/O request to the physical disk location.

For example the virtualized device may:

- Receive a read request for vdisk LUN ID=1, LBA=32
- Perform a metadata look up for LUN ID=1, LBA=32, and finds this maps to physical LUN ID=6, LBA0, and physical LUN ID=7, LBA0
- Sends a read request to physical LUN ID=6, LBA0 and physical LUN ID=7, LBA0

- Receives the data back from the physical LUNs
- Sends the data back to the initiator as if it had come from vdisk LUN ID=1, LBA32

Virtualization benefits–availability: Non-disruptive data migration

- The host only knows about the logical disk (the mapped LUN) and so any changes to the metadata mapping is transparent to the host. This means the actual data can be moved or replicated to another physical location without affecting the operation of any client. When the data has been copied or moved, the metadata can simply be updated to point to the new location, therefore freeing up the physical storage at the old location.
- Improved availability by increasing fault tolerance of system.

Storage virtualization benefit–improved utilization

- Utilization can be increased by virtue of the pooling, migration, and thin provisioning services.
- When all available storage capacity is pooled, system administrators no longer have to search for disks that have free space to allocate to a particular host or server. A new logical disk can be simply allocated from the available pool, or an existing disk can be expanded.
- Storage can be assigned where it is needed at that point in time, reducing the need to guess how much a given host will need in the future.
- Virtual volume expand and shrink

Storage virtualization risks

Metadata becomes critical:

- Once virtualized, the metadata are the glue in the middle. If the metadata are lost, so is all the actual data as it would be virtually impossible to reconstruct the logical drives without the mapping information.

Complexity increases:

- **Management of environment**: Although a virtual storage infrastructure benefits from a single point of logical disk and replication service management, the physical storage must still be managed. Problem determination and fault isolation can also become complex, due to the abstraction layer.
- **Infrastructure design**: Traditional design ethics may no longer apply, virtualization brings a whole range of new ideas and concepts to think about.
- Every data that arrives at a virtualized array is torn into multiple pieces, as it has to be written on to all drives. Thus, in general, I/OPS become a bottleneck rather than bandwidth at frontend.

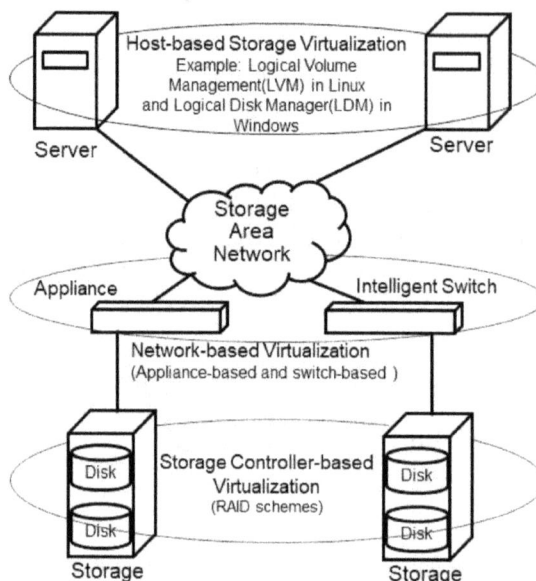

Figure 3.34: Storage virtualization and different level

Logical Volume Management

Host-based volume management is a software RAID solution implemented within host OS. **Logical Volume Management (LVM)** is an example of storage virtualization at host level. Today most modern Linux distributions are LVM-aware.

LVM provides administrator to take advantage of storage virtualization by abstracting the physical layout of storage devices for easier and flexible administration. RAID volume can be configured with striping and mirroring to achieve better fault tolerance and performance. Data can be spread across underlying heterogeneous storage devices and migrated online from one storage type to another. Volumes can be resized dynamically. LVM also offers advanced storage features like snapshotting, cloning, expand and shrink.

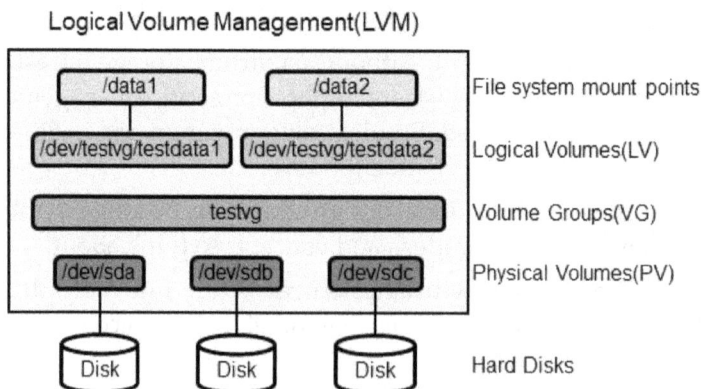

Figure 3.35: LVM architecture

LVM terminologies and architecture

- **Physical volume (PV)**: Physical block device, created for each physical disk, and used by LVM as the raw building material for higher levels of abstraction. This physical disk can also be a logical disk of a host-based RAID controller or virtual disk of an RAID storage array.

- **Volume group (VG)**: Combination of PVs into storage pools known as **VG**.

- **Logical volume (LV)**: A VG can be sliced up into any number of logical volumes. Each LV is used to create file system and mount for storing data.

- **Extents**: VG is segmented into small, fixed-size chunks called **extents**. Logical volumes are expanded or shrunk by adding required number of extents to or removing extents from the VG.

Configuring LVM in Linux

As a first step to configure, physical devices need to be marked as PVs using the pvcreate command.

An example command:

```
# pvcreate /dev/sda /dev/sdb /dev/sdc
```

Second step is to add the PVs into a VG:

```
# vgcreate testvg /dev/sda /dev/sdb
```

And the last step is to create LV from VG:

```
# lvcreate -L 20G -n testdata1 testvg
```

```
# lvcreate -L 30G -n testdata2 testvg
```

Following commands can be used to create file system on LV and mount them

```
# mkfs.ext4 /dev/testvg/testdata1
# mkfs.ext4 /dev/testvg/testdata2

# mkdir /data1
# mkdir /data1

## mount /dev/testvg/testdata1 /data1

# mount /dev/testvg/testdata2 /data2
```

Entries for each mount point can be added in /etc/fstab file to make the mounts persistent across reboot of the system.

Refer LVM documentation specific to the OS for detailed information.

Conclusion

Multiple controllers in a storage system provide load balance and fault tolerance. Based on storage system model and its design, there are different controller mode of operation, active/standby, active/passive and Asymmetrical Active-Active and True Active-Active.

Among these modes True Active-Active is the mode that is implemented most of the modern storage systems. This ensures all controllers in the storage system, equally loaded for I/O operations.

Caching techniques are implemented in most storage system to have improved performance. Data is temporality stored in cache memory DIMM for faster read/write requests. There are several techniques available–write-back, read-ahead, write-through, and adaptive caching.

RAID is also another popular technology that is implemented in all storage system. RAID is basically hard disk configuration during creation virtual volume for host server to access. Host server is unware of physical drives that are used to configure the virtual volume. It treats the volume like single disk. Depending of various RAID level, it influences performance, availability of data, space efficiency. For instance, RAID 0, stripes the data across all the drives that are configured, it provides better performance and space efficiency, but no fault tolerance. On the other hand RAID 6 or RAID 1 with many drive members, provides best fault tolerance, but performance may not be as good as RAID 0. In summary RAID configuration is a tradeoff among performance, data availability, and space efficiency.

No RAID level increases efficiency of data storing capability, meaning there is no RAID level that can store more data on less space. For example, more than 100GB data cannot be stored on 10 number of 10GB disk. All RAID level reduces the usable capacity except RAID 0. Only RAID 0 configuration will allow to store maximum 100GB on 10 number of 10GB disks, RAID 1+0 will allow you to store maximum 50GB.

Comparing RAID Levels

	RAID 0	RAID 1	RAID 3	RAID 5	RAID 6
I/O performance	Highest	High	Medium	Medium	Low
Fault tolerance	None	Highest	Medium	Medium	High
Space efficiency	Highest	Low	Medium	Medium	Medium

Table 3.6: RAID level comparison

* For large, sequential I/O requests

** Lower than Raid 3 and 5

Space efficiency vs. availability vs. performance

Selection of a RAID level is always a tradeoff among three aspects of a storage space efficiency, availability and performance. For example, RAID 0 has maximum space efficiency and provide better performance, but fault tolerance is extremely low. Failure of any disk can cause data loss of the volume. On the other hand, RAID 1 provides better fault tolerance and performance, but has poor space efficiency. Therefore it is important for storage administrator to select appropriate RAID level based on business requirement.

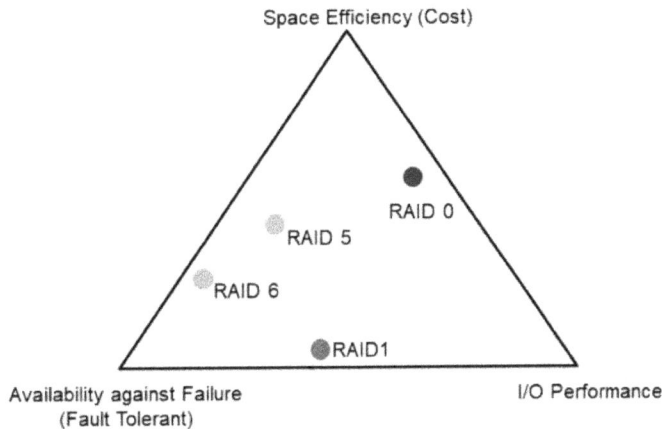

Figure 3.36: RAID level tradeoffs

RAID technology also evolved over the time and currently modern storage systems, combines multiple RAID virtual volumes to construct another layer of virtualization. Though this increases complexity of implementation and troubleshooting, but enhance performance and data availability further. This is called **Virtual RAID**.

Storage virtualization is commonly implemented technology in every storage solution. RAID is an example of a virtualization within a storage system. Similarly virtualization can also be implemented across multiple storage system, or at network level or host server level. This enhances performance and space utilization efficiency.

Case studies
Case Study 1: Performance and space efficiency are critical

Let us look at performance and space efficiency:

Requirement

An organization requires storage volume for testing a software product. Performance and usable capacity is most important for them. They can copy the test data again, if it is lost. What solution can be proposed for this requirement?

Analysis

As shown in *Figure 3.35: RAID Level tradeoffs*, all RAID levels provide data protection against any disk failure except RAID 0. RAID 0 also provides maximum performance, as all drives, underlying to RAID 0 volume, are involved in read/write requests. Since there is no parity or mirroring of data involved in RAID 0, entire space of all drives are used for storing data. Therefore RAID 0 provides maximum usable capacity.

Solution

RAID 0 virtual volume is recommended for this requirement. The *Figure 3.15: Striped disk array without fault tolerance* can be referred to understand how RAID 0 is implemented.

Case Study 2: Testing of disk failures in Virtual RAID enabled storage system

Let us look at the testing of disk failures in Virtual RAID enabled storage system:

Requirement

A company recently purchased a latest storage system with 120 disks. The storage system supports Virtual RAID. Administrator wants to test pattern of disk failures when Virtual RAID 1 is configured with all the disks.

Analysis

Virtual RAID breaks down each physical disk into smaller physical chunk, which is a miniature of a physical disk. When a Virtual RAID 1 is created out of all 120 disks, hundreds of logical disks are formed based on those chunks and then concatenated them to form a virtual volume. Each RAID 1 logical volume chunk is formed from physical chunk resides on different physical drives. At larger view, layout of the Virtual RAID 1 is something similar to RAID 1 + 0, but at granularity of smaller physical chunk, instead of considering whole disk in traditional RAID levels.

Therefore there is going to be total 60 pairs of disk. For testing, administrator can pullout maximum of 60 disks together, but each drive can be one member of each pair. But if he pulls out just two drives and they happen to be part of same pair then virtual volume would go into failed state.

Solution

Refer production document to determine the RAID layout. Once it is understood, one member from each pair can be failed or pulled out together without impacting virtual volume.

However pulling out two drives of same pair may impact the volume.

Learning check
Objective questions

1. **Consider a RAID array consisting of four 750 GB disks, What is the usable capacity if a RAID 5 volume is created:**

   a. 3 TB

   b. 1.5 TB

   c. 2.25 TB

   d. 1 TB

2. **If your application does write operation most of the time, which RAID from below you would not prefer:**

   a. RAID 5

   b. RAID 1

   c. RAID 0

   d. RAID 1 + 0

3. **Why do we need RAID to be configured to store data(Select all choices that apply)**

   a. Cost effective

   b. Better performance

   c. Fault tolerance

   d. Space efficiency

4. **For better performance which option would you choose, if RAID is implemented at:**

   a. Software level

   b. Hardware level

   c. Both levels

   d. Any levels

5. **What is major disadvantage with RAID 1?**

   a. Poor performance

   b. Low fault tolerance

   c. Cost ineffective

   d. All of the above

6. **You have configured RAID 1+ 0 with 16 drives, for testing how many maximum drives you can pull at the same time without losing data:**

   a. 2

   b. 4

   c. 8

   d. 16

7. **RAID influences:**

   a. Fault tolerance

   b. Performance

   c. Space efficiency

   d. All of the above

8. **How many maximum drives can fail at the same time from a RAID 6 volume, without impacting access to data on it:**

   a. 1

   b. 2

   c. 3

   d. 4

9. **What is major disadvantage with RAID 4:**

   a. Byte level striping

   b. The parity drive becomes the bottleneck

   c. Block level striping

   d. Parity is distributed

10. **Which statement is true; if a user copies a file of 12 MB size on a RAID 0 (Striped) volume of two 10 MB disks:**

   a. First 10 MB would be written to first disk and then 2 MB on to the second disk

   b. 10 MB to first disk and 2 MB to second disk would be written simultaneously

   c. 6 MB of data would be written on to both the disks simultaneously

   d. First 6 MB would be copied to first disk and then 6 MB on to the second disk

11. **Which RAID level is not fault tolerant?**

   a. RAID 0

   b. RAID 1

   c. RAID 5

   d. RAID 6

12. **Disadvantages of Virtual RAID are:**

    a. Lower performance

    b. Low fault tolerant

    c. Implementation complexity

    d. Complex data recovery in case of failure

13. **How many maximum drive of a Raid 0 volume can fail without any data loss?**

    a. 3

    b. 2

    c. 1

    d. 0

14. **In a three member RAID 1 volume, how many maximum drive can fail together without any data loss?**

    a. 3

    b. 2

    c. 1

    d. 0

15. **In a three member RAID 5 volume, how many maximum drive can fail together without any data loss?**

    a. 3

    b. 2

    c. 1

    d. 0

16. **Virtual RAID is implemented in a storage system with 20 disk drives installed, user created a RAID 5 volume with data and parity ratio 4:1. How much maximum drive can fail together without impacting data access of the virtual volume, assuming no two drives from same logical volume chunk?**

    a. 8

    b. 4

    c. 10

    d. 5

17. **You have bought a disk array with 20 disks. You have two options: Option-1: Create a single RAID 5 volume using all 20 disks, Option-2: Create 4 different RAID 5 volumes using 5 disks in each Which are the following statements true:**

    a. As a whole, more space would be lost in Option-1 compared to Option-2

    b. Probability of entire data loss would be higher in Option-1, compared to Option-2

    c. Comparatively performance would be expected more in option Option-2

    d. All of the above

18. **How many minimum physical drives are necessary to create a RAID 5?**

    a. 2

    b. 3

    c. 4

    d. 5

19. **How many minimum physical drives are necessary to create a RAID 6?**

    a. 3

    b. 4

    c. 5

    d. 6

20. **Can there be hot spare disks configured for a RAID 0 array?**

    a. Yes

    b. No

21. **You have a video streaming application, which does mainly large block sequential read/write operations, which RAID level would you like to choose:**

    a. RAID 3

    b. RAID 4

    c. RAID 5

    d. RAID 6

22. **Your application demands more storage performance, You have configured a 4 member RAID 0 volume, still application is failing with storage timed out, what you can think next:**

    a. Convert the volume to RAID 1+0

    b. Convert the volume to RAID 5

    c. Add more disks to the existing RAID 0 volume

    d. Remove some disks from the existing RAID 0 volume

23. **Assuming a RAID volume has 10 disks, which of the following RAID levels is the most faults tolerant**

    a. RAID 5

    b. RAID 6

    c. RAID 1+0

    d. RAID 0+1

24. **Assigning a hot spare to a RAID 0 volume is:**

    a. Meaningful

    b. Meaningless

25. **My manager is planning to store some extremely critical data and given me just 4 disks. Which RAID level should I go for:**

    a. RAID 1+0

    b. RAID 0+1

    c. RAID 6

    d. RAID 5

26. **In storage virtualized environment, location of the data on physical storage is known through:**

    a. Cabling

    b. Metadata

    c. Controller

    d. Cache memory

27. **Which is not a benefit of storage virtualization?**

    a. Improved data availability

    b. Simple implementation

    c. Improved storage utilization

    d. Non-disruptive data migratio

28. **Which statement is not true for an active/passive storage**

    a. Owning controller accepts the host I/O request for the LUN

    b. LUN gets transferred to non-owning controller, if owning controller fails

    c. Non-owning controller accepts host I/O request for the LUN

    d. Mirrored cache can be disabled for a LUN

29. **Which statement is not true for an Active-Active storage?**
    a. Owning controller accepts the host I/O request for the LUN
    b. LUN gets transferred to non-owning controller, if owning controller fails
    c. Non-owning controller accepts host I/O request for the LUN
    d. Mirrored cache can be disabled for a LUN

30. **Battery backup is required mainly for:**
    a. Write cache
    b. Read cache
    c. Read and write both
    d. Read or write cache

31. **Which one of the following are true. Data read from the physical disks is also stored into read cache, because:**
    a. For faster processing of current read request
    b. In case, data is lost, can be found in cache
    c. If the host requests the same data again, the data can be supplied from cache
    d. If one controller fails, other controller can find the data in its cache

32. **In write-through technique, data is stored in cache, because:**
    a. For faster processing of write request
    b. In case, data is lost, can be found in cache
    c. If host does read request for the same data, the data can be supplied from cache
    d. If one controller fails, other controller can find the data in its cache

33. **In mirrored write-back mode, The I/O is considered to be completed once the data is written:**
    a. In owning controller's cache
    b. In non-owning controller's cache
    c. In both controller's cache
    d. To backend disks

34. **Which of the following statements is true for an active/standby storage:**
    a. Data is written to the primary controller's cache, then to the secondary controller's cache, complete status is sent to the host and then data is written to the disk
    b. Both controllers accept host requests, but only owned controller interacts with backend disks

    c. One of two controllers is in always idle state and wakes up when other controller dies.

    d. Both controllers serve I/O, but only for the LUNs that they own

35. **Which two of the following statements are true for an Asynchronous Active-Active Storage?**

    a. Data is written to the primary controller's cache, then to the secondary controller's cache, complete status is sent to the host and then data is written to the disk

    b. Both controllers accept host requests for a given LUN, but only owned controller interacts with backend disks

    c. One of two controllers is always in idle state and wakes up when other controller dies.

    d. Both controllers read and write I/O for all the LUNs irrespective of their ownership

36. **Which of the following statements are true for 'True' Active/ Active Storage?**

    a. Both controllers accept host requests for a given LUN, but only owned controller interacts with backend disks

    b. Both controllers read and write I/O for all the LUNs irrespective of their ownership

    c. One of two controllers is in idle state and wakes up when other controller dies

    d. Both controllers serve I/O, but only for the LUNs that they own

37. **Which statement is incorrect in a non-virtualized storage environment?**

    a. Entire disk is mapped to a host. This may be larger than requirement, thus wasting space

    b. Unused space cannot be used by another host

    c. Improved storage performance achieved

    d. If the disk fails, data is lost

38. **Where virtualization can be done?**

    a. At host level

    b. At network level

    c. At storage level

    d. Any of the above levels

39. **Challenges in storage virtualization implementation compared to traditional non-virtualized storage are (choose two).**

    a. Multiple level of virtualization – host, network, and storage levels

    b. Fault isolation

    c. Components are at multiple layers–hosts, network, storage controller, disks

    d. Metadata design

40. **What is hot-sparing?**

    a. A spare device to remove and replace a device manually.

    b. A spare device is available in the subsystem operation without having to remove and replace a device.

    c. A spare device to be removed and inserted into a subsystem without turning off the system.

    d. A spare device to be removed and inserted into a subsystem, when its tuned off.

41. **A technique that splits up the stored data among the available drives is called what?**

    a. Error checking and correcting

    b. Parity

    c. Striping

    d. Mirroring

42. **Mirror cache is implemented in a storage system mainly to improve:**

    a. Fault tolerant

    b. Performance

    c. Space efficiency

    d. All of the above

43. **Which of the following two statements are true for an active/passive storage?**

    a. Data is written to the primary controller's cache, then to the secondary controller's cache, complete status is sent to the host and then data is written to the disk

    b. Both controllers accept host requests for a given LUN, but only owned controller interacts with backend disks

    c. One of two controllers is always in idle state and wakes up when other controller dies.

    d. Both controllers serve I/O, but only for the LUNs that they own

44. **Which one is the default SCSI ID for SCSI HBA?**

    a. 0

    b. 1

    c. 2

    d. 7

45. **If you lose the data in cache due to some reason, what impact would you like to expect?**

    a. Your application would not read the data for sure

    b. Your application may or may not be able to read the data; depending on the lost data is just an update of existing data or a portion of required data

    c. No impact at all

46. **When metadata gets corrupted or lost, what impact would you like to expect?**

    a. Read/write operations would be prevented–storage device would become inaccessible

    b. You would not be able to read the right and expected data and write the data on right location of the physical disks

    c. No Impact at all

47. **Is it possible to have a storage device from heterogeneous storages at host-based virtualization?**

    a. Yes

    b. No

48. **One of the disks in a mirrored volume set has been removed due to drive failure. What will be the status of the volume?**

    a. Degraded

    b. Failed

    c. Missing

    d. Healthy

49. **Which of the two statements are true about stripe size?**

    a. Granularity of data that is rebuilt in case of any drive failure.

    b. Amount of data that is divided and then stored on all the drives of the array.

    c. Granularity at which data is stored on one drive of the array before subsequent data is stored on the next drive of the array.

    d. Stripe size is recommended to be close to the size of the system I/O request.

50. **LUN is logical unit of number, which represents:**
    a. The storage controller
    b. The target port of storage controller
    c. A path to a physical disk
    d. A unit of storage disk

51. **Hot-swapping is basically?**
    a. Devices are not allowed to be removed and inserted into a system
    b. Devices are allowed to be removed and inserted into a system without turning off the system
    c. Devices are only allowed to be removed and inserted into a system, when its tuned off

52. **Match the following:**

i. Virtual volume	1. JBOD
ii. LUN	2. Host server
iii. Physical disk	3. Storage system

    a. (i) - (1), (ii) - (2) and (iii) - (3)
    b. (ii) - (1), (i) - (2) and (iii) - (3)
    c. (iii) - (1), (ii) - (2) and (i) - (3)
    d. (iii) - (1), (i) - (2) and (ii) - (3)

53. **Physical disk for an LVM PV can be:**
    a. Physical disk attached directly to host via SCSI controller
    b. Logical disk of a host-based RAID controller
    c. Virtual disk carved out from an SAN based storage array.
    d. All of the above

54. **Which of the following sequence is appropriate abstraction layers of LVM:**
    a. PV -> LV -> VG -> Physical disk
    b. LV -> VG -> Physical disk -> PG
    c. Physical disk -> PV -> VG -> LV
    d. VG -> Physical disk -> PV -> LV

Descriptive questions

1. Explain advantages and disadvantages of a storage virtualization.
2. Highlight advantages of Virtual RAIDs compared to traditional RAID levels.

Quiz questions

1. What is a storage virtual volume? Why do we need it?
2. Which RAID level, between RAID 1+0 or RAID 0+1, provides better fault tolerance and why?
3. If 300 blocks of data written on a RAID 0 virtual volume with three underlying physical disks, are 1-100 blocks written to first disk, then 101-200 blocks to second disk and 201-300 blocks to third disk.
4. An organization has 14TB data to store. They bought 10 number of 1TB disks. Which RAID level administrator should select?

Glossary and key terms

- **RAID**: Redundant Array of Inexpensive Disks, a technology to enhance storage fault tolerance and performance.
- **Virtual volume**: A simulated disk drive created by storage controllers as storage for one or more hosts. The host computer sees the virtual volume as real, with the characteristics of an identical physical disk.
- **Host**: A logical entity in storage system that represents a host server. Virtual volumes are provided access to it.
- **LUN**: Logical unit number. A SCSI convention used to identify a SCSI device. The host sees a virtual volume as a LUN. The LUN number is assigned at the time of export or assigning a virtual volume to a host. The LUN at which that host will see the virtual volume. Some cases virtual volume is also referred as LUN.
- **ALUA**: Asymmetric Logical Unit Access enabled OS can determine optimized and non-optimized paths.

Join our Discord space

Join our Discord workspace for latest updates, offers, tech happenings around the world, new releases, and sessions with the authors:

https://discord.bpbonline.com

CHAPTER 4
Storage Communication Protocols

Introduction

Host systems communicate with storage systems using a standard communication protocol. **Small Computer System Interface (SCSI)** protocol is widely used by operating systems for **input/output (I/O)** operations to disk drives. Though, **Fibre Channel (FC)**, **internet SCSI (iSCSI)** and **FC over Ethernet (FCoE)** protocols are designed for storage networks, operating systems still use SCSI protocol to communicate with the disk drives over these storage network protocols.

File level NAS storage is usually accessible using common file level protocols such as SMB/CIFS and NFS.

Structure

Upon successful completion of this chapter, you will be able to learn following key areas of storage communication protocols:

- SCSI protocols
- Fabre Channel basics
- iSCSI concept
- FCoE overview
- File access protocols

Objectives

A protocol is a set of rules and guidelines for communicating data between host servers and storage systems. In this chapter, you will learn about various standard storage protocols, such as SCSI, FC, iSCSI and FCoE, NFS, and CIFS/SMB. This includes how data gets transferred between host server and storage system during read and write operation using each protocol.

SCSI protocol

SCSI, is a set of *American National Standards Institute* (*ANSI*) standard electronic interfaces that allow host servers to communicate with storage device.

T10 (**https://www.t10.org/**) is responsible for SCSI architecture and SCSI command set standards. These standards are used by almost all the modern I/O interfaces.

In SCSI communication, host server is always initiator and storage is target. Any single request is initiated by host server. Storage being target always responds to initiator's request.

- **Initiator**: An initiator issues requests for service by the SCSI device and receives responses. Initiators come in a variety of forms and may be integrated into a server's system board or exist within a **host bus adapter** (**HBA**).

- **Target**: SCSI target is typically a storage device. The target can be a hard disk or an entire storage array.

SCSI command descriptor block

The SCSI **command descriptor block** (**CDB**) is a block of information that describes the SCSI command. Commands are sent from SCSI initiators to SCSI targets, which are controllers of some type of storage device (hard disk, tape drive, and so on). Almost every CDB contains three parts:

1. What field
2. Where field and
3. How Much field

For some commands, these fields are implied or not required.

The **What** field is called the **operation code** (**opcode**) and tells the target what the command is supposed to do. A couple of examples would be READ or WRITE. The READ command moves data from the storage device to the host system, while the WRITE command moves data to the storage device for later access.

The **Where** field tells the target where to begin the operation and is expressed as a **Logical Block Address** (**LBA**). This address ranges from zero (0) to the maximum address of the device. Some commands, such as INQUIRY, do not require this field.

The **How Much** field tells the target, how many blocks (or bytes) or data to move. The block size of most storage devices is 512 bytes, but in certain storage devices, the block size can be different. This field is expressed as either transfer length (in blocks), allocation length (bytes moving to the host), or parameter list length (bytes moving to the device). Which name is used, depends on the command itself?

SCSI addressing

In SCSI bus each device is identified with a unique address such as **Bus, Target and LUN** (**B.T.L**). Following is an example simple DAS:

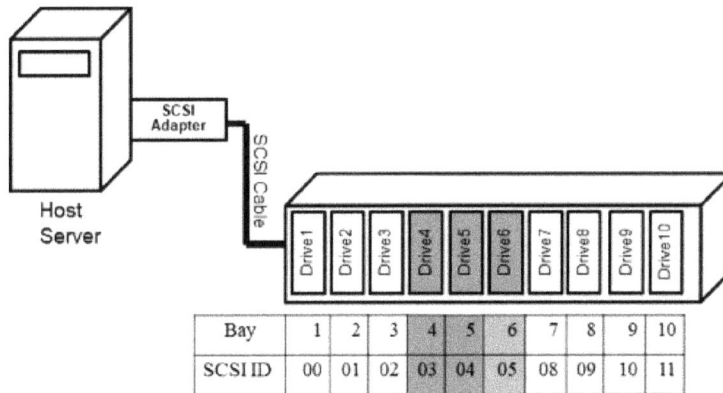

Bay	1	2	3	4	5	6	7	8	9	10
SCSI ID	00	01	02	03	04	05	08	09	10	11

Figure 4.1: SCSI address in a DAS

If only filled highlighted slots have disks drive installed:

```
> show device list (Equivalent command)
```

Device	Name	Bus	Target	LUN
Disk1		1	03	0
Disk2		1	04	0
Disk3		1	05	0

- Bus value is assigned by the operating system based on PCI slot order of the server
- SCSI ID 6 and 7 are reserved for SCSI adapter. Typically SCSI adapter has default SCSI ID 7 assigned.

In case of SAN environment, bus value is assigned based on PCI slot, in which HBA is installed. Target values are based on controller port and LUN ID are the values assigned during presentation or export of the storage volume using management software.

Some SCSI adapter or HBA have more than one port, called **channel**. To support this, some operating system or SCSI driver use four parameters for SCSI addressing **Host:Channel:Target:LUN (H:C:T:L)**. In this case, bus is referred as **channel**.

Channel value is zero, if its not applicable. In that case, the host number becomes the bus.

There are three primary phases of an SCSI operation:

- **Command**: Initiator sends commands and parameters via CDB.

- **Exchange data**: Transfer data. Mainly used during read or write operations. There are some SCSI commands, such as **Test Unit Ready (TUR)**, do not use data stage.

- **Status**: Receive confirmation of the command executed.

SCSI protocol write request example

A server communicates with a storage array via a protocol known as the **SCSI protocol**:

1. Server sends a SCSI write request to the array. The write request tells the array, what size the I/O will be.

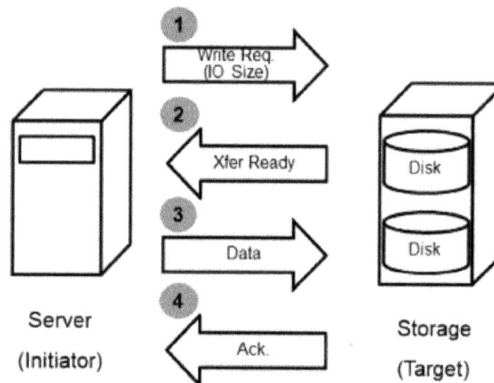

Figure 4.2: SCSI write request

2. When the array is ready to receive the data, it sends a transfer ready to the server.
3. The server sends the data.
4. The array acknowledges the receipt of the data.

SCSI protocol: Read request example

A server communicates with a storage array via a protocol known as the SCSI protocol:

1. Server sends SCSI read request to the array (the read request telling the array what size the I/O will be and what data is being requested via a block address range).

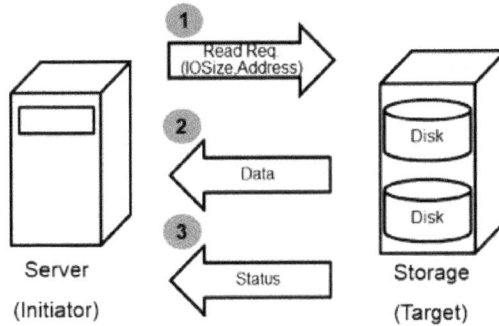

Figure 4.3: *SCSI read request*

2. The array retrieves the data and sends it to the server.

3. Array returns status upon completion.

Host I/O timeout

Host applications and operating systems are designed to retry read/write I/O requests in case of delay in response from storage system. These retries are performed for a specific period of time. This time period is called host I/O timeout for the application or the operating system.

Parallel SCSI vs. serial SCSI

Two major disadvantages with parallel SCSI are, at a faster bus speed, it becomes more difficult to manage the complex signaling and prevent data corruption. When you send signals across a parallel bus, there is no guarantee that they will all arrive at their destination at the same time. Hence, 80MHz of Ultra320 SCSI is the highest achievable transmission rate in parallel SCSI. Secondly, to ensure data integrity, the maximum cable length for single-ended SCSI decreases by half each time the signal speed doubles.

In serial SCSI , changing from 8 bit or 16 bit data transfer widths to one bit at a time might seem like a step backwards. However, the dramatic increase in speed allowed by serial communication reverses this bandwidth loss.

Serial SCSI includes the SAS and **Serial Advanced Technology Attachment (SATA)** solutions. Following are some differences between parallel SCSI and serial SCSI:

	Parallel SCSI	**Serial SCSI (Serial attached SCSI–SAS)**
Architecture	Parallel, all devices connected to share bus.	Serial, point-to-point, discrete signal paths. Port expander 1 used for fan-out.

	Parallel SCSI	**Serial SCSI (Serial attached SCSI–SAS)**
Performance	Max speed 320 MBps (Ultra320 SCSI). Performance degrades as devices added to shared bus. Speed shared across the entire multi-drop bus.	The basic speed is 3 Gbps, the equivalent of 300 MBps data pathway, which can be doubled to the equivalent of 600 MBps since the SAS channel is full-duplex. In addition, you can use several pathways per device to multiply the available bandwidth. Performance is maintained as more drives are added.
Scalability	Number of devices per cable limited by SCSI IDs to 8 or 16 on a single channel.	Up to 128 devices. 16,384 devices with fan-out expander.
Compatibility	Incompatible with all other drive interfaces.	Compatible with SATA.
Maximum cable length	12 meters total. Can use SCSI repeaters to exceed this limit but they are expensive.	8 meters per discrete connection; total domain cabling thousands of feet.
Cable Form Factor	Multitude of conductors adds bulk an cost.	Compact connectors and cabling save space and cost.
Device identification	Manually set; user must ensure no ID number conflicts on bus.	Worldwide unique ID set at time of manufacture uniquely identifies devices; no user action required.
Termination	Manually set; user must ensure proper installation and functionality of terminators.	Discrete signal paths enable devices to include termination by default; no user action required.

Table 4.1: Parallel SCSI vs. Serial SCSI

Fibre Channel basics

FC is a networking technology which is designed to facilitate high-speed data transfer between host servers and storage devices. T11 (**http://www.t11.org**) is a technical committee of the *InterNational Committee for Information Technology Standards* (*INCITS*) defines and maintains technical standards of FC specifications.

FC supports several common transport protocols including IP and SCSI. The support for multiple protocols allows FC to merge high-speed I/O with networking functionality in a single package. To understand FC, we must discuss the concept of a network vs. a channel.

FC carries, or encapsulates, other communication protocols, such as SCSI-3, FICON (SBCCS), IP, HiPPI, and so on. FC is like building block of a road, where SCSI-3, FICCON and others are vehicles that move the data cargo down the road.

- FC can carry multiple protocols simultaneously to support a variety of applications.
- FC is to SANs what Ethernet is to LANs and more:
  - o Ethernet just defines how data is physically transmitted
  - o Protocols like IP define the logical network
  - o FC defines both physical and logical aspects

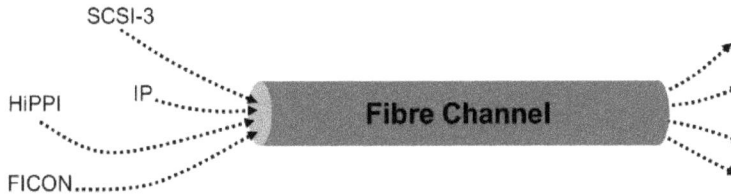

Figure 4.4: FC

Fibre Channel topologies

Fabric is logical FC network that is formed using nodes of one or two switches. There are three topologies for FC fabrics:

Point-to-point:

- Two node ports have the same signaling rate and class of service. For example, this topology gets formed when host server directly connected to storage system.

Figure 4.5: Point-to-point topology

Switched fabric:

It is the most commonly used FC topology. 16 million node ports can be interconnected. One or more FC switches can be used to build a switched fabric.

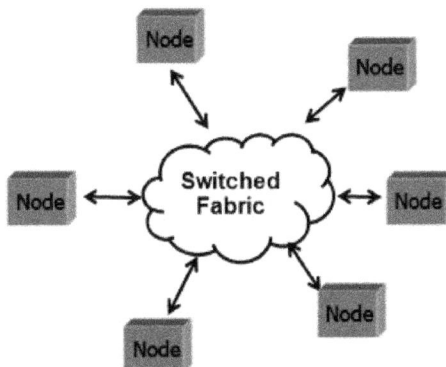

Figure 4.6: Switched fabric topology

A switched fabric can have one or more number of switches connected.

Arbitrated loop:

- Organizes up to 127 FC ports on a ring, and distributes the routing functions among them.

- **Arbitrated Loop Physical Address (AL_PA)** is 1 byte assigned during loop initialization.

- Loop initialization required when a new device is added to a loop requiring an AL_PA to be assigned to it.

- In most FC-AL hub, a bypass circuit removes the FC device out of FC-AL loop topology when signaling is lost.

- It is used less than the switched topology. Some storage systems are designed to have AL to connect all physical disks in its backend.

- It also costs less than switched topology.

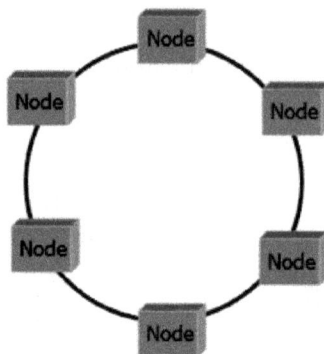

Figure 4.7: AL topology

Fibre Channel node and port type

Short name	Descriptive name	Device type	Port function
N_Port	Node port	Node	Port used to connect a node to a FC switch
F-port	Fabric port switches	Switch	Port used to connect the FC fabric to a node
L-port	Loop port nodes	Node	Port used to connect a node to a FC loop
NL-port	Node loop	Nodes	Node port which connects to both arbitrated loops and switches

Short name	Descriptive name	Device type	Port function
FL-port	Fabric + loop port	Switches	Switch port which connects to both arbitrated loops and switches
E-port	Expansion port	Switches	Used to cascade FC switches together
G-port	General port	Switches	General purpose port which can be configured to emulate other port type
U-port	Universal port	Switches	Initial port state on a switch before anything has connected and it changes personality to an operation state (E-port, F-port, FL-port) or a transitional state like a G-port

Table 4.2: FC node and port type

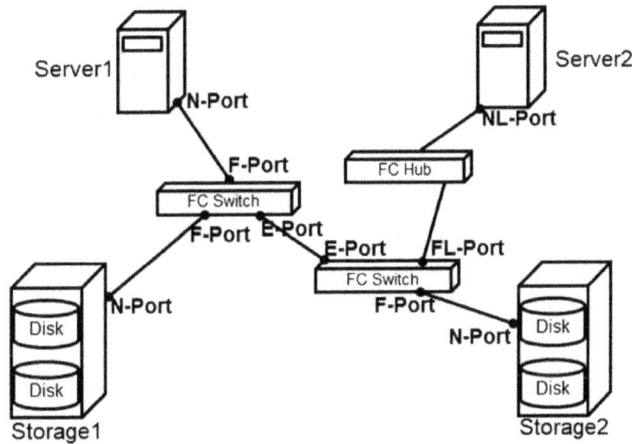

Figure 4.8: FC node and port types

Fibre Channel login processes

When N_Port device (server or storage) is connected to a switch, it sends a **fabric login (FLOGI)** request to switch to obtain **Fibre Channel ID (FCID)**. FCID in FC is like an IP address in TCP/IP network, using which it communicates with other devices in the fabric. FLOGI request is similar to DHCP client request for an IP address.

An IP address has two parts, network ID and host ID. Similarly, FCID also has two parts, domain ID, which is unique for all devices that are connected to a switch, and the port ID, which is unique to each N_Port device connected to the switch.

Login server process running in switch provides a unique FCID to each device connected to it. Similar to DHCP, server provides each network device a unique IP address.

WWPN in FC is equivalent to MAC address in network.

N_Port	F_Port	Sequence	Result
	NOS	Link not operational	
OLS→		N_Port powered-up-offline state	
	LR←	**Link reset (LR)**	
LRR→		**LR response (LRR)**	Link active
FLOGI→		Fabric login	
	ACC←	Fabric login accept	Address obtained

Table 4.3: Link reset and fabric login

After the N_Port begins the initialization process by sending OLS, the F_Port then tries to reset the port by sending a sequence of LR. The N_Port responds with a sequence of LRR. From this point on, the link is active and idles flow in both directions on the link.

Idle frames are sent continuously when no frames are being transmitted to maintain synchronization and to make the link active. In an idle transmission word the first character is a K28.5, the second is the idle character, and the last two characters are any characters that satisfy disparity. Idles are transmitted between frames.

After N_Port device completes the FLOGI process, it requires to reach other devices connected to the fabric. A service run in is called **name server**. PLOGI is used by one N_port to log in to another N_Port, open a session, and exchange service parameters. LOGO is used to terminate a login session and free its associated resources.

N_Port	F_Port	Sequence	Result
PLOGI→		Port login to name server	
	ACC←	Port login accept	
FCS→		Request directory	
	Directory←	Directory services response	
LOGO→		Logout from name server	
	ACC←	Logout accept	Directory obtained

N_Port	F_Port	Sequence	Result
PLOGI→		Port login to another N_Port	
	ACC←	Port login accept	Parameters exchanged

Table 4.4: Port login

Now, the N_Port can log in to each of the other ports and exchange service parameters. The initiator sends a PLOGI with its operating parameters. The target N_Port responds with ACC frame that specifies its own operating parameters. N_Port informs the name server of its personality and capabilities.

N_Port	F_Port	Sequence	Result
PRLI→		Process login	
	ACC←	Process login response	Communication established

Table 4.5: Process login

After successful PLOGI, N_Port knows about each of the other ports and the driver has stored their details in a parameter block, the driver in this node can open a channel with each of the other drivers associated with each node. When a channel has been successfully opened, like in the case of a SCSI initiator, opening a channel with a SCSI target, an image pair is established and communication can take place while the channel is open. If an image pair is closed by the driver when it logs out (PRLO), the image pair must be established again before further communication can take place.

PRLI establishes an FC-4 session between the originator and responder ports so that the driver's process service parameters can be exchanged between process image pairs.

PRLO terminates an existing session between an image pair and releases driver resources.

Fibre Channel layers

FC-0: Physical interface, transmission, signalling, cables/connectors

FC-1: 8b/10b encode/decode, link control, ordered set specifications

FC-2: Framing, flow control, classes, exchange/sequence management

FC-3: Application-specific layer for encryption, compression, RAID striping

FC-4: Protocol mapping of existing protocols and native FC protocols

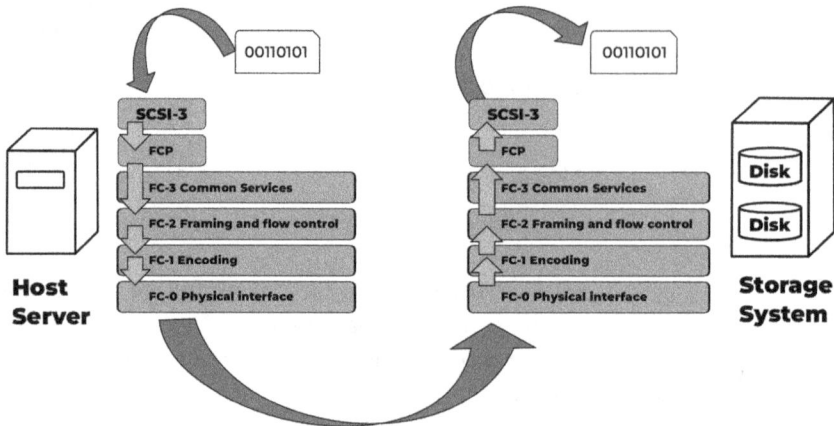

Figure 4.9: FC layers

- OX_ID   Unique 16-bit ID set by the exchange originator
- RX_ID   Unique 16-bit ID set by the exchange responder

There are multiple exchanges active at any time.

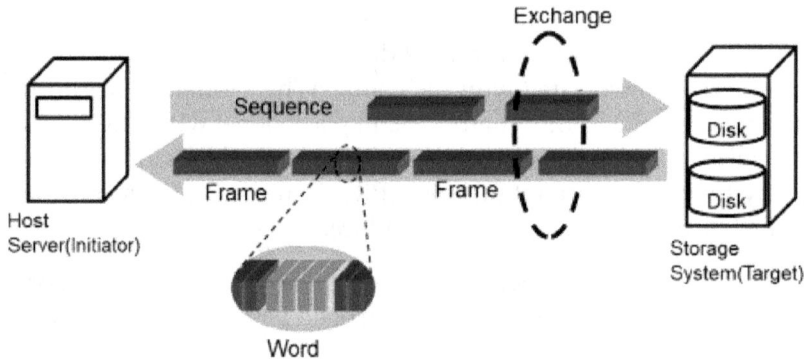

Figure 4.10: FC exchange, sequence, frame and word

Upper layer protocols (**ULPs**), such as SCSI , ESCON, and IP are mapped to the FC-4 layer for transmission:

- Information units are ULP units that are mapped into FC sequences.
- Sequences are uni-directional collections of frames making up a single group of information from one FC client to another.
- Information units consist of one or more chunks that are mapped onto frames.
- A frame consists of SOF, header, payload, CRC and EOF.
- Frames are individual units of transfer that can typically contain mapped commands or data packets from ULPs.

- The maximum frame payload size is 2112 bytes (including optional headers) with a typical maximum data payload of 2048 bytes.

- The receiving port may only be able to handle 2KB or 1KB frames, so the FC-4 layer must break up information units into correctly sized chunks for delivery by FC.

Exchanges are bi-directional groups of sequences which describe a conversation between the two nodes.

FC constructs can be compared to grammatical equivalents in the following way:

- Words are the basic unit of conversation in both speech and FC.

- Frames are complete collections of words, and relate to complete thoughts, or sentences.

- Sequences are the collection of frames in a transmission by a single sequence initiator, represented as a paragraph in written speech.

Exchanges are conversations between nodes that consist of multiple sequences:

- The exchange is the mechanism used by two FC ports to identify and manage an operation between them.

- An exchange is opened whenever an operation is started between two ports. The exchange is closed when this operation ends.

In summary, FC constructs are similar to grammatical equivalents. Word is also similar to word in any language. FC frame (36 to 2148 bytes) is equivalent to Sentence. Sequence (uni-directional) is like paragraph and exchange (bi-directional) is like conversation.

Classes of service

FC-2 provides different **classes of service** (**CoS**) for different levels of delivery guarantee, bandwidth, and connectivity. Different applications require different levels of these services.

- **Class 1**:

  Characteristics: Exclusive connection-oriented, 100% reserved bandwidth, in order frame delivery of frame, confirmed delivery

  Usage: Specialized applications; not widely supported

- **Class 2**:

  Characteristics: Frame-switched, meaning a frame or packet of data is routed to a destination based on the address in the frame or packet header, connectionless, confirmed delivery

  Usage: Clustering, OLTP

- **Class 3**:

  Characteristics: Frame-switched, connectionless, no delivery confirmation, controlled environments

  Usage: Most commonly implemented in FC fabrics today

- **Class 4**:

  Characteristics: Fractional or shared bandwidth, connection-oriented through virtual circuit, in order frame delivery and confirmed delivery

  Usage: Specialized applications, best recommended for a multi-media, such as video/audio application, not widely supported

  Note: **Class 5 is not defined.**

- **Class 6**:

  Characteristics: Multicast, meaning sending a copy of the same transmission from a single source device to multiple destination devices on a fabric, connection-oriented, in order frame delivery and confirmed delivery

  Usage: Specialized applications, not widely supported multiple CoS can co-exist within a fabric

Flow control

The concept of flow control deals with the problem where a device receives frames faster than it can process them. As a result, device is forced to drop some of the frames. In other words, flow control is a mechanism for ensuring that traffic (frames) only move when there is somewhere for them to go.

Using flow control, the receiving port indicates to the transmitting port that it can accept the next frame. The transmitting port will not transmit the next frame until it knows that the receiving port has a buffer available to accept the frame. The receiving port is always in control.

FC uses two types of built in flow control mechanisms that is **buffer-to-buffer** (**BB**) and **end-to-end** (**EE**) flow control.

- **BB**:
  - o Deals only with N_Port to F_Port or N_Port to N_Port in peer-to-peer.
  - o BB_Credit is established during login.
  - o Each port also keeps track of BB_Credit_CNT, which is initialized to 0. For each frame transmitted, BB_Credit_CNT is incremented by 1.
  - o The value is decremented by 1 for each **receiver ready** (**R_ RDY**) primitive signal received from the other port.

- o Transmission of an R_RDY indicates the port has processed a frame, freed a receive buffer, and is ready for one more.

- o If BB_Credit_CNT reaches BB_Credit, the port cannot transmit another frame until it receives an R_RDY.

- **EE**:

  - o EE flow control is not concerned with individual links, but rather the source and destination N_Ports.

  - o For all classes of service except Class 3.

  - o When the two N_Ports log into each other they exchange EE_Credit.

  - o EE_Credit_CNT is set to 0 after login and increments by 1 for each frame transmitted to the other port. It is decremented upon reception of **acknowledgement (ACK)** link control frame from that port.

  - o ACK frames can indicate the port has received and processed 1 frame, N frames, or an entire sequence of frames

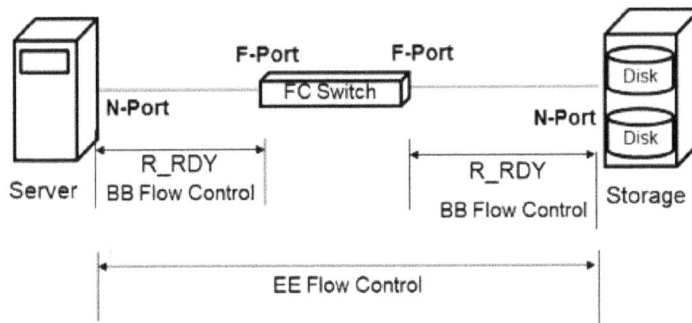

Figure 4.11: BB and EE flow control

iSCSI overview

iSCSI is an emerging industry-standard that allows SCSI block I/O protocols to be transmitted over a network using the TCP/IP protocol. Due to recent advancement of Ethernet and significant increase of operating speed, iSCSI is becoming very popular and commonly used storage communication protocol.

- IP storage networking provides solution to carry storage traffic within IP
- Uses TCP which is a reliable transport for delivery
- Applicable to local data center and long-haul applications
- Three primary protocols within IP:

  - o **Internet-SCSI (iSCSI)**: Used to transport SCSI CDBs and data within TCP/IP connections.

o   **Fibre Channel over IP (FCIP)**: used to transport FC frames within TCP/IP connections—any FC frame—not just SCSI.

o   **Internet FC Protocol (iFCP)**: Used to transport SCSI CDBs and data within TCP/IP connections.

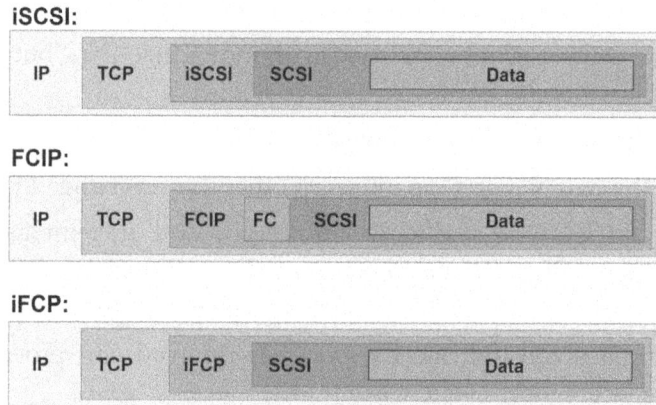

iSCSI:

IP	TCP	iSCSI	SCSI	Data

FCIP:

IP	TCP	FCIP	FC	SCSI	Data

iFCP:

IP	TCP	iFCP	SCSI	Data

Figure 4.12: iSCSI , FCIP and iFCP packets

iSCSI, FCIP and iFCP all three protocols have common IP as a network transport protocol for moving block data over IP based networks. However, iSCSI is fundamentally different from FCIP and iFCP. iFCP and FCIP are primarily used for interconnecting **storage area network (SAN)** devices to support data movement. FCIP encapsulates the entire FC frame in a TCP frame and iFCP breaks out the payload of the FC frame and encapsulates it in a TCP frame, whereas iSCSI encapsulates SCSI commands and data in a TCP frame. It does not use FC.

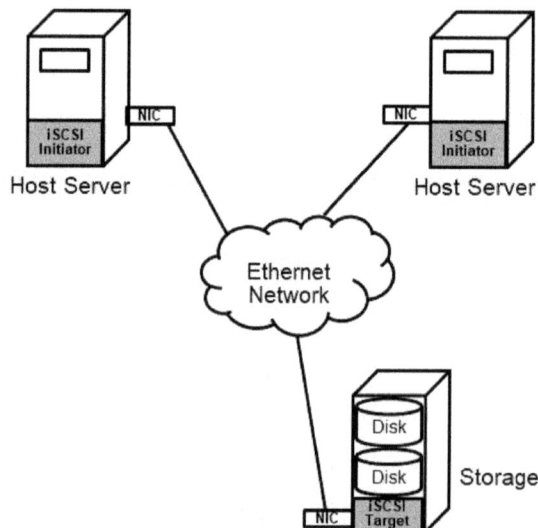

Figure 4.13: IP storage

iSCSI enables server host applications to perform traditional block-level transactions over a common IP network. It is built on two of the most commonly understood protocols: SCSI and Ethernet, the dominant standards for storage and networking. Using an ordinary IP network, iSCSI transports block-level data between an iSCSI initiator on a server and an iSCSI target on a storage device. iSCSI protocol encapsulates SCSI commands and assembles the data in packets for the TCP/IP layer. Packets are sent over the network using a point-to-point connection.

Upon arrival, the protocol translates data back to SCSI:

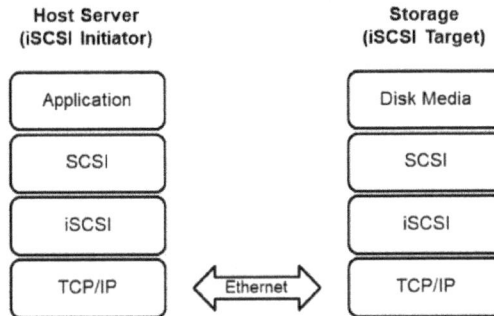

Figure 4.14: iSCSI target and initiator

iSCSI naming

Initiator and target require iSCSI names. This is also referred as iSCSI node name and SCSI device name of iSCSI device, and uses up to 255 bytes displayable strings.

There are two iSCSI name types:

- iSCSI qualified name (IQN)
- **Extended Unique Identifier (EUI)** IEEE EUI-64-also used for FC **worldwide name (WWNs)**

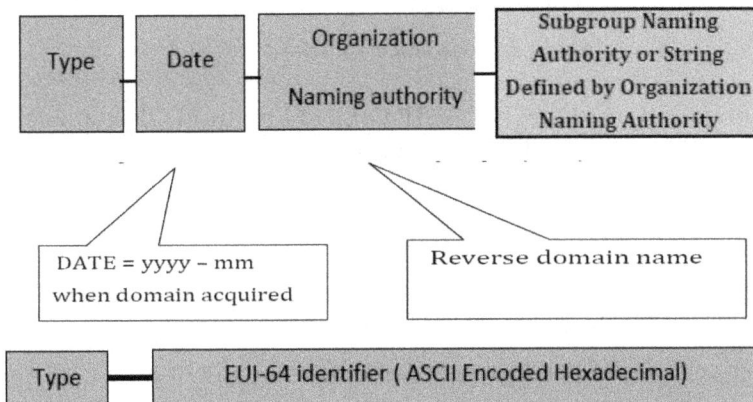

Figure 4.15: iSCSI names

Example:

- iqn.1987-05.com.domain.1234abcdef987601267da232.bet

- iqn.2001-04.com.domain.storage.tape.sys1.xyz

- eui-02004567a425678d

iSCSI initiator

There are primarily two type of iSCSI initiator:

- **Software iSCSI initiator with regular NIC**: iSCSI stack is implemented within software and runs on host server. This is a effective solution but requires more CPU and memory resources of the host. iSCSI traffic consumes CPU resources that can be utilized by the application. Most modern operating systems have in-built software iSCSI initiator built.

- **Hardware iSCSI initiator with iSCSI HBA**: iSCSI stack is implemented within adapter hardware. The adapter is called **iSCSI HBA**. All of the work associated with iSCSI is performed by the iSCSI HBA, instead of host server resources. iSCSI HBAs are more expensive than regular NIC.

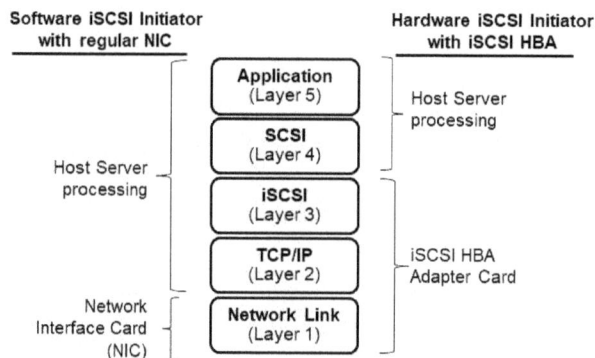

Figure 4.16: Hardware and software iSCSI

Some vendors make NIC card that is **TCP/IP Offload Engine** (**TOE**) capable, in which part of the iSCSI stack (layer 2) is implemented within the hardware.

iSNS

Internet Storage Name Service (**iSNS**) is a name registration service for IP storage devices. This is like DNS for iSCSI devices. It has the following features:

- Provides centralized management capabilities.

- iSNS server is a repository of currently active iSCSI nodes, as well as their associated portals, entities, and so on.

- Nodes can be initiators, targets, or management nodes.
- Typically, initiators and targets register with the iSNS server, and the initiators query the iSNS server for the list of available targets.

iSCSI security

There are several levels of iSCSI security available. The basic level is based on the **Challenge-Handshake Authentication Protocol (CHAP)**. CHAP is a protocol that is used to authenticate the peer of a connection and is based upon the peers sharing a secret (a security key that is similar to a password). IPsec is a protocol that enforces authentication and data encryption at the IP packet layer, which provides an added level of security.

- **One-way CHAP authentication**: With this level of security, only the target authenticates the initiator. The secret is set just for the target and all initiators that want to access that target need to use the same secret to start a logon session with the target.

- **Mutual CHAP authentication**: With this level of security, the target and the initiator authenticate each other. A separate secret is set for each target and for each initiator in SAN.

- **IPsec**: With this level of security, all IP packets sent during data transfers are encrypted and authenticated. A common key is set on all IP portals, allowing all peers to authenticate each other and negotiate packet encryption.

Non-Volatile Memory Express

Non-Volatile Memory Express (NVMe) has revolutionized the storage industry by drastically reducing latency and improving throughput. Most storage vendors have redesigned their storage systems to use EE NVMe protocol at the frontend and as well as at the backend.

Chapter 2, Storage Infrastructure, explained more about usage of NVMe protocol for disk drive interfaces at the backend of a storage system.

Majorly two transport protocols, FC and IETF **Transport Control Protocol (TCP)**, are used in the frontend to transfer data and commands between an initiator host server and a target storage system.

NVMe over FC is referred as **NVMe-oFC** or **NVMe/FC** and NVMe over TCP as **NVMe-oTCP** or **NVMe/TCP**.

Supported FC HBA and NIC with updated drive is to support NVMe/FC and NVMe/TCP respectively.

Modern enterprise storage systems support a total of four host protocols , that is, FC, iSCSI, NVMe/FC and NVMe/TCP. The following figure depicts infrastructure for all types of hosts, though an organization may not have requirement of deploying all types of hosts together.

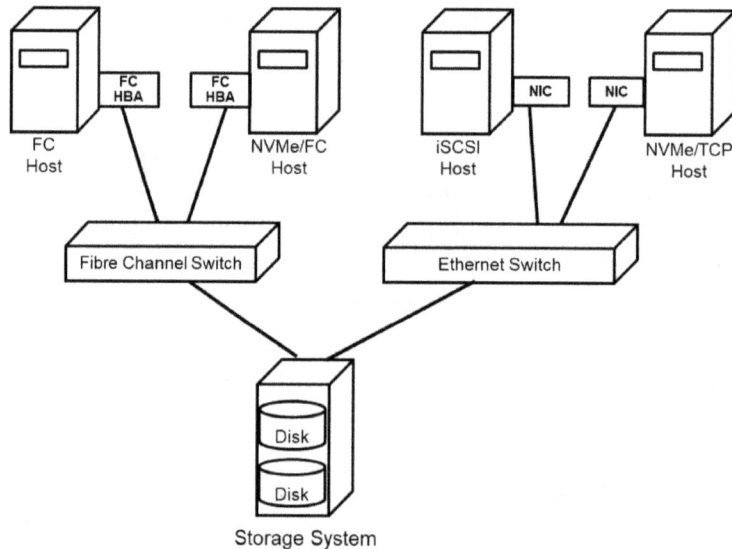

Figure 4.17: *Host types based on communication protocol*

Host type	Infrastructure	Transport protocol	Data protocol	Initiator and target identification	Storage volume identification
FC	FC	FC	SCSI (FCP)	WWN	**Logical unit number ID (LUN ID)**
iSCSI	Ethernet	TCP	SCSI	IQNs	LUN ID
NVMe/FC	FC	FC	NVMe	NQNs	**Namespace ID (NSID)**
NVMe/ TCP	Ethernet	TCP	NVMe	NQNs	NSID

Table 4.6: *Transport and data communication protocols*

NVMe is an emerging technology. The main advantage of NVMe is 64K queues per controller, which reduces latency. Since, it does not need any additional infrastructure, most organizations are migrating to NVMe environment.

FCoE overview

FCoE solves the problem of organizations having to run parallel network infrastructures for their Lans and their SANs. As a result, they have to operate separate switches, HBAs, NICs and cables for each of these networks. Even utilizing a virtualization solution like

VMware can actually increase the number of network adapters required to carry traffic out of the servers.

FCoE reduces cards and cabling

With so many NICs, HBAs, switches and cables to deal with, both capital and operational costs to run a data center can increase significantly. FCoE represents a way to drastically reduce the number of cards, switches, adapters, and assorted cabling by running LANs and SANs over the same infrastructure. According to analyst firm, **Enterprise Strategy Group (ESG)**, FCoE works out considerably cheaper to deploy than traditional networks due to reduced hardware costs.

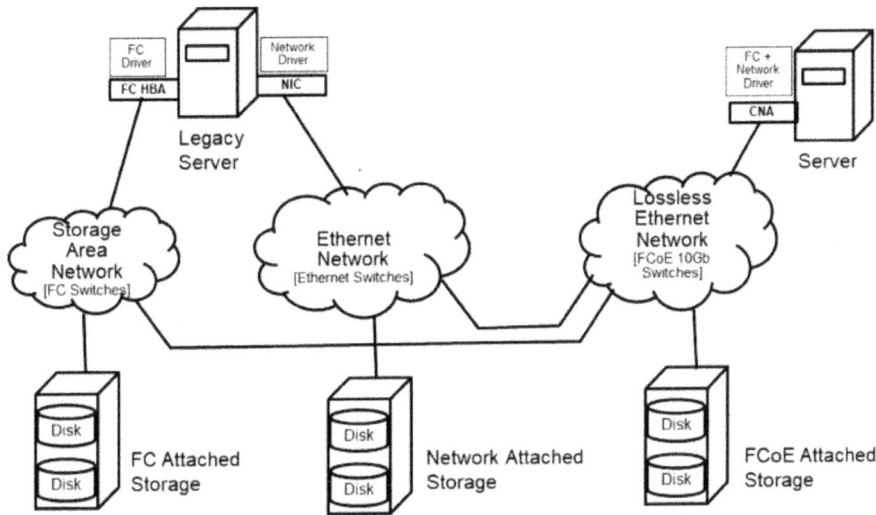

Figure 4.18: *FC/iSCSI vs. FCoE*

To look at it in another way, FCoE is a standard for using the FC protocol (which is the mainstay of the SAN) over Ethernet networks (the mainstay of the computer networks, both wired and wireless). FCoE provides a way to transport FC SAN traffic over Ethernet, eliminating the need for a separate storage network.

To understand FCoE, it is important to grasp the two key definitions that form the terms FC and Ethernet.

Fibre Channel

FC is a serial data transfer protocol and standard for high-speed enterprise-grade storage networking. It supports data rates up to 10 Gbps and delivers storage data over fast optical networks. Basically, FC is the language through which storage devices such as HBAs, switches and controllers can communicate.

Ethernet

Ethernet is an architecture developed almost 40 years ago for LANs. In its early days, it supported up to 10 Mbps. However, more recently this has been extended to 1 Gbps, 10 Gbps and more. Ethernet is essentially a transfer medium enabling data to travel along cables or wirelessly in units known as **frames**.

FCoE technology

FCoE is basically a way to map FC over full-duplex Ethernet networks based on the *Institute of Electrical and Electronic Engineers* (*IEEE*) 802.3 standard. As well as consolidating I/O, it is an effective way of reducing complexity by eliminating the necessity of establishing and running parallel networks for storage and networking.

The technology can be deployed in a **top-of-the-rack** (**ToR**) configuration: FCoE-enabled switch sits on the top of the rack and takes the place of FC switch and an Ethernet switch. This configuration would assume the use of **converged network adapters** (**CNAs**) or a universal **LAN on motherboard** (**LOM**) that is capable of supporting FCoE.

If warranted, redundant connections can be established using at least two FCoE connections for each server to the ToR FCoE switch. This would take the place of two FC and two Ethernet connections per server for redundancy purposes. The ToR switch would then send the Ethernet traffic to the LAN and the FC traffic to the SAN.

As well as ToR switches, FCoE is also available in other formats, such as blades that plug into the storage backbone. and at the server level, CNAs for FCoE can replace FC HBAs and Ethernet NICs, along with associated cabling. Both protocols can be supported on the same port. In terms of the overall network stack, FCoE routes FC traffic at the link layer, and also uses Ethernet to transmit the FC protocol.

Overall, the move toward FCoE is seen as part of an overall trend toward network convergence. In recent times, we have seen convergence in such areas as voice and data. Formerly, telecom utilized one network to carry phone lines and another line for computerized data traffic. This has converged using **Voice over Internet Protocol** (**VoIP**) as a means of cutting down on network clutter and unifying traffic.

The same basic trend is now beginning to take effect in storage, where more and more hardware can accommodate converged networks. Servers, for example, are available with universal connectivity adaptors that are able to handle almost any Ethernet-based protocol either via chips on the motherboard or through adapter cards. Eventually, storage networks may converge completely with Ethernet. but for now, both converged and dedicated storage networks remain widely.

File access protocols

NAS devices typically leverage existing IP networks for connectivity, enabling companies to reduce the price of entry for access to shared storage.

RAID and clustering capabilities inherent to modern enterprise NAS devices offer greatly improved availability when compared with traditional DAS.

It is because NAS devices control the file system, they offer increased flexibility when using advanced storage features such as snapshots.

With 10GE connectivity, NAS devices can offer performance on par with many currently installed FC SANs.

NFS/CIFS (NAS) storage protocol are designed to accept host requests like **create-file-Mywork.doc** or **read-file-Office.xls**.

NFS is a distributed file system protocol originally developed by *Sun Microsystems* in 1984, allowing a user on a client computer to access files over a network in a manner similar to how local storage is accessed. On the contrary, CIFS is its Windows-based counterpart used in file sharing.

NFS using advisory locks locking implementation, a process can read and write to a file while it is locked. However, there is a way for a process to check for the existence of a lock before a read or write.

NAS, in contrast to SAN, uses file-based protocols such as NFS or SMB/CIFS, where it is clear that the storage is remote, and computers request a portion of an abstract file rather than a disk block. The key difference between DAS and NAS is that DAS is simply an extension to an existing server and is not necessarily networked. NAS is designed as an easy and self-contained solution for sharing files over the network.

Scale out NAS is a type of file level storage that incorporates a distributed file system that can scale a single volume with a single namespace across many nodes. Scale out NAS file level storage solutions can scale up to several PBs all while handling thousands of clients. As capacity is scaled out, performance is scaled up.

Conclusion

Host system and storage systems are designed to use standard protocol to communicate each other. Host systems and storages can be from the different vendor as long as they both support the standard protocol, like SCSI , FC, iSCSI , and FCoE for block storage and NFS and CIFS/SMB for file storage. Though, over the network client system uses NFS or CIFS to read or write shared files, within the file storage, SCSI protocol used to eventually write data on to the disk drive.

SCSI is the fundamental protocol used for initiator to perform read/write, FC, iSCSI and FCoE are transport protocol that encapsulate the SCSI packet with it for transporting the data.

FC is a carries for other protocols like SCSI, FICON, IP or HiPPi. FC is like Ethernet in LAN. It defines how data needs to be transmitted. It supports both media option that is copper cables or optical cables. There are two types of fibre cables that is multimode and single-mode.

Multimode cables are used usually for short distance, for example, connecting equipment within a rack, whereas single-mode cables are used for long distance, for example, two building within a city or a locality.

iSCSI is an emerging industry-wide popular SCSI block I/O protocols to be transmitted over a IP network. It encapsulate SCSI packet inside IP frame and transmits data between instar and target devices.

File level NAS storage use file level protocols such as SMB/CIFS and NFS for I/O operation within shared files.

Case studies

Case study 1: Identifying SCSI disks in Linux host with DAS solution

Let us identify SCSI disks in Linux host with DAS solution:

Requirement

In DAS solution, JBOD is connected to Linux host server via SCSI adapter. JBOD has total four disk drives in alternate bay starting from first bay. Disk in first bay has OS installed. Provide steps to identify disk in operating system, so that file system can be configured on them.

Analysis

As described in following figure, each disk connected via SCSI adapter has a unique SCSI ID. SCSI ID depends on the bay position in JBOD.

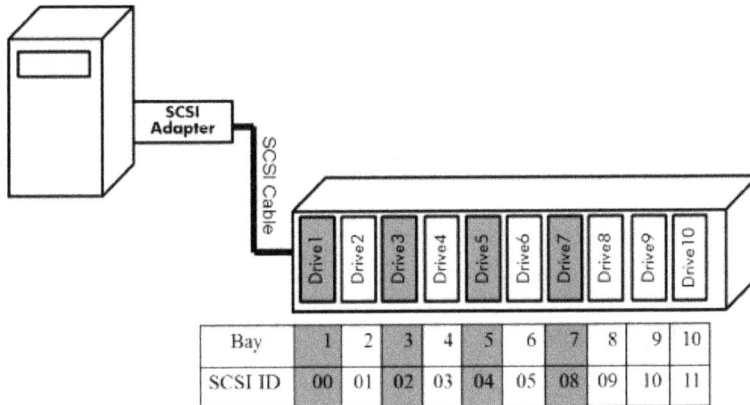

Figure 4.19: *Identifying disks in a DAS*

There are several ways to list storage devices in Linux. lsscsi is one of the a commonly used utility to get details of SCSI devices along with their B.T.L details.

Solution

```
[root@ localhost ~]# lsscsi
```

```
[2:0:0:0]disk VENDORNAME MK5061GS MF00 /dev/sda [2:0:2:0] disk VENDORNAME
MK6072FH MF00 /dev/sdb [2:0:4:0] disk VENDORNAME MK5033KS MF00 /dev/sdc
[2:0:8:0] disk VENDORNAME MK5034KS MF00 /dev/sdd
```

```
[root@localhost ~]#
```

As channel value is 0, here, bus value is 2 for the SCSI adapter installed in host server. Bus value depends on PCI slot of the host server in which this SCSI adapter is installed. If second SCSI adapter was installed in the server, another bus value would have got assigned to it.

0, 2, 4 and 8 are target values. Target value is also referred as SCSI ID. It depends on bay position of the disk in the JBOD. 0 corresponds to disk in bay # 1, 1 for bay 2, and so on. SCSI ID 6 and 7 are reserved for SCSI adapter.

Case study 2: Fibre Channel node and port types for storage devices in SAN environment

Let us look at fibre channel node and port types for storage devices in SAN environment:

Requirement

Two FC switches connected via a cable. Host server connected to first switch and storage to second switch. A tape device connected to FC hub, switch connected to second switch. Draw the SAN diagram along with FC node and port type.

Analysis

As per *Table 4.2* FC port type depends on the device type and the network type to which it is connected. For example, 2 FC switches are connected via E-ports. N_Port is a node port that is connected to a FC switch. F-port is a switch port that is connected to FC fabric. Again L-port is node port that is connected to FC loop.

Solutions

Following figure shows all devices mentioned along with their connectivity. FC each port is labeled with the FC port type.

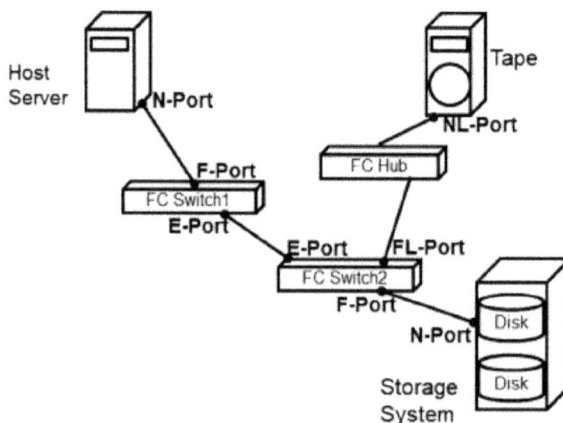

Figure 4.20: FC node and port type

Case study 3: Cost effective high performance storage solution

Let us look at cost effective high performance storage solution:

Requirement

Your company is looking for a cost effective high performance storage solution for database application. Primarily looking for leveraging existing network infrastructure. Describe the solution that is suitable for this requirement.

Analysis

Block storage systems are most suitable for database application. High performance block storage can only be implemented either with FC or iSCSI transport protocol. There are three primary reasons that iSCSI storage environments have become popular in recent days.

- iSCSI uses Ethernet as its underlying communications fabric. Leveraging this technology avoids the need to build separate infrastructures, including switches, cables connectors, and so on.

- iSCSI is much less expensive than FC and operates at speeds of 10Gbps, 25Gbps and 40Gbps, and 100Gbps.

- iSCSI advances along with Ethernet.

Solution

iSCSI storage solution can be proposed for high performance block level storage access. It is also a cost effective solution. It uses standard Ethernet switches and cabling. Refer to *figure 4.13* for schematic diagram of the proposed solution.

Learning check
Objective questions

1. **N_Port device can be member of two separate zones:**
   a. Yes
   b. No

2. **Sequence of login for FC login processes:**
   a. Process login (PRLI), port login (PLOGI), fabric login (FLOGI)
   b. Port login (PLOGI), process login (PRLI), fabric login (FLOGI)
   c. Fabric login (FLOGI), port login (PLOGI), process login (PRLI)
   d. Fabric login(FLOGI), process login(PRLI), port login (PLOGI)

3. **During which Login process N_Port informs the fabric name server of its personality and capabilities?**
   a. Port login (PLOGI)
   b. Process login (PRLI)
   c. Fabric login (FLOGI)
   d. Process logout (PLOGO)

4. **Process login can only be between:**
   a. Two switch ports
   b. Two initiators
   c. Two targets
   d. One pair of initiator and target

5. **As per standard, maximum of how many bytes can be accommodated within a FC frame?**

   a. 2048 bytes

   b. 2112 bytes

   c. 2011 bytes

   d. 1024 bytes

6. **Which of the following statements is related to an exchange is incorrect?**

   a. Multiple exchanges are active at any given time between initiator and target

   b. An exchange has unique identification number

   c. Always two exchanges are active at any given time between initiator and target

   d. Multiple exchanges may occur within a single login session

7. **Originator exchange ID (OX_ID) and responder exchange ID (RX_ID) are:**

   a. 16 bit

   b. 32 bit

   c. 64 bit

   d. 128 bit

8. **Fibre Channel address has:**

   a. 16 bit

   b. 24 bit

   c. 32 bit

   d. 40 bit

9. **During speed negotiation, each port starts with:**

   a. Lower speed, then steps up to higher

   b. Higher speed, then steps down to lower

   c. Randomly selects the speeds

   d. Depends on vendor's implementation

10. **Which of the following statements related to an idle is incorrect?**

    a. Idles are sent continuously when no frames are being transmitted to maintain synchronization and to make the link active

    b. Idle frame has all zero bits

    c. In an idle transmission word, the first character is K28.5, the second is the idle character, and the last two characters are any characters that satisfy disparity

d. Idles are transmitted between frames

11. **Which one of the following list the three FC topologies used with storage systems solutions?**

a. Parallel-to-serial, SCSI IDs, and switched fabric

b. Point-to-point, arbitrated loop, and switched fabric

c. Point-to-point, arbitrated loop, and RAID 0

d. Point-to-point, fabric arbitrated loop, and storage fabric

12. **Which port type can connect nodes to other nodes in an arbitrated loop?**

a. NL-port

b. FL-port

c. G-port

d. E-port

13. **A unique 8 byte (64 bit) address that is encoded into each port by the manufacturer is called:**

a. AL_PA

b. Port ID

c. WWN

d. Simple name server

14. **What is the function of E_port on FC switch?**

a. Contains the Link_Control_Facility

b. Contains the arbitrated loop functions

c. Acts as a generic switch port

d. Connects fabric switches together

15. **Which FC topology supports up to 127 nodes on a single loop?**

a. Point-to-point

b. Switched fabric

c. Arbitrated loop

16. **What are the two methods of electrical signaling in a SCSI environment?**

a. Single-ended and differential

b. Single-ended and external

c. Single-ended and low voltage

d. Low voltage and differential

17. **What is the maximum data transfer rate of Wide Ultra3?**

    a. 20 Mbps

    b. 40 MBps

    c. 60 MBps

    d. 160 MBps

18. **Performance and security provided by FC is better than iSCSI:**

    a. True

    b. False

19. **Data transfer across FC is achieved through use of packets, instead of frames of data:**

    a. True

    b. False

20. **iSCSI , through Ethernet and IP, allows enterprises to deploy a single network infrastructure that is ubiquitous, widely understood, and costs less than FC:**

    a. True

    b. False

21. **Which technical committee within INCITS is responsible for FC standards development?**

    a. T-11

    b. T-10

    c. ANSI

    d. T-13

    e. IEEE

22. **Which statement is true during read operations?**

    a. I/O size is communicated by storage during sending data

    b. Storage sends transfer ready to the server before sending data

    c. Server tells storage the block address range of data during initial SCSI read request

    d. The server acknowledges receive of data from storage

23. **The Internet SCSI (iSCSI) protocol defines a means to enable _____ storage applications over TCP/IP networks.**

    a. Block

    b. File

    c. Disparate

    d. Highly available

24. **iSCSI is an emerging industry-standard that allows _____ to be transmitted over a network using the TCP/IP protocol.**

    a. SCSI file I/O protocols

    b. SCSI block I/O protocols

25. **Which entity consists of software drivers that initiate the SCSI request over IP to a target server**

    a. iSCSI initiator

    b. iSCSI target

    c. iSCSI terminator

26. **The basic system model for iSCSI is that of an extended virtual cable, connecting a SCSI initiator device to a SCSI target device.**

    a. True

    b. False

27. **What two elements generate a unique network address for iSCSI device?**

    a. The MAC address and the node IP address

    b. The node IP address and the TCP port number

    c. The TCP port number and the MAC address

28. **How many parts are there in the standard IQN iSCSI name?**

    a. Two

    b. Three

    c. Four

29. **How far apart can FC devices be, if optical fibre is used as the physical medium?**

    a. 1 km

    b. 5 km

    c. 10 km

    d. 15 km

30. **Which FC layer transfers frame formats, performs sequence and exchange management, controls the flow of data, and administers the topologies?**

    a. FC-1

    b. FC-2

   c. FC-3

   d. FC-4

31. **What is the maximum FC frame size?**

   a. 512 bytes

   b. 1024 bytes

   c. 2148 bytes

   d. 4296 bytes

32. **In which topology, SAN devices are connected in the form of a ring?**

   a. Point-to-point

   b. Arbitrated loop

   c. Switched fabric

33. **What are the components of a frame?**

   a. SOF, header, payload, CRC, and EOF

   b. SOF, header, SCS, CRC, and EOF

   c. SOF, CLS, payload, CRC, and EOF

34. **What is the size of the AL_PA address that identifies a port?**

   a. 8 bit

   b. 16 bit

   c. 24 bit

   d. 32 bit

35. **What process must be executed when a new device is added to a loop requiring AL_PA to be assigned to it?**

   a. Loop master selection

   b. AL_PA assignment

   c. Position mapping

   d. Loop initialization

36. **What is a public loop?**

   a. A loop that is inaccessible to other nodes that are not a part of the loop

   b. A loop that is not a part of the SAN fabric

   c. A loop that is not connected to any other loop

   d. A loop with an active FL_Port

37. **How many NL_Ports can a private loop accommodate?**

    a. Up to 32

    b. Up to 64

    c. Up to 127

    d. Up to 252

38. **A switched fabric can connect up to how many nodes?**

    a. 127

    b. 227

    c. 8 million

    d. 16 million

39. **Which statement correctly describes fabric login?**

    a. This is performed on every N_Port in the environment with which the N_Port communicates.

    b. This determines network parameters and is done once or twice depending on whether the fabric can assign port identifiers.

    c. This is performed on every L_Port in the environment with which the NL_Port communicates.

40. **Which is the correct statement when comparing serial SCSI with parallel SCSI?**

    a. To ensure data integrity, the maximum cable length for serial SCSI decreases by half each time the signal speed doubles.

    b. When you send signals across a parallel bus, there is no that they will all arrive at their destination at the same time. Hence, at a faster bus speed, it becomes more difficult to manage the complex signaling and prevent data corruption.

    c. In serial SCSI, all devices connected to a shared bus. Whereas in parallel, communication is mainly based on point-to-point.

    d. In Serial SCSI, device identification is manually set; user must ensure no ID number conflicts on bus. In parallel SCSI, the worldwide unique ID set at time of manufacture; no user action required.

41. **CIFS is an abbreviation of which of the following?**

    a. Converged Infrastructure File System

    b. Close Interface File System

    c. Cisco Internet File System

    d. Common Internet File System

42. **Which are two most commonly implemented file I/O protocols in NAS storage system?**

    a. NFS

    b. NTFS

    c. CIFS

    d. UFS

43. **Which protocols provide file locking mechanism to ensure that two or more users do not attempt to modify the same file simultaneously?**

    a. CIFS

    b. NFS

    c. UFS

    d. NTFS

44. **In which locking implementation, a process can read and write to a file while it is locked. However, there is a way for a process to check for the existence of a lock before a read or write?**

    a. CIFS using ACLs

    b. NFS using advisory locks

    c. UFS using ACL

    d. NTFS using ACL

45. **Which is not used as a file access protocol in NAS?**

    a. Network File System

    b. Common Internet File System

    c. Unix file system

    d. Netware communication protocol

    e. AppleTalk filing protocol

46. **What is the real difference between NAS and NFS or, why pick a NAS device over mere NFS?**

    a. Better performance

    b. Enhanced file security

    c. Much better scalability

    d. All of the above

47. **Which of the following statements is false about iSCSI?**

    a. iSCSI PDU can span multiple IP packets

    b. Two iSCSI PDU's can be sent in a single IP packet

    c. iSCSI session can span multiple TCP connections

    d. All of the above statements are false

48. **Which of the following SCSI bus phases is used to select the LUN to which a SCSI command is sent from initiator to target on a SCSI bus?**

    a. ARBITRATION

    b. SELECTION

    c. MESSAGE OUT

    d. COMMAND OUT

    e. STATUS IN

    f. DATA IN

49. **For an initiator host, iSCSI has more CPU utilization compared to FC. This statement is:**

    a. True

    b. False

50. **Which of the following statements is false about iSCSI?**

    a. iSCSI node name is independent of it is IP address

    b. iSCSI node can have multiple IP addresses

    c. IP address in iSCSI node cannot be changed

    d. In iSCSI network entity, there can be multiple iSCSI nodes, each node representing a target

51. **Which of the following is generally not true about NFS?**

    a. NFS can run both over TCP and UDP

    b. NFS security is weak

    c. NFS advisory locking is not enforced by operating system

    d. NFS is a stateful protocol

52. **Which of the following is not the role of SCSI target device?**

    a. May arbitrate and reselect an initiator for purpose of continuing SCSI operation that was previously suspended

    b. Controls the entire process after being successfully selected by initiator

    c. Originates SCSI command operations after arbitrating for the SCSI bus

    d. Returns the status byte for every SCSI operation that requests data to be transferred

53. **Which of the following statements is true about SAS and SATA drives?**

    a. SAS drives offer high performance, high reliability for mission critical environments

    b. SATA drives are ideal for non-mission critical, low workload environments

    c. Systems are capable of supporting both SATA and SAS drives on a single SAS backplane

    d. All of the above

54. **Verify the statement: In serial protocols like SATA or SAS, the clock is part of the data am compared to parallel SCSI bus where the clock is a separate line on the bus.**

    a. True

    b. False

55. **Which of the following statements is false about SAS?**

    a. SAS is a point-to-point architecture

    b. SAS has scalable performance

    c. SAS provides a data transfer speed of up to 6 Gbps

    d. SAS does not support worldwide name addressing

56. **Which of the following statements is false about SATA?**

    a. SATA is a serial version of the IDE/ATA specification and it uses the ATAPI command specs

    b. SATA devices are hot-pluggable

    c. SATA is a point-to-point architecture

    d. SATA devices can accept SCSI commands

57. **Which storage protocol can accept host requests like FileA.doc or FileB.xls?**

    a. iSCSI

    b. NFS/CIFS (NAS)

    c. FC-SAN

    d. All of the above

58. **Which two storages from the following can accept host requests like read-block-fifty-five or write-block-four-thousand-and-three?**

    a. iSCSI

    b. NFS/CIFS (NAS)

    c. FC-SAN

59. **iSCSI initiator cannot connect to an iSCSI target's network portal. What could be the problem? Select all choices that apply.**

    a. Wrong IP address or TCP port number

    b. No IP route from the initiator to the target portal

    c. No IP route from the target portal back to the initiator

    d. Initiator is not on the access control list of the target

60. **iSCSI initiator connects to an iSCSI target network portal but does not find any targets. What could be the problem? Select all choices that apply.**

    a. No targets are configured on the storage array

    b. Initiator is not on the access control list of any targets in the array

    c. None of the above

61. **An Active-Active storage array has two storage controllers. Each storage controller has 2 iSCSI ports. Controller A's ports are SA0 and SA1. Similarly controller B's ports are SB0 and SB1. An iSCSI target node is defined on this system with just one portal group.**

    Which portals could be defined in this portal group to ensure redundant multipathing for a host that needs to access this target? Select all choices that apply.

    a. SA0, SB0

    b. SA0, SB1

    c. SA0, SA1

    d. SB0, SA1

62. **Which CoS is most commonly implemented in FC fabrics today?**

    a. Class 1

    b. Class 2

    c. Class 3

    d. Class 4

63. **What functionality is provided in both Class 2 and Class 3 classes of service in FC? Select all choices that apply.**

    a. Connectionless

    b. Acknowledged

    c. In order delivery of frames guaranteed

    d. Bandwidth is guaranteed

64. **What is the difference between Class 1 and Class 4 services in FC? Select all choices that apply.**

    a. Class 1 uses dedicated circuit, Class 4 uses virtual circuit

    b. Class 1 uses 100% bandwidth of an N_Port, Class4 allows sharing of bandwidth of an N_Port for multiple connections

    c. Class 4 does not support in-order delivery of frames

    d. None of the above

65. **If all classes of services were implemented by FC vendor in their switches, which of the following could be best recommended for a multi-media (video/audio) application while at the same time not wasting bandwidth?**

    a. Class 1

    b. Class 2

    c. Class 3

    d. Class 4

66. **Which of the following classes of service in FC could be best recommended for an application requiring multi-cast functionality?**

    a. Class 2

    b. Class 3

    c. Class 4

    d. Class 6

67. **With FC-AL Hub, if one of the nodes ports on the loop malfunctions or is shut down, will the arbitrated loop be broken?**

    a. Yes

    b. No

68. **What process must be executed when a new device is added to a loop requiring AL_PA to be assigned to it?**

    a. Loop master selection

    b. AL_PA assignment

c. Position mapping

d. Loop initialization

69. **BB flow control is used in FC between:**

    a. N_Ports

    b. E-ports

    c. N_Port and F-port

    d. All of the above

70. **End-to-end flow control is used in FC between:**

    a. N_Ports

    b. E-ports

    c. N_Port and F-port

    d. All of the above

71. **Properties of a storage LUN in an OS shows B.T.L as 3-2-1. Due to some reason, PCI slot of the server where HBA was installed is not working, you had to put it in different PCI slot. Now, when system boots up, which of the B.T.L value you expect to have different because of changing the HBA slot?**

    a. Bus

    b. Target

    c. LUN

    d. None of the above

72. **FC-iSCSI Router or iFCP router:**

    a. Puts whole FC frame into TCP/IP packet

    b. Takes out payload from FC frames and encapsulate into TCP/IP packet

    c. Sends FC frame as-is

73. **Maximum number of devices in FC arbitrated loop topologies are:**

    a. 64

    b. 127

    c. 256

    d. 512

74. **Maximum number of devices in FC point-to-point topologies are:**

    a. 16

    b. 8

   c. 4

   d. 2

75. **Theoretical maximum number of devices in FC switched fabric topologies are:**

   a. 2^8

   b. 2^{16}

   c. 2^{24}

   d. 2^{48}

76. **For which two of the following requirements, iSCSI can be recommended?**

   a. High performance and high availability for business-critical applications, usually in the corporate data center

   b. An environment consisting of midrange or low-end servers, a solution that delivers the most appropriate price/performance

   c. An environment consisting of high-end servers that require high bandwidth or data center environments with business-critical data

   d. Business applications in smaller regional or departmental data centers

77. **An iSCSI initiator discovers an iSCSI target but cannot login to the target. What might be the problem? Select all choices that apply.**

   a. No LUNs configured for the iSCSI target

   b. The maximum session count for the target may have exceeded

   c. CHAP logon information improperly configured in the iSCSI initiator

   d. The target portal might be configured on a different IP network with no network access for the initiator

78. **What is the SCSI addressing components handled by the SCSI protocol?**

   a. SCSI bus, logical unit

   b. SCSI bus, target ID, logical unit

   c. SCSI bus, target ID, adaptor number

   d. SCSI bus, adaptor number, logical unit

79. **N_Port A connected to a fabric during the fabric login process it queries the name erver provided by the directory service of the switch.**

   If the N_Port sends a request to the name server to get the list of port addresses or port names in the fabric, then the response to this request depends on the N_Ports that are soft zoned to this N_Port A.

   Is the preceding statement true?

a. Yes

b. No

80. **What is bypass circuitry in FC technology?**

a. A circuit that automatically removes the FC device out of switched fabric topology when signaling is lost

b. A fabric management service to zone out a device from an existing zone

c. A circuit that automatically removes the FC device out of FC AL loop topology when signaling is lost

81. **What advantages would using iSCSI SAN give to your organization over using DAS?**

a. Traditionally expensive SCSI controllers and SCSI disks no longer need to be used in each server, reducing overall cost

b. Increased utilization of storage resources

c. Expansion of storage space without downtime

d. All of the above

82. **The LUN is basically:**

a. An address for host operating system to communicate to the device

b. A unique number that is assigned to each storage device or partition of the storage that the storage can support

c. An address that is hard coded into a FC HBA and is used to identify individual port (N_Port or F_Port) in the fabric

d. An address to communicate FC devices

83. **WWN is basically:**

a. An Address for host operating system to communicate to the device.

b. A unique number that is assigned to each storage device or partition of the storage that the storage can support.

c. An address that is hard coded into a FC HBA and is used to identify individual port (N_Port or F_Port) in the fabric

d. An address to communicate FC devices

84. **WWN address that is encoded into each port by the manufacturer is of:**

a. 16 bit

b. 24 bit

c. 48 bit

d. 64 bit

85. **What are the services provided by fabric to all the nodes?**

    a. Fabric login

    b. Fabric address notification

    c. Registered state change notification

    d. All of the above

86. **What is the smallest unit of information transfer in FC?**

    a. Packet

    b. Frame

    c. Sequence

    d. Exchange

Descriptive questions

1. Describe different phases of an SCSI command and also describe SCSI protocol write and read request sequences.

2. When a server or storage is connected to a fabric, describe each login process that take place to establish the communication.

3. Describe and highlight purposes of iSCSI , FCIP and iFCP protocols

Quiz questions

1. What are SCSI initiator and target?

2. If an IP address is equivalent to FCID, MAC address is equivalent to WWPN, then what are equivalent to DHCP client and server?

3. FC construct is similar to grammatical equivalents of any language. FC word is also similar to word in any language. FC frame is equivalent to sentence then, what are equivalent to paragraph and entire conversation?

4. What is analogous to iSNS server for iSCSI?

5. Explain difference between host I/O timeout and latency.

Glossary and key

- **SAS**: Serial attached SCSI interface protocol for disk drive.
- **SATA**: Serial Advanced Technology Attachment interface protocol for disk drive.
- **HBA**: Host bus adapter. An adapter used to connect the host server to the fabric.
- **SFP**: Small Form Factor Pluggable transceiver, converts the electrical signal into an optical signal.

- **WWN**: World wide name is a unique FC identifier consisting of a 16 character hexadecimal number. WWN is required for each FC communication port.
- **WWNN**: Worldwide node name is a globally unique 64 bit number that identifies a node process.
- **WWPN**: Worldwide port name is a globally unique 64 bit number that identifies a node port.
- **ISL**: Inter site link, a connection from one FC switch to another FC switch.
- **FC**: Fibre Channel, a high-speed network technology mainly used to connect storage to host servers. FC supports several common transport protocols including IP and SCSI.
- **FCoE**: Fibre Channel over Ethernet. Consolidates LANs and SANs.
- **Fabric**: A network of FC switches or hubs and other devices.
- **FCID**: Fibre Channel ID, 24 bit FC address obtained during Fabric login (FLOGI).
- **iSCSI**: Internet SCSI interface protocol, used for block-level access of IP storage devices.
- **IQN**: iSCSI qualified name, a unique name in IP storage system used for accessing iSCSI devices.
- **iSCSI HBA**: Hardware iSCSI initiator adapter card.
- **iSNS**: Internet Storage Name Service, a name registration service for IP storage devices.
- **CHAP**: Challenge-Handshake Authentication Protocol, for providing security to iSCSI storage volume.
- **CNA**: Converged network adapter that functions like FC HBAs and Ethernet NICs both.
- **NQN**: NVMe qualified name, which is similar to an iSCSI qualified name, a unique name in NVMe storage system used for accessing NVMe devices.

Join our Discord space

Join our Discord workspace for latest updates, offers, tech happenings around the world, new releases, and sessions with the authors:

https://discord.bpbonline.com

CHAPTER 5
Storage Networking to Share Storage

Introduction

When computer networking evolved, industry trend had changed to multiple cluster servers hosting different applications. So, an additional requirement of centralized storage for sharing data evolved. Therefore, a new network, called **SAN**, for sharing storage systems came into picture.

In other words, a computer network is a communication network which allows exchanging data among host servers and storages.

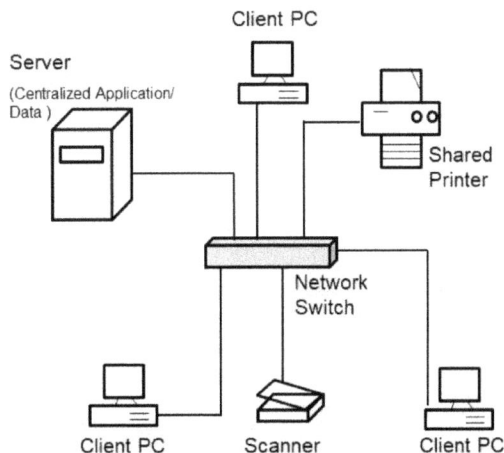

Figure 5.1: *Computer networking*

Refer to the following *Figure 5.2:*

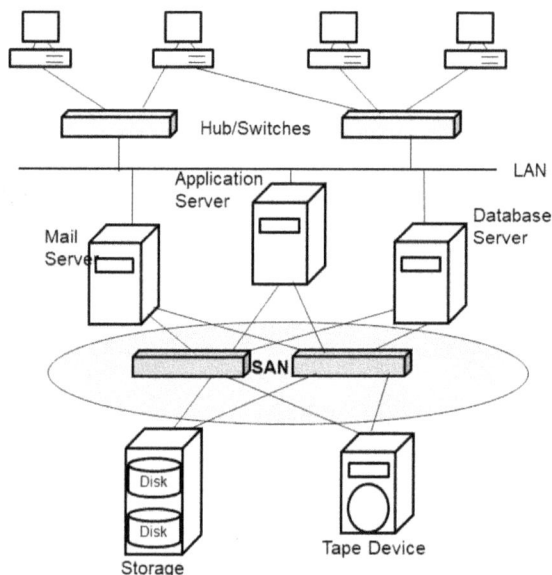

Figure 5.2: Storage networking to share storage

SAN fabric is a logical entity that consists of multiple FC switches connected together. Connection between two switches is called **inter-switch link (ISL)**.

Structure

Upon successful completion of this chapter, you will be able to learn following key areas of storage networking:

- SAN topology
- Zoning
- LUN masking
- Multipath

Objectives

In this chapter, you will learn different network topologies through which host servers and storage systems are connected. You will also learn about network configurations to control various access of storage system by the host servers, such as zoning and LUN masking.

It is because of some specific network physical connectivity and access configuration multiple paths get created between host server and storage system, in this chapter you will also learn about how virtual volumes are accessed over multiple path along with load balance and failover.

SAN topology

At the time of designing SAN, topology is one of the most important considerations. Topology is mainly driven by the requirement on how big or small the network is going to be, how many host servers and storage storages are going to be connected to it, and so on.

One or two switches are connected to each other to form a fabric. Again, one or two fabrics together is called a **SAN**.

Following figure shows single fabric and dual-fabric SAN. At least two fabrics are needed to have **no single point of failure** (**NSPOF**) environment, in which any fabric failure does not impact host server communication to storage.

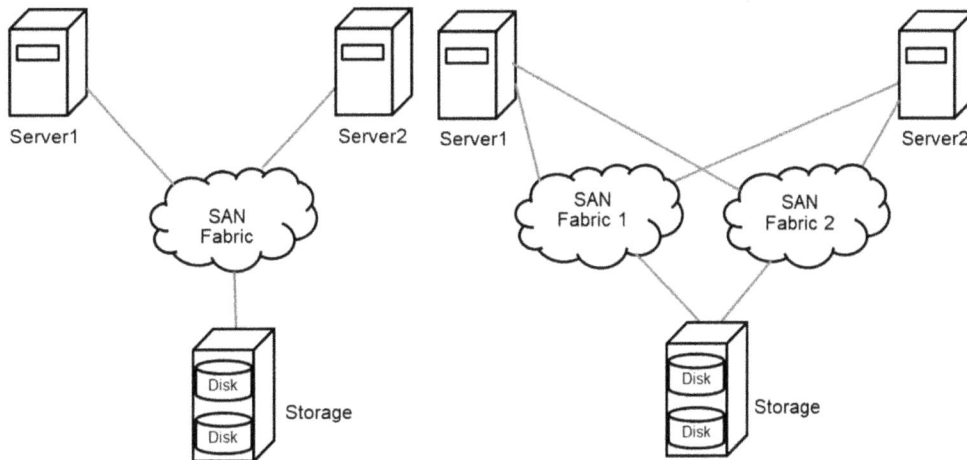

Figure 5.3: Single fabric and dual fabric SAN

To have redundancy, best practice is to have two fabrics and devices connect to both. This ensures availability of one path in the event of a fabric failure.

There are three types of topologies available in a SAN fabric:

- **Single switch topology**:

    Only one switch is used to form the fabric and to connect host server to storage system. This is mainly used for entry level storage solution with few number of host servers connected to a storage system.

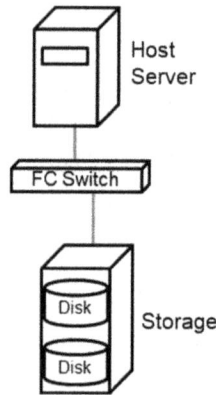

Figure 5.4: *Single switch topology*

Though, this is cost effective solution, failure of the switch will cause communication failure between host server and the storage.

- **Mesh fabric**:

In a mesh fabric, switches are connected to other switch using ISL.

Mesh fabric is of two types, that is, full mesh and partial mesh. In full mesh topology, every switch is connected to every other switch using ISLs. Host traverse a maximum of one hop to access its storage. The hop count is defined as the number of switches in the path between the host server and storage system. Most switch vendors support maximum of 7 hops.

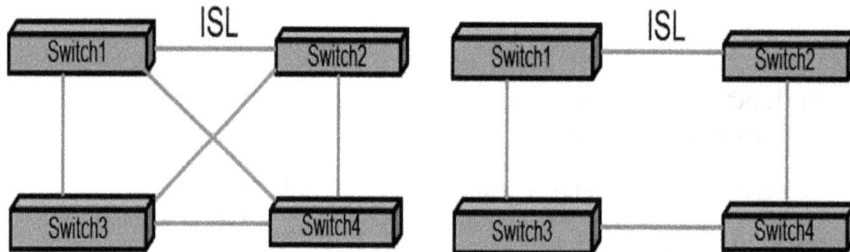

Figure 5.5: *Full and partial mesh topology*

In a partial mesh topology, not all the switches are connected to every other switch. Compared to full mesh, in this topology, hop count may increase, depending on connection of host server and storage, but number of ports used by ISLs can be saved.

- **Mesh fabric**:

The core-edge topology has two types of switch tiers: edge and core. The edge tier is usually composed of low-end switches in which host servers are connected.

These edge-tier switches are not connected to each other; instead they are core tier switches.

The core tier is usually composed of high-end director switches. Generally, one or two storage systems are shared by many host servers, hence this topology helps better distribution of bandwidth for all host servers to the storage system with minimum number of hop count.

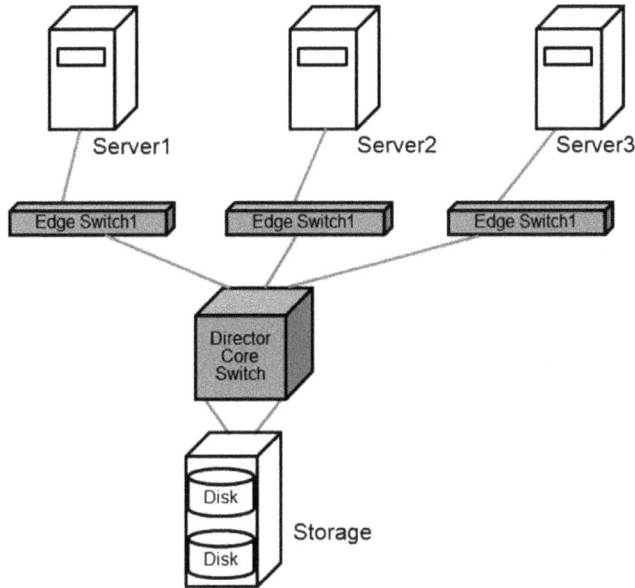

Figure 5.6: Core-edge or tiered topology

This topology also reduces the port utilization by the ISLs.

Core-edge topology is typically used in enterprise storage solution.

Zoning

Zoning is logical partitioning of SAN fabric into smaller subsets. In the following figure, although both servers and storages are connected to same fabric, because of Zone1, and Zone2, Server1 can only access Storage1, and Server2 can access Storage2. Zoning is required to restrict interference, add security, and simplify management.

Zoning can offer a number of benefits:

- **Security**: Zoning keeps users from accessing information they do not need.
- **Performance**: Blocks unwanted fabric broadcasts, which improves I/O. performance.
- **Manageability:** By splitting the SAN up into chunks, zoning makes it easier to keep track of devices, storage, and users.

- **Separation by purpose:** Setting up zones to reflect operational categories, such as engineering or human resources, organizes storage logically. It also makes it easy to establish specialized networks for testing or other purposes.

- **Separation by operating system:** Putting different OSs in different zones reduces the possibility of data corruption.

- **Allowing temporary access:** Administrators can remove the zone restrictions temporarily to allow tasks such as nightly backup.

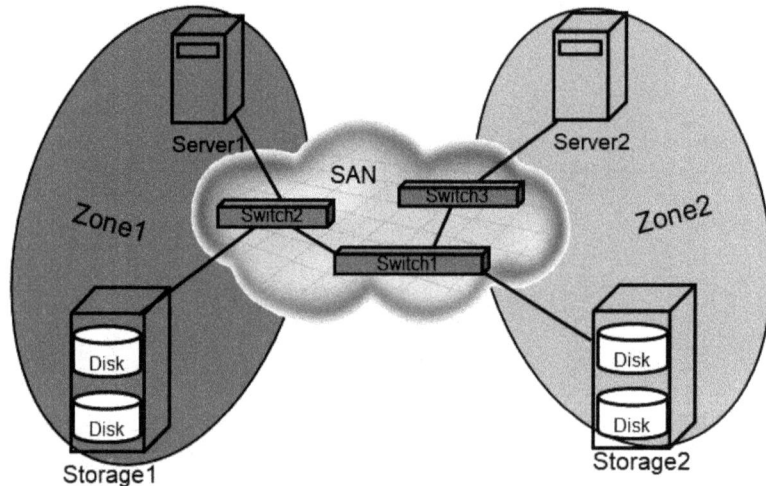

Figure 5.7: Zoning: Logical partitioning

Refer to the following figure:

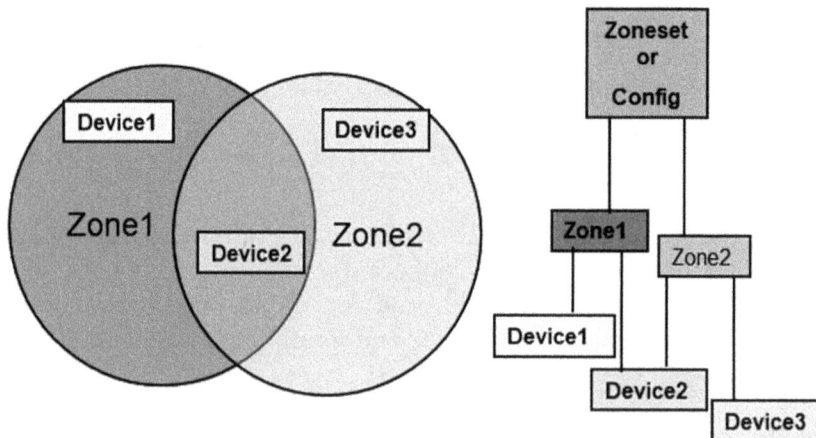

Figure 5.8: N_Port devices, zone, and zone set or Configuration

- Device1 and Device2 can see each other in Zone1
- Device2 and Device3 can each other in Zone2.

- Device1 and Device3 will not be able to see each other.

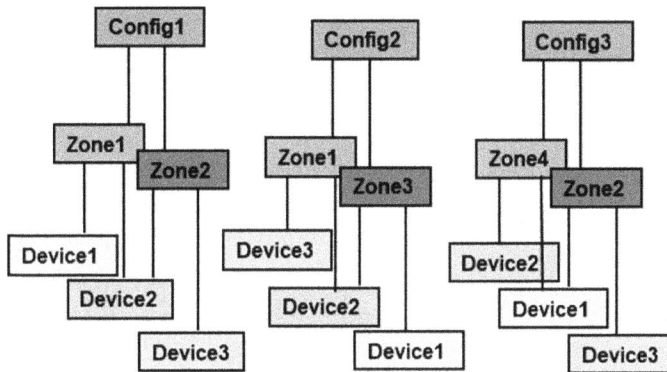

Figure 5.9: *Multiple zone configurations*

Only one configuration can be enabled at any given time, For example, If Config3 is enabled, Device2 and Device1 can see each other in Zone4 and Device1 and Device3 can see each other in Zone2.

There is no difference between Config1 and Config2.

Notes:

- When zoning is not configured, all devices connected to a fabric can see each other.
- If zoning is configured, but some devices are not included in any zone, no device can see them. They also cannot see each other.
- If zoning is configured and modified, zone configuration replicates to other switches automatically in the fabric
- Fully NSPOF environment requires at least two fabrics. Zoning required to be implemented in each fabric separately.
- A unique 8 byte (64 bit) address is encoded into each FC adapter by the manufacturer is called **worldwide name (WWN)**, and the unique address for each port is called **worldwide port name (WWPN)**.
- WWN based zoning: Zone/alias definition by wwn name. Downside: if an HBA fails and has to be replaced you have to change zoning information, too.
- Port-based zoning: Zone/alias definition by switch domain ID/port number. Downside: you cannot simply plug a cable into another port.

Hard zoning vs. soft zoning

- Hard zoning physically blocks access to a zone from any device outside of the zone.
- Soft zoning uses filtering implemented in FC switches to prevent ports from being seen from outside of their assigned zones. The security vulnerability in soft zoning

is that the ports are still accessible if the user in another zone correctly guesses the FC address.

- Soft zoning is to think in terms on your unlisted home phone number. However, your phone will still ring if someone dialed the correct number. For hard zoning, think of caller ID blocking. Even if you do know the number, there is no access.

- Hard zoning maps devices physically to a port, and soft zoning maps them logically. If you use the WWN of the device for zone definition, you are using soft zoning. If you use the physical port number, you are using hard zoning.

- Brocade's hardware zoning was only enabled when port-level zoning was used. This is not the case with all the vendors, as many have port zoning, which is still based on software and not secure.

- Soft zoning is much more flexible and easier to implement, especially in very large, complex SANs. If your SAN is not as large and complex, or a company has the resources available, hard zoning provides greater security.

Typical zone configuration steps

1. Identify each device and its WWNs or the port where the device is connected.

2. Assign meaningful alias name for each device or port. Alias creation is optional, but recommended step. If alias is not created, WWN can be directly used while creating zone.

3. Create zones and include the desired devices in them.

4. Create configuration or zone set and include required zones in it.

5. Enable the configuration or the zone set.

Zone conflict

Zone conflict is an error condition that occurs when multiple zone configuration exist in same fabric. This primarily happens when zone configuration in two different switches in same fabric are different. Following potential causes for the zone conflict:

- Link between the two switches went down, and zone configuration modified and then the link restored.

- Configurations are changed simultaneously from multiple switches.

- Zone configuration modified from lower model of switch in a mix switch model SAN Procedure to fix it, is as follows:
  o Identify the switch which has valid zone configuration.
  o Disconnect the ISL links.
  o Clear the zone configuration from other switches.
  o Reconnect the links back to replicate the configuration to all the switches.

Zoning guidelines

There are several best practices that need to be followed while creating zone. Every vendor highlights guideline in their product documentations. Following are some generic best practices for zoning:

- Always implement zoning.
- Apply zoning changes during off-peak hours
- All type of operating systems, Tape and Storage Arrays must be in different zone. All cluster nodes must be separated by their cluster configuration.
    - o   Linux1, Linux2 in Zone1 and Windows1 in Zone2
    - o   Tape_Lib1, Host1 in Zone1 and Storage1, Host1 in Zone2
    - o   Cluster1_Member1, Cluster1_member2 in Zone1, Cluster2_ Member1, Cluster2_member2 in Zone2, and Host1 in Zone3
- Use single initiator zoning.
- Single initiator (host) and single target (storage) is recommended in a zone.
- WWN based zoning is recommended because of interoperability and MPR configuration in the future.
- Pure port-based and WWN-based zoning handledby ASIC (Hardware).
- Mixed zoning (Port and WWN) handled by name server (processor).
- Alias must be created for each device with a meaningful name.
- Zoning configuration modification is recommended to do on the principal switch.
- Clear unused zoning elements.
- Do not have tapes and disks defined in the same zone.

LUN masking

A method to allow and restrict server access to storage LUN, in the other words this can also be described as allocation of storage LUN to that server. This is the step performed to provide access LUN to a host server after the creation of virtual volume. LUN masking is similar to zoning but is implemented in the storage array, not in the switch.

Different vendors use different terminologies for allow and restrict server access to storage LUN, some of them are present and unpresent or export and unexport or assigned and unassigned, LUN binding, and so on.

A unique LUN ID is assigned at the time of providing access of a virtual volume to a host. When multiple volumes are presented to a host, they are assigned unique LUN ID. Same virtual volume should not be presented to multiple hosts if they are not in cluster. This is to avoid data corruption by simultaneous write operations on a virtual volume.

Some operating systems identify storage device based on their LUN ID, after cluster failover, application to refer correct storage volume, device naming must be consistent across all cluster members. Therefore for cluster solution, each volume must be presented to all cluster members with same LUN ID.

Multipath

Multipath technique is implemented in host server to utilize the multiple paths of a redundant network to provide high availability and bandwidth between host server and storage devices.

There are primarily two reasons to have multiple paths to storage LUN:

1. NSPOF, if one path fails, I/O continues using other available paths.
2. Higher bandwidth, using load balance across all available paths.

Multipath is applicable and implemented for both iSCSI and FC environments.

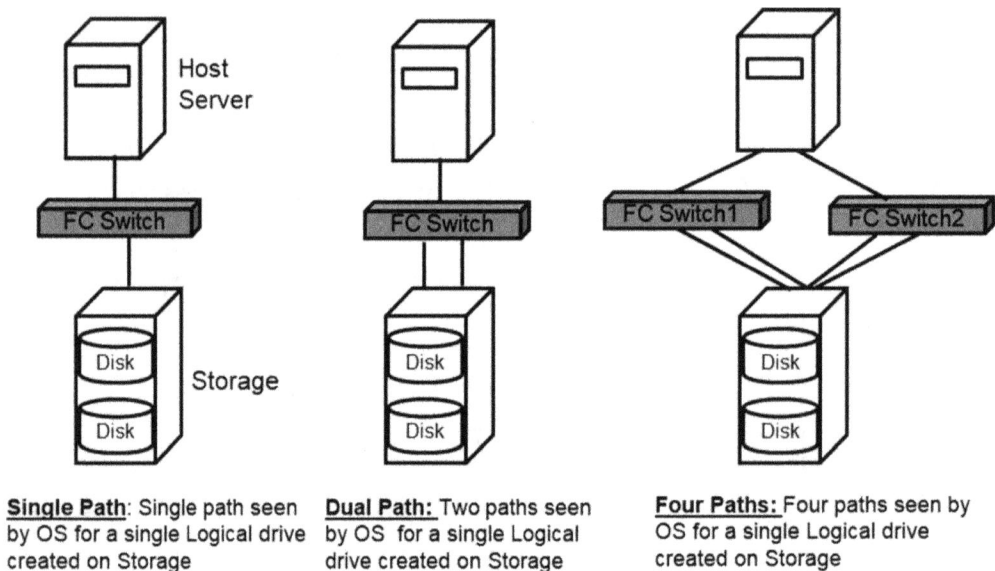

Single Path: Single path seen by OS for a single Logical drive created on Storage

Dual Path: Two paths seen by OS for a single Logical drive created on Storage

Four Paths: Four paths seen by OS for a single Logical drive created on Storage

Figure 5.10: Formation of multipath

Physical cabling and zoning, both the configurations impact number of paths. For example, in *Figure 5.10*, if all the target ports are zoned with all the initiator ports, the server would get to access each LUN with multiple paths but in this setup, if zoning is done between only one target port and one initiator port, then, only one path would be available for server to access LUN.

Number of paths = Number of paths from host server to switch X

Number of paths from storage system to switch.

All modern operating systems have multipath driver in-built into it. Previously storage vendor used to supply multipath application for each operating system. There are still some storage vendors who develop and sell multipath as a separate software component which provides more intelligent load balancing and path failover mechanism.

Without multipath software, one device for each path would be visible. For example, if a LUN has four paths, there would be total four devices being seen from operating system.

Writing data simultaneously on to different devices for same LUN may also result in data corruption.

For easy device management some multipath software hides all device except one per LUN.

Why do we need single device appearance in operating system? Without Multipath driver, each path from a host server to a storage system is treated by the operating system as a separate device. For example, if a virtual volume presented to a Linux host with four paths, operating system finds four device: `/dev/sdb`, `/dev/sdc`, `/dev/sdd` and `/dev/sde`, one corresponds to each path. Multipath driver creates a single multipath device on top of these underlying devices and balances I/O paths across these available paths. Some multipath driver, such as Windows MPI/O, hides devices corresponds to each path to avoid confusion and simultaneous writes via different paths that may lead to data corruption.

Load balancing policies

The objective of load balancing is to maximize workload throughput, reduce I/O latency and optimize resource utilization. To have better control on load balancing, multipath driver allows administrator to set user defined polices. Though different vendor designs and implements different set of policies, fundamentally they are more or less similar. Following are the typical list of load balancing policies:

- **Round robin (RR)**: All I/O requests are distributed across all active paths to the device in a RR manner. RR is most commonly used and default load balancing policy but it does have much intelligence, it uses all the available paths in a balanced way.

- **Shortest queue requests (SQR)**: Each I/O request is routed to the active path with the least number of outstanding requests.

- **Shortest queue bytes (SQB)**: Each I/O request is routed to the active path with the least number of outstanding data bytes.

- **Shortest queue service time (SQST)**: Each I/O request is routed to the active path where the total outstanding time for pending I/O requests is the least.

- **No load balance (NLB)**: All I/O requests are routed through a chosen active path.

Conclusion

Depending on the requirement and complexity of storage solution, SAN topology is designed. There are three different type SAN fabric topology such as single switch, mesh, and core-edge topology. Typically single-switch topology is used in entry level storage solution, and mesh topology is used in mid-range solution. And enterprise storage solution uses core-edge tiered topology.

Zoning and LUN masking are more of configuration of restriction and better management of storage access. Zoning is done between two ports that is, one from host server (initiator) and other from storage system (target) and LUN masking is about providing access to a virtual volume to host server.

Both the functionalities in storage solution are important consider for better management and stability of the storage solution

Multipath is operating system level intelligence to determine and distribute all I/O request across all available paths. Thus enhances performance and as well fault tolerance aspect in storage solution.

To summarize, following three important configuration checks must be met for a host server to access storage LUN:

a) Physical cabling between server and storage

b) Configuring zoning to allow access

c) Configuring LUN masking to allow access to LUN

Case studies

Case study 1: Steps to configure zoning in a fabric with Brocade FC switch

Let us look at the steps to configure zoning in a fabric with Brocade FC switch:

Requirement

Your company is planning to deploy a SAN environment that consists of a Linux and a Windows host server connected to a storage system via Brocade FC switch. The solution also includes a tape device connected to same SAN. Windows server is going to run a backup application that requires FC access to the tape device. WWPN details of FC adapters are as follows:

Linux host: 50:01:43:80:24:27:5a:a8

Windows host: 10:00:70:10:6f:e8:77:6f

Storage controller 1: 20:11:00:02:ac:01:84:ea

Storage controller 2: 21:11:00:02:ac:01:84:ea

Tape device: 50:01:43:80:28:ce:4a:7e

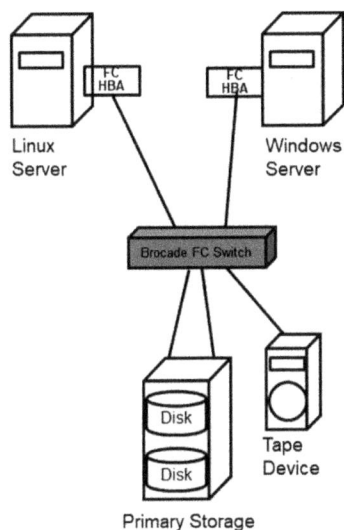

Figure 5.11: *Host servers and storage systems*

Analysis

Both initiators and target devices are connected to single fabric involving single switch. Zoning is required to be implemented only in this switch. Two host servers are not in the cluster and running different operating systems. Therefore, they need to be in the different zone. Separate zones are needed to be created for target devices. As per the requirement, the storage system is needed to be accessible by both Linux and Windows hosts and tape device by only windows host.

There are three zones needed:

1. Zone for Linux host and storage system
2. Zone for Windows host and storage system
3. Zone for Windows host and tape device

For better management of zone configuration, each device can have meaningful alias name. Those devices with alias name can be member of respective zone. and then finally all zones can be part of a zone configuration.

Solution

Every switch vendor designs switch interfaces differently. Brocade switch has GUI and **command line interface** (**CLI**) interface. Zone configuration can be done using any of these interfaces. Product documentation can be referred to understand command and their syntaxes.

CLI commands and syntaxes for Brocade FC switches are as follows:

Alias creation:

```
Usage: alicreate "<Alias Name>", "<WWPN>"
```

```
Switch> alicreate "Linux_Host","50:01:43:80:24:27:5a:a8"
```

Linux_Host is the alias name assigned to the WWPN of the HBA installed in Linux host server:

```
Switch>alishow Linux_Host
    alias: Linux_Host
50:01:43:80:24:27:5a:a8
Switch>
Switch> alicreate "Windows_Host","10:00:70:10:6f:e8:77:6f"
Switch> alicreate "Storage_Ctrl1","20:11:00:02:ac:01:84:ea"
Switch> alicreate "Storage_Ctrl2","21:11:00:02:ac:01:84:ea"
Switch> alicreate "Tape","50:01:43:80:28:ce:4a:7e"
```

Zone creation:

```
Switch> zonecreate "Linux_Storage","Linux_Host;Storage_Ctrl1; Storage_Ctrl2"
```

Linux_Storage is the name assigned to the zone:

```
Switch> zoneshow
zone: Linux_Storage
        Linux_Host; Storage_Ctrl1;
Storage_Ctrl2
Switch>
Switch> zonecreate "Windows_Storage","Windows_Host;Storage_
Ctrl1;Storage_Ctrl2"
Switch> zonecreate

    "Windows_Tape","Windows_Host;Tape"
Switch>
```

Configuration creation:

```
Switch> cfgcreate
"Zone_Config","Linux_Storage;Windows_Storage;Windows_Tape"
```

Zone_ Config is the name assigned for the configuration:

```
Switch> cfgshow Zone_Config
    cfg: Zone_Config
        Linux_Storage;Windows_Storage;Windows_Tape
Switch>
```

Saving configuration:

```
Switch> cfgsave
```

Enabling the configuration:

```
Switch> cfgenable "Zone_Config"
```

Listing the configuration:

```
Switch> cfgshow
Defined configuration:
cfg: Zone_Config
        Linux_Storage; Windows_Storage; Windows_
Tape
zone: Linux_Storage
        Linux_Host; Storage_Ctrl1; Storage_Ctrl2
zone: Windows_Storage
        Windows_Host; Storage_Ctrl1; Storage_Ctrl2
zone: Windows_Tape
        Windows_Host; Tape
alias: Linux_Host
    50:01:43:80:24:27:5a:a8
```

```
alias: Windows_Host
   10:00:70:10:6f:e8:77:6f
alias: Storage_Ctrl1
   20:11:00:02:ac:01:84:ea
alias: Storage_Ctrl2
        21:11:00:02:ac:01:84:ea
alias: Tape 50:01:43:80:28:ce:4a:7e
Effective configuration:
cfg: Zone_Config
zone: Linux_Storage
        50:01:43:80:24:27:5a:a8
        20:11:00:02:ac:01:84:ea
        21:11:00:02:ac:01:84:ea
zone: Windows_Storage
        10:00:70:10:6f:e8:77:6f
        20:11:00:02:ac:01:84:ea
        21:11:00:02:ac:01:84:ea
zone: Windows_Tape
      10:00:70:10:6f:e8:77:6f
      50:01:43:80:28:ce:4a:7e
Switch>
```

As per effective configuration listed above, now, Linux and Windows both hosts can access the storage system and only Windows system can access the tape device.

Case study 2: Modifying existing zone configuration of a fabric with Brocade FC switch

Let us modify existing zone configuration of a fabric with Brocade FC switch:

Requirement

After a few months of operation, your company decided to deploy a VMWare vSphere ESXi host into the existing SAN. The new host will share storage space of the existing storage system. Due to shortage of port of the existing switch, a new Brocade switch is also procured.

WWN details of the FC adapter in ESXi host is **10:00:00:90:fa:55:9c:8b**.

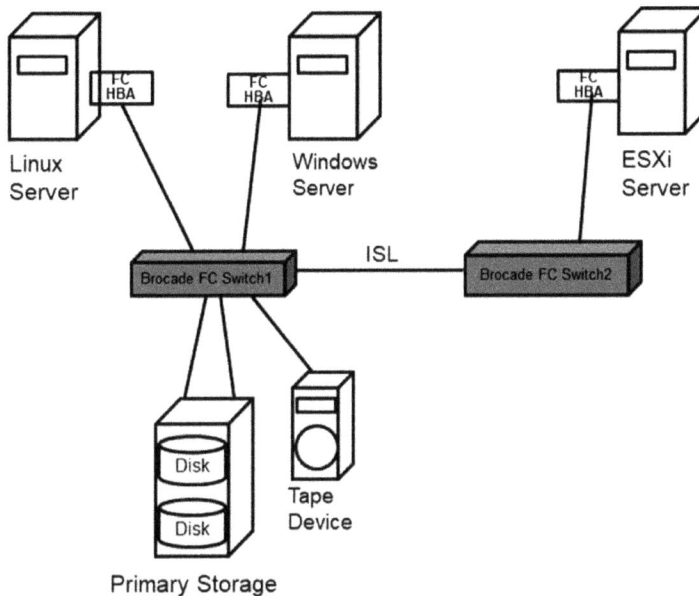

Figure 5.12: Adding a host server in existing SAN via an ISL

Analysis

Since the company already has an operational SAN. To include a host server to it, an available port is needed in the fabric. The new switch must be connected to existing switch using an ISL. The ESXi host can be connected to new switch.

New alias and zone must be created for the new host and added into the existing zone configuration. Finally, the zone configuration must be enabled to have new zone in effect.

Solution

Connect the new switch using a FC cable. This is called **ISL connection**. This will automatically replicate the zone configuration to new switch.

Alias creation:

```
Switch> alicreate "ESXi_Host","10:00:00:90:fa:55:9c:8b"
Switch> alishow ESXi_Host
    alias: ESXi_Host
        10:00:00:90:fa:55:9c:8b"
Switch>
```

Zone creation:

```
Switch> zonecreate "ESXi_Storage","ESXi_Host;Storage_
Ctrl1;Storage_Ctrl2"
Switch> zoneshow
zone: ESXi_Storage
        ESXi_Host; Storage_Ctrl1; Storage_Ctrl2
Switch>
```

Zone addition into an existing configuration:

```
Switch> cfgadd "Zone_Config","ESXi_Storage"
```

Saving configuration:

```
Switch> cfgsave
```

Enabling the configuration:

```
Switch> cfgenable "Zone_Config"
```

Zone enable must be done during off-peak hours, as host read/write traffic may get impacted.

Listing the configuration:

```
Switch> cfgshow
Defined configuration:
cfg: Zone_Config
        ESXi_Storage; Linux_Storage; Windows_
Storage; Windows_Tape
zone: ESXi_Storage
        ESXi_Host; Storage_Ctrl1; Storage_Ctrl2
zone: Linux_Storage
        Linux_Host; Storage_Ctrl1; Storage_Ctrl2
zone: Windows_Storage
        Windows_Host; Storage_Ctrl1; Storage_Ctrl2
zone: Windows_Tape
        Windows_Host; Tape
```

```
alias: ESXi_Host
                10:00:00:90:fa:55:9c:8b
alias: Linux_Host
                50:01:43:80:24:27:5a:a8
alias: Windows_Host
                10:00:70:10:6f:e8:77:6f
alias: Storage_Ctrl1
                20:11:00:02:ac:01:84:ea
alias: Storage_Ctrl2
                21:11:00:02:ac:01:84:ea
alias: Tape      50:01:43:80:28:ce:4a:7e
Effective configuration:
cfg: Zone_Config
zone: ESXi_Storage
                10:00:00:90:fa:55:9c:8b
                20:11:00:02:ac:01:84:ea
                21:11:00:02:ac:01:84:ea
zone: Linux_Storage
                50:01:43:80:24:27:5a:a8
                20:11:00:02:ac:01:84:ea
                21:11:00:02:ac:01:84:ea
zone: Windows_Storage
                10:00:70:10:6f:e8:77:6f
                20:11:00:02:ac:01:84:ea
                21:11:00:02:ac:01:84:ea
zone: Windows_Tape
                10:00:70:10:6f:e8:77:6f
                50:01:43:80:28:ce:4a:7e
Switch>
```

As per effective configuration listed above, now Linux and Windows both hosts can access the storage system and only Windows system can access the tape device.

Case study 3: Virtual volume presentation in a host server cluster environment

Let us look at virtual volume presentation in a host server cluster environment:

Requirement

An organization is planning to have four host servers in the cluster. Oracle database would be configured on all of them. Space requirement for database is 10 TB for data files, 2 TB for archive log and 500 GB for redo logs.

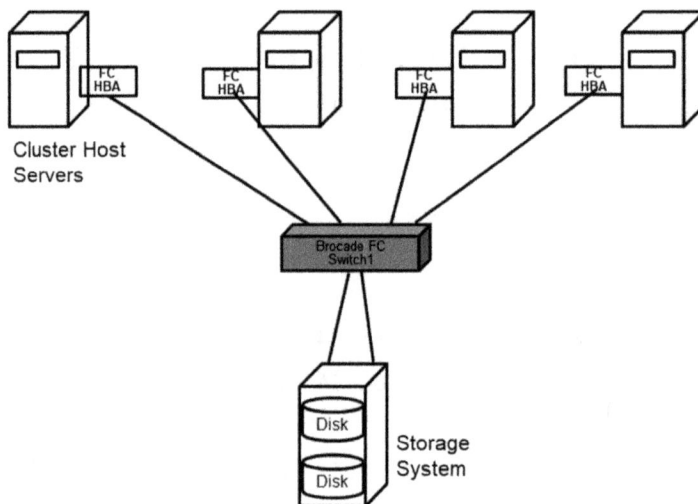

Figure 5.13: Host server cluster environment

Analysis

Since application running on cluster members are going to access same database, same storage volumes requires to be presented to all four cluster members. As a best practice of zoning, all the host servers and storage can be in single zone.

Solution

Following steps can be followed to implement storage solution as described in the requirement:

1. Create a single zone with WWPN of all four host server members and storage system.

2. Create three virtual volumes in storage system:

   a. **DataVol**: 10 TB

b. **ArchVol**: 2 TB

c. **RedoVol**: 500 GB

3. Present each volume to all four host servers with same LUN ID. For example, DataVol with LUN ID 1, ArchVol with LUN ID 2 and RedoVol with LUN ID 3.

4. Rescan the LUNs in each member and configure file system.

5. Configure Oracle application.

Case study 4: Identifying device files and I/O paths for Linux and Windows hosts

Let us identify device files and I/O paths for Linux and Windows hosts:

Requirement

A Linux host has single HBA connected to fabric. A storage system with two controllers connected to fabric via two FC cables. All three N_Ports are zoned together. Two virtual volumes 20 GB and 30 GB are presented to the host with LUN ID 0 and 1 respectively. Draw SAN diagram along with identification path and device files.

Analysis

There is single path from host to fabric and two paths from storage system to fabric; therefore number of paths from host is expected to be 1 x 2 = 2 paths per device.

LUN ID of 20 GB volume is expected to have 0 and for 30 GB its 1.

Solution

From Linux Kernel version 2.6 onward, following command shows list of WWPN for the adapters available in the host server:

```
[root@DV-S563 ~]# cat /sys/class/fc_host/host?/port_name
0x100070106fe8776f
[root@DV-S563 ~]#
```

These example commands are to bring more clarity on the concept discussed in the earlier part of this chapter. Output may vary depending on the environment, software component versions and configuration.

Device mapped multipath software component is needed to be installed in host, if not installed already.

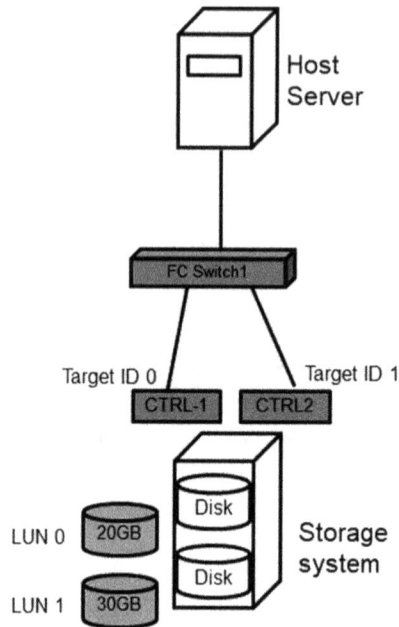

Figure 5.14: *Host server in SAN environment*

List of available paths for all the devices:

```
[root@DV-S563 ~]# multipath -ll
mpatha (360002ac0000000000d00728e000184eb) dm-2
Vendorname,Virtual Volume
size=20G features='1 queue_if_no_path' hwhandler='0' wp=rw
`-+- policy='round-robin 0' prio=1 status=active
|- 3:0:0:0 sdb 8:16 active ready running
`- 3:0:1:0 sdd 8:48 active ready running
mpathb (360002ac0000000000d007290000184eb) dm-3
Vendorname,Virtual Volume
size=30G features='1 queue_if_no_path' hwhandler='0' wp=rw
`-+- policy='round-robin 0' prio=1 status=active
|- 3:0:0:1 sdc 8:32 active ready running
`- 3:0:1:1 sde 8:64 active ready running
[root@DV-S563 ~]#
[root@DV-S563 ~]# lsscsi
[1:0:0:0] cd/dvd NECVMWar VMware IDE CDR10 1.00 /dev/
sr0
[2:0:0:0] disk VMware Virtual disk 1.0 /dev/
```

```
sda
[3:0:0:0] disk Vendorname Virtual Volume
2.0 /dev/sdb
[3:0:0:1] disk Vendorname Virtual Volume
2.0 /dev/sdc
[3:0:0:254] enclosu Vendorname SES 2.0 -
[3:0:1:0] disk Vendorname Virtual Volume
2.0 /dev/sdd
[3:0:1:1] disk Vendorname Virtual Volume
2.0 /dev/sde
[3:0:1:254] enclosu Vendorname SES 2.0 -
[root@DV-S563 ~]#

[root@DV-S563 ~]# lsblk
NAME MAJ:MIN RM SIZE RO TYPE
MOUNTPOINT
sr0 11:0 1 1024M 0 rom
sda 8:0 0 30G 0 disk
├─sda1 8:1 0 500M 0 part /
boot
└─sda2 8:2 0 29.5G 0 part
├─vg_b2host1-lv_root (dm-0) 253:0 0 25.6G 0 lvm /
└─vg_b2host1-lv_swap (dm-1) 253:1 0 4G 0 lvm
[SWAP]
sdb 8:16 0 20G 0 disk
└─mpatha (dm-2) 253:2 0 20G 0 mpath
sdc 8:32 0 20G 0 disk
└─mpathb (dm-3) 253:3 0 20G 0 mpath
sdd 8:48 0 20G 0 disk
└─mpatha (dm-2) 253:2 0 20G 0 mpath
sde 8:64 0 20G 0 disk
└─mpathb (dm-3) 253:3 0 20G 0 mpath
[root@DV-S563 ~]#
[root@DV-S563 ~]# ls /dev/mapper/* | grep -i /dev/mapper/m
/dev/mapper/mpatha
/dev/mapper/mpathb
[root@DV-S563 ~]#
```

The first virtual volume of size 20 GB with LUN ID 0 has been assigned with device file / dev/mapper/mpatha, underlying devices / dev/sdb and /dev/sdd. The path corresponds to /dev/sdb is via Controller 0 as the Target ID of [H:C:T:L] = [3:0:0:0] is 0. The path corresponds to /dev/sdd is via Controller 1, as the Target ID of [3:0:1:0] is 1.

Similarly, the second virtual volume of size 30 GB with LUN ID 1 has been assigned the device file /dev/mapper/mpathb, underlying devices /dev/sdc and /dev/sde.

Learning check

Objective question

1. **A customer bought storage with a controller pair, each controller has only single host port. He wants have 4 path for each LUN of that storage. What would be your solution?**

   a. Not possible

   b. Install one single ported HBA in server and connect it to same fabric where both storage host ports are also connected

   c. Install two single ported HBAs in server and connect them to same fabric where both storage host ports are also connected

   d. Install two single ported HBAs in server and connect them to two different fabrics where each of storage host ports are connected

2. **Number of paths from server to a device can be controlled by:**

   a. Changing physical cabling (Server–switch–storage)

   b. Changing zone configuration

   c. Changing number of HBA in the server

   d. Any of the above

3. **Number of paths to a device can be controlled by:**

   a. Changing physical cabling between server and switch

   b. Changing physical cabling between switch and storage

   c. Any of the above

4. **LUN is showing total 8 paths to storage via fabric. Storage has two controllers, each controller has 4 ports. All ports are connected to a fabric. No zone configuration. How many HBA the server has?**

   a. 8

   b. 4

   c. 2

   d. 1

5. **A server with two single-ported HBAs connected to storage via fabric. Storage has two controllers, each controller has 4 ports. All storage ports are connected to a fabric. No zone configuration. One of the cables from storage to switch is faulty. How many paths would you expect for each LUN presented from storage to this server?**

   a. 16

   b. 14

   c. 12

   d. 10

6. **A server with two single-ported HBAs connected to storage via fabric. Storage has two controllers, each controller has 4 ports. All storage ports are connected to a fabric. No zone configuration. One of the FC cables from server to switch is faulty. How many paths would you expect for each LUN presented from storage to the server?**

   a. 16

   b. 8

   c. 4

   d. 2

7. **Inter-switch link (ISL) is:**

   a. Connection between servers to switch

   b. Connection between switch to storage

   c. Connection between switches

   d. Connection between servers to storage

8. **SAN might contain both heterogeneous servers and heterogeneous storage:**

   a. True

   b. False

9. **Which component initiate initialization to FC devices?**

   a. HBA

   b. Disk array

   c. SAN management

   d. SAN switch

10. **Multipath I/O is (Choose two):**

    a. A fault tolerant technique

    b. A scalable technique

    c. A cost effective solution

    d. A performance improvement technique

11. **Multipath I/O is:**

    a. More than one I/O requests, even via single physical path between the CPU in the computer systems and its main storage devices

    b. More than one logical path between the CPU in the computer systems and its main storage devices through zoning, storage virtualization

    c. More than one physical path between the CPU in the computer systems and its main storage devices through the buses, controllers, switches and other bridge devices connecting them

    d. More than one storage devices between the CPU in the computer systems and storage disk Array

12. **What are the two major classification of zoning?**

    a. Software zoning

    b. Hardware zoning

    c. WWN zoning

    d. Port zoning

13. **Zoning is (Choose two):**

    a. Fabric management service to enable communication between switches

    b. Fabric management service that can be used to create logical subsets of devices within a SAN

    c. This enables portioning of resources for management and access control purpose.

    d. To monitor health of devices connected to fabric

14. **Two separate FC switches are having a zone set configured in them. An ISL is now cabled between the 2 switches. Both the switches contain a zone with the same zone name, but the members of the zone are different in the two switches. Which of the following statements is true after an ISL is attempted between the 2 switches?**

    a. The active zone set between the 2 switches is successfully merged and the ISL is established.

    b. The active zone set between the 2 switches cannot be merged and the ISL is isolated.

15. **LUN Masking is method to create:**

    a. A LUN

    b. Access control to a LUN

    c. More number of LUNs

    d. Replication between two LUNs

16. **Match the following:**

    i.   Zoning   1. Host server

    ii. Multipath   2. Switch

    iii. LUN masking   3. Storage system

    a. (i) - (1), (iii) - (2) and (ii) - (3)

    b. (i) - (1), (ii) - (2) and (iii) - (3)

    c. (ii) - (1), (i) - (2) and (iii) - (3)

    d. (ii) - (1), (iii) - (2) and (i) - (3)

17. **Which one of the following list is the default load balancing policy in most multipath driver:**

    a. Round robin (RR)

    b. Shortest queue requests (SQR)

    c. Shortest queue bytes (SQB)

    d. Shortest queue service time (SQST)

18. **Match the following:**

    i.   Single switch fabric topology   1. Mid-range storage solution

    ii. Mesh topology   2. Entry level storage solution

    iii. Core-edge topology   3. Enterprise storage solution

    a. (i) - (1), (iii) - (2) and (ii) - (3)

    b. (i) - (1), (ii) - (2) and (iii) - (3)

    c. (ii) - (1), (i) - (2) and (iii) - (3)

    d. (ii) - (1), (iii) - (2) and (i) - (3)

19. **How many hops are supported by most of FC switch vendors?**

    a. 1

    b. 7

    c. 8

    d. 16

Descriptive questions

1. Explain different type of SAN topologies and their pros and cons.

2. Describe purpose and benefits of zoning.

3. Why do we need single device appearance in operating system when there are multiple paths exist?

4. Describe all levels of configuration and restrictions of storage LUN access by host server.

Quiz questions

1. Physical cabling between a storage system and host server is done to get total 8 paths for each LUN. Is it possible to configure zoning to increase number of paths to 16?

2. Is multipath implemented only to have NSOF solution?

3. Is LUN masking configured at host side?

4. State the formula to determine total number of paths for storage device, when number of from host and storage to switch is known?

Glossary and key terms

- **No single point of failure (NSPOF)**: A storage solution configured in such a way that one hardware or link failure would not impact I/O operation of the storage system

- **Multipath**: Two or more data path between host server and storage system. Multipath gets created based on how cables are connected between host server and storage via a switch and how ports are zoned.

- **Load balance policies**: Various policies provided by multipath driver in the operating. Based on requirements, this user configurable polices directs paths utilization by the I/O requests.

- **LUN masking**: Storage system functionality to configure and restriction virtual volume access to host servers

- **Zoning**: Logical partition with SAN fabric for better management, security and performance

- **Hard zoning**: Physically blocking access to a zone from any device outside of the zone.

- **Soft zoning**: Filtering out a device from zone just prevent visibility in it.

CHAPTER 6

Storage Performance

Introduction

The storage system is not only used to store data, but it is important how fast application can write and read the data. Therefore, storage performance is an important aspect of all storage systems. All storage vendors put significant effort to enhance their storage systems and as well as the solutions to get faster access to the data. Several features are implemented to ensure data can be accessed as fast as possible from a storage system.

Although some of the features, such as controller operation mode, caching techniques, multipathing, RAID levels, let us recap those feature briefly in this chapter on how these impacts storage performances.

Multipath: Unlike the above three features within a storage system, multipath is an operating system level intelligence that can determine and distribute the I/O requests across all available paths between the storage system and host system. Multipath gets created based on the number of cables connected and zoned. Multipath also has a great impact on performance, especially if each path does not have much bandwidth to support the host server's demand and storage system's capability.

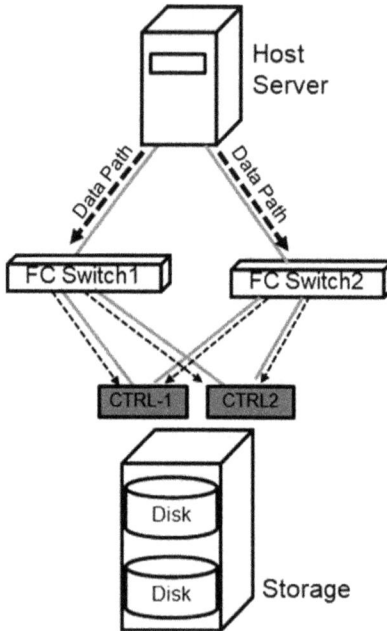

Figure 6.1: Multipath solution

Controller operating mode: In *Chapter 3, Storage Disk Array*, we learned the different mode of controller operations, such as active/passive, Active-Active. Most storage vendors make storage system with two or more controllers, with the maximum of eight controllers. If all controllers operate at the same time in parallel, the storage system can process this should come together request pretty fast. Therefore multiple controllers in a storage system have added advantages to enhance the performance.

Caching techniques: Physical disk drives are much slower than cache memory DIMM in the storage system. Therefore, for write operation data is temporarily stored in high-speed and faster accessible memory DIMM. Later point in time, data is flashed into the disk for permanent storage. because of this technique, host server receives a faster response from storage system while writing data. Similarly, for reading storage systems can intelligently predict next data to be read, it read beforehand from disk keeps in the cache memory.

Disk Enclosures with dual path: Disk enclosures, connected to the backend of the storage controller, are designed to have two paths to transfer data more efficiently to and from physical disks.

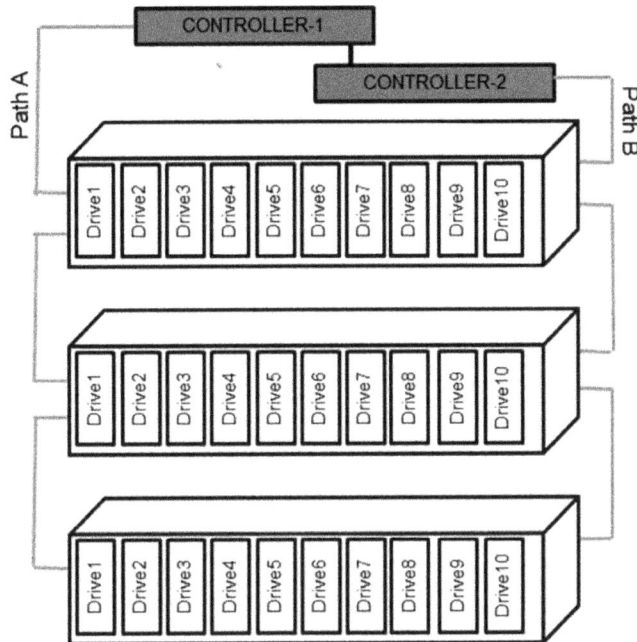

Figure 6.2: Disk enclosures with dual paths

RAID level: As discussed in *Chapter 3, Storage Disk Array*, there are RAID levels, for example, RAID 0 and RAID 1+0 that stripes and mirrors the data and involves more number of disk in parallel to improve the performance.

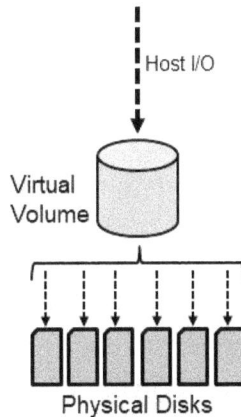

Figure 6.3: RAID implementation

Physical disk count and type: Virtual RAID implementation in modern storage system enables the involvement of all physical disks for read/write operations, thus enhances performance drastically. Therefore, storage system having hundreds of physical disks perform much faster, compared to a system with just a few tens of drives.

Type of disks also plays a major role in storage performance. There three type of disks used in storage system today are SSD, SAS, and SATA. SATA drives are typically low cost, 7.2K RPM and known for high capacity and efficient power consumption. Mainly used for data archival purpose. SAS drives more reliable, high-speed, 15K RPM, and used for business-critical enterprise applications. Seek times approximately two times faster than SATA drive. SSD drives known for performance, offer up to 100 times faster than traditional hard drives, as there are no moving parts and seek time is near to zero.

Structure

At the end of this chapter you will learn the following:

- Storage performance basics
- Measuring storage performance
- Storage system features that enhance performance

Objectives

In this chapter, you will learn about storage performance basics that include the definition of key factors to measure storage performance. How to determine whether storage is performing slow or faster? You will also learn about the important features which are implemented within a storage system to enhance the performance.

Performance terminologies

Storage performance is measured primarily with load and the delay. I/O the storage is processing in per unit time. There are primarily two ways to measure load:

- **Throughput**: Number of jobs (usually I/O requests) completed per unit time (usually per second). In other words, the number of I/O requests processed per unit time. Unit to measure throughput is **I/O per sec** (**IOPS**). Some storage vendors refer throughput directly as IOPS.

- **Data transfer rate**: Amount of data being transferred between two systems, per unit time. Unit to measure data transfer rate is KBps, MBps, GB/h, and so on. It is also known as **bandwidth**. Some storage vendors also refer it as **throughput**.

In the following figure, throughput = 5 IOPS and data transfer rate = 7 MBps.

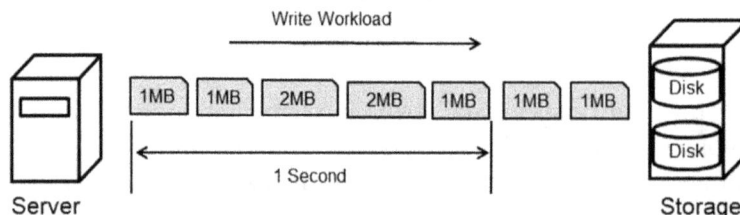

Figure 6.4: *Data transfer rate and throughput*

If all I/O transfer length (request size) are equal, then Throughput can be derived from data transfer rate and vice versa.

Data transfer rate = Throughput X Average I/O size

Delay: Indicates how much trouble the array is going through, to process the request, in other words, how much time it is taking to complete each request. This is a measure of how fast a storage system responds to read and write requests. Storage serving faster I/O is considered to be high performing storage; therefore latency is expected to be as low as possible.

Latency: Time is taken to complete a single I/O operation. This is also known as **response time** or **service time**. This is typically measured in **milliseconds (ms)**.

Queue depth: The number of jobs (I/O requests) waiting in a queue in order to get processed. This is called the **queue length**. Concurrency is achieved by providing multiple paths to the storage system and using system memory as a cache to queue transactions. This leads to this measurement. This indicates how many I/O requests a device can handle simultaneously.

This matches with an analogy of doctor checking patients. If the doctor takes more time to complete checking a patient and demand is high, queue length will keep on increasing. Time to check a patient is similar to latency here and the number of patients being checked is similar to throughput and number of patient waiting is queue length.

A single disk drive may have a queue length in single or double figures, whereas a large Storage system will provide a queue depth into the tens or hundreds per LUN, per port or a combination of both.

Load and delay are exponentially related. Latency increases exponentially along with an increase of throughput on a storage system. Following figure is an example to show how throughput and latency are related to each other.

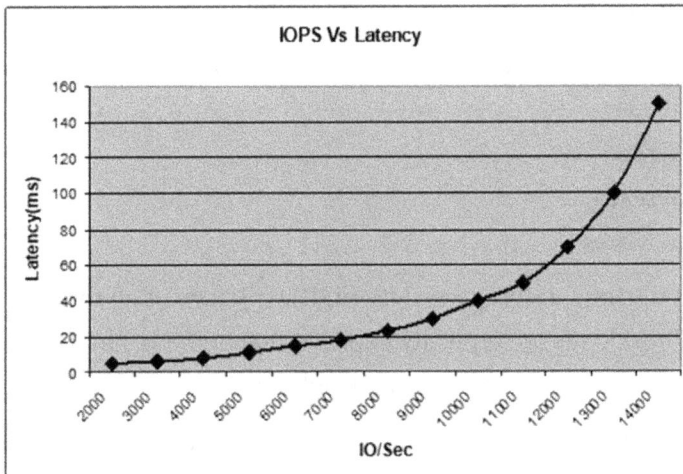

Figure 6.5: Throughput and latency

Host I/O timeout: The amount of time for an initiator host waits for unresponsive disk I/O operations. This is typically measured in **seconds** (**sec**).

Most operating systems and applications have their default I/O timeout set and allow them to configure it. Host I/O timeout and latency are two different measurements. The former one is measured from host server or application perspective, and it indicates level tolerance level, whereas latter primarily indicates how fast received I/O requests are being processed within the storage system.

Performance bottleneck: Bottleneck is a situation that can occur within or outside of a storage system that impedes data flow. When processing is faster than transport and load touches its maximum allowed capability and when transport is faster than processing and the delay prevents the increase of load. Therefore, on a loaded system bottleneck always exist.

Workload and its pattern

Workloads are I/O operations that are generated by host applications on to a storage system.

Workload is characterized mainly using three factors:

- **I/O block size**: Size of the data block sent or received as part of read/write requests. Example 4 KB, 8 KB, 16 KB, 32 KB, 64 KB, and so on.

- **Read/write** %: Percentage of Read and Write request. for example 70% Read indicates host reads 70% of time whereas writes 30% of time.

- **Random vs. sequential** %: Sequential access pattern is something in which next block for read/write operation is predictable. For example, Block 5, Block 6, Block 7, and so on. Random is something in which next block is hard to predict. For example, Block 3, Block 16, Block 8, and so on.

There are four basic access patterns of workloads that an array can encounter:
- Random reads
- Random writes
- Sequential reads
- Sequential writes

In reality, most of the time a storage system finds a mixture of all four of these workloads:
- Random workloads are typically expected to consist of small block I/Os
- Small block workloads are workloads where the I/O size is between 2k–16k

Small block random workload is also called as **online transaction processing** (**OLTP**), generally database generates such workload.

Generally backup operation, HD video streaming generates sequential workload and typically these application uses large block size, larger than 64 KB

Example of a server's sequential I/O requests can change to a random request due to file system effects, especially if file system fragmented.

Reads, especially of random, are generally more time-consuming than write operations. This is because data for all write get written into cache and acknowledges completion to host, whereas data for random read access have to fetch directly from disk.

Tiered storage

Most of the storage features create a tradeoff among performance, fault tolerance and space efficiency. For example, if you configure RAID 0, you lose fault tolerance aspect, but you gain performance and space efficiency. Another example, with data compression, you gain space efficiency, but lose performance. To gain one aspect, you lose other.

Data tiering feature helps to achieve your objective by automatically toggling characteristic of your storage volume based on set of policies that are defined by end user as well as within storage system.

If you have a storage system SSD, and SAS HDD with 15K RPM and SATA HDD with 7.2K RPM drives, generally storage vendor defines SSD as Tier 0 and 15K HDD as Tier 1 and 7.2K HDD as Tier 2. User now defines some policies based on IOPS and latency of the virtual volume based on which storage system automatically moves the volumes from one tier to other. Volumes which are mostly accessed would typically be moved to higher tier and less access volumes to lower tier.

In summary, tiered storage is a tradeoff between performance (IOPS) per unit price and space (GB) per unit price.

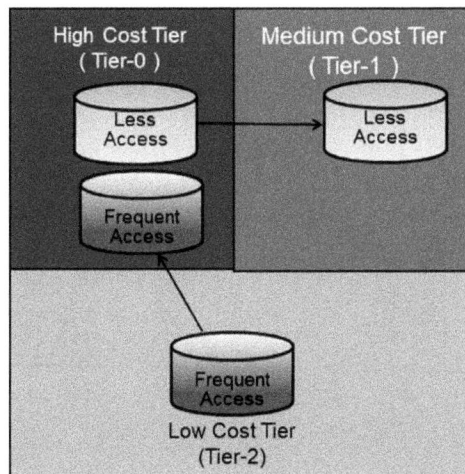

Figure 6.6: Tiered storage with different access level of volumes

Quality of service

With popularity of SAN and virtualization, storage systems are now shared by multiple servers and applications. Typical challenge in shared environment, any workload intensive application that consumes maximum available storage resources and bandwidth makes other applications to starve.

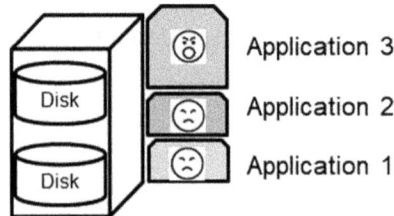

Figure 6.7: QoS implementation

QoS is set of policies defined in the storage system, based on **service level agreements** (**SLA**) for different application's incoming I/O requests. This is to ensure an application gets its predefined share of resources when there is a demand for it. QoS policies are typically implemented for virtual volume or group of virtual volumes, host or group of hosts and at system level. Policies mainly set minimum and maximum IOPS, bandwidth and latency for different workload pattern.

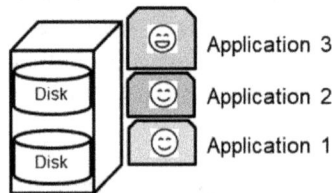

Figure 6.8: QoS implementation

Clone file blocks and zero file blocks

During usual copy data from one volume to other, server first reads the data and then writes to destination volumes.

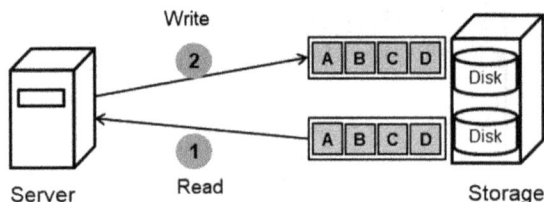

Figure 6.9: Regular copy operation

The clone file blocks feature allows an initiator to copy a large number of disk blocks without needing to transfer the data between the storage volume and the server.

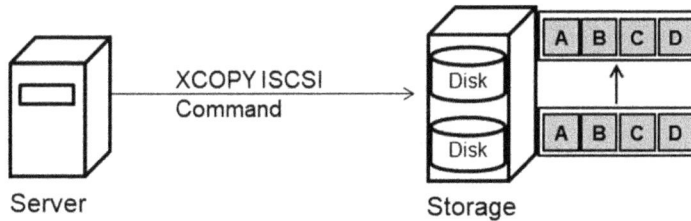

Figure 6.10: *XCOPY operation*

T10 SCSI **EXTENDED COPY (XCOPY)** specification describes this feature in detail.

Similarly the zero file blocks feature allows an initiator to zero a large number of disk blocks without needing to transfer a large number of zeroed buffers. This is based on T10 SCSI **WRITE SAME (WSAME)** specification.

Operating systems, such as Microsoft Windows 2012 or later and VMWare vSphere ESXi internally uses these storage features that accepts these SCSI commands to offload specific data copy and storage management operations to improve performance.

Conclusion

Storage performance is an important aspect of a storage system, meaning how fast storage system can respond to host server's read/write requests.

Storage performance is determined using throughput and latency. Throughput is number of I/O requests processed per unit time. And latency is time taken to complete a single I/O operation.

Data transfer rate, amount of data transferred per unit time, is also another way to measure load on the storage system. MBps, TB per hour are the units of data transfer rate.

Generally storage systems are designed to have more number of controllers, so that it can perform host server's read/write request quite fast. Data caching is another technique that temporary keeps data in faster accessible DIMM to add value to the performance. RAIDs are also configured to perform parallel read/write on to multiple disks together.

Apart from this, clone file blocks XCOPY and zero file blocks WRITE SAME are also implemented in a storage system to improve data copy performance within the system itself.

Case studies

Case study 1: Throughput, data transfer rate and latency of a storage volume for a given workload

Let us look at throughput, data transfer rate and latency of a storage volume for a given workload:

Requirement

Generate workload of the following characteristics on a storage volume:

Block size: 8KB

Read/write %: 70% read, 30% write

Access: Random

Determine throughput, data transfer rate and latency.

Analysis

Although, performance result depends to many other factors such as host configuration, network bandwidth and other workload parameters, this test can be performed only on available environment with given workload parameters.

There are several tools available to generate workload and measure performance of storage devices. I/OMeter is widely accepted free tool for workload measurement and characterization, available to download from www.iometer.org web site.

I/OMeter can be used to generate the specified workload and measure throughput, data transfer rate, and latency.

Solution

Following steps can be performed to determine throughput, data transfer rate and latency of a storage volume:

1. Download the Iometer tool from **http://www.iometer.org** website and install it on a Windows host.

2. Create a virtual volume in storage system, present to the host and scan for the new device in the operating system.

3. Open the tool and go to **Access Specifications** tab. Click on **New** button.

4. Specify a name and the parameters, that is, 8 KB block size, 70% read and 30% write and 100% Random.

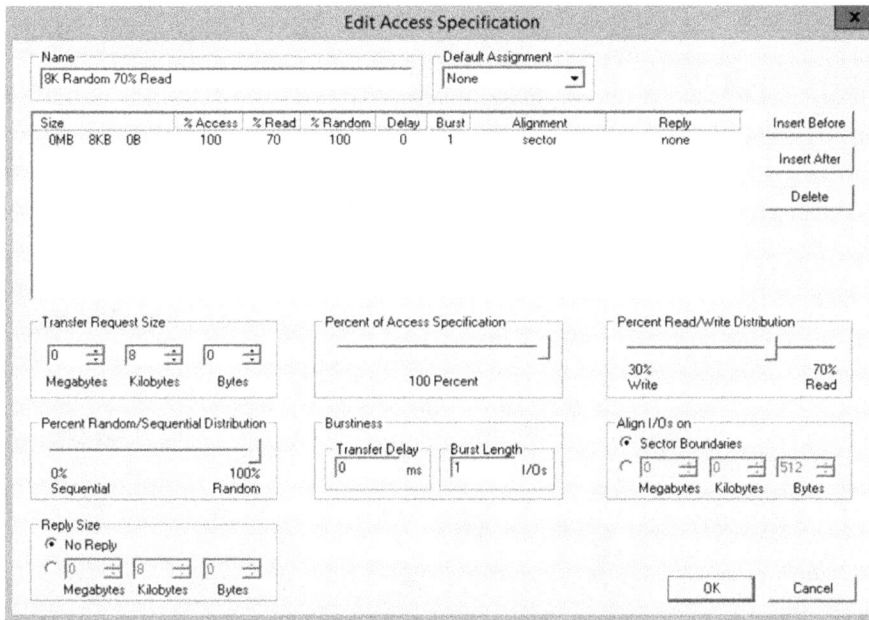

Figure 6.11: *Diameter Access configuration*

5. Assign this access specification.

6. Go to **Disk Targets** tab, select the disk and then click on green flag from toolbar to initiate the workload.

7. Now, go to **Test results** tab, move update frequency to 1 or 2 seconds to view current workload status.

8. Note throughput (I/Os per second), data transfer rate (MBps) and Latency (Average I/Os response time) (ms).

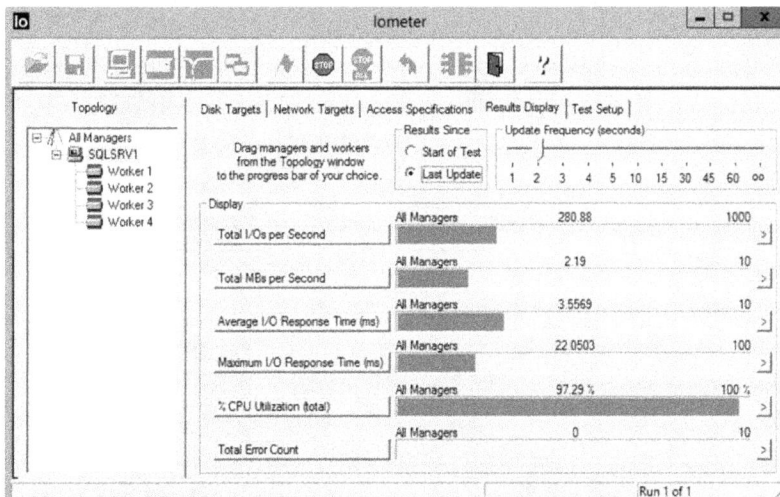

Figure 6.12: *Throughput and data transfer rate in diameter*

Case study 2: Identifying possible bottleneck for the given configuration

Let us identify possible bottleneck for the given configuration:

Requirement

Your company has purchased a high-end file storage system with SSD drives in it. VMware ESXi server access the storage via NFS protocol. ESXi host is also a higher model server. But to migrate a virtual machine of size 200 GB to this storage takes about half an hour.

Analysis

200 GB VM takes approximately 30 minutes to migrate, therefore data transfer rate is approximately = *(200 X 1024) / (30 x 60) = 113 MBps*

113 MBps = 113 x 8 Mbps = 904 Mbps

904 Mbps is very close to 1 Gbps bandwidth speed.

Most likely something in the network is causing bottleneck and dropping the data transfer rate to 1 Gbps.

To investigate any performance issue, it is important to understand the environment in detail. When information is collected, it is understood that the company is using existing LAN for connecting ESXi host to file storage. Though, both systems are connected to two different 10 Gb Ethernet switches, but both switches are connected via a 1 Gb switch. Hence this component is the bottleneck in data transfer. Host server and storage both high-end with SSD drives, therefore processing is faster than transport and load touching its maximum in the network.

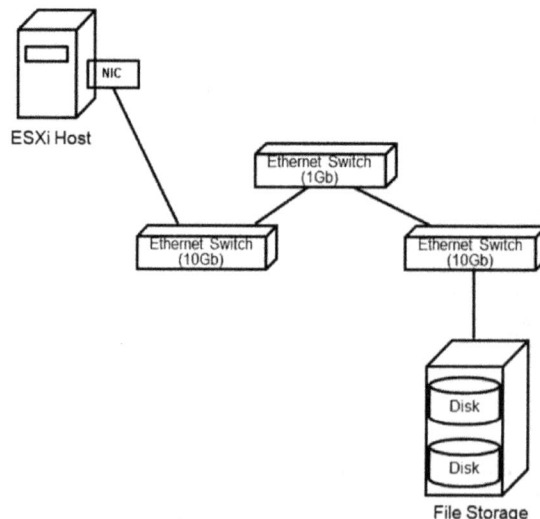

Figure 6.13: *Multi-switch SAN solution*

Solution

1 Gb switch in between host and storage communication can be avoided to eliminate the bottleneck. Storage system and host server can be connected to same 10 Gb switch.

Case study 3: Speeding up month-end closure activities

Let us look at speeding up month-end closure activities:

Requirement

An organization recently purchased a hybrid storage system which has SSD and SAS both type drives. They have configured two set of virtual volumes–one set on SSD for hosting application that their customers access and another set on SAS for their internal reporting and analysis. During end of every month, they generate huge number of report from second application.

Analysis

Demand for accessing data on second set of volumes is high during the end of month. Data tiering feature can be used to move second set of volumes on to SSD drives during month. Once the activities are completed, they can be moved back to home drives.

If sufficient space on SSD drive is not available, first set of volumes can be moved to SAS before moving second set of volumes to SSD.

Solution

Create schedule to move first set of volumes to SAS disk just before month-end activities. Also create another schedule to move second set of volumes to SSD.

After completion of the activities the volumes can be reverted as per their original disk location.

Learning check

Objective questions

1. **Your application demands more storage performance, basically means the requirement is:**
   a. More response time
   b. More number of I/O requests
   c. More number of I/O requests at less response time
   d. Any of the above

2. **What is the measuring unit of data transfer rate?**

   a. Megabytes (MBs)

   b. Gigabits per second (Gbps)

   c. I/O per second (IOPS)

   d. Millisecond (ms)

3. **What is the measuring unit of throughput?**

   a. Megabytes (MBs)

   b. Gigabits per second (Gbps)

   c. I/O per second (IOPS)

   d. Millisecond (ms)

4. **What is the measuring unit of latency?**

   a. Megabytes (MBs)

   b. Gigabits per second (Gbps)

   c. I/O per second (IOPS)

   d. Millisecond (ms)

5. **Which statement related to storage performance terminology is true:**

   a. Throughput is number of jobs (usually I/O requests) completed per unit time (IOPS)

   b. Data transfer rate is amount of data being transferred between two systems per unit time (e.g., KBps, MBps, GB per hour, etc.)

   c. Latency is time required to complete a job (I/O request)

   d. All of the above

6. **Which storage would you buy, if cost and capacity is same?**

   a. The one provides 10000 IOPS at 10ms latency

   b. The one provides 10000 IOPS at 15ms latency

   c. Both are same

   d. Any of them

7. **Cache memory is used in a storage system mainly to improve:**

   a. Fault tolerant

   b. Performance

   c. Space efficiency

   d. All of the above

8. **Which of the following terminology is not used in the context of storage performance?**

   a. Throughput

   b. Space per unit price

   c. Data transfer rate

   d. Response time

9. **Which of the following terminology is used in the context of smart data categorization or tiered storage?**

   a. Performance (IOPS) per unit price

   b. Space (GB) per unit price

   c. Solid state drive (SSD) type

   d. All of the above

10. **A customer observes few IOPS, in the range of 100-200, on an high-end enterprise storage; he wants to know the possible reasons:**

    a. His host is not demanding enough I/Os from storage

    b. Frontend of his storage is not capable of processing 100-200 IOPS

    c. Backend of his storage is not capable of processing 100-200 IOPS

11. **Which of the two among the following impact the performance of storage:**

    a. Dynamic capacity management (LUN shrink/expansion) feature

    b. Thin provisioning feature

    c. Disk type

    d. RAID implementation

    e. Remote replication

12. **Quality of service mainly deals with:**

    a. Distributing load across of the physical disks

    b. Fair share of optimal storage space

    c. Fair share of resources for optimal storage performance

    d. All of the above

13. **Which of the following features that impact workload performance, but not implemented within a storage system?**

    a. Data tiering

    b. Quality of service (QoS)

c. XCOPY/WSAME

d. Multipath

14. **Which are the terminologies used in context of data tiering?**

    a. Performance per unit price (IOPS/$)

    b. Level of fault tolerance per unit price (Surviving from number of failures/$)

    c. Space per unit price (GB/$)

    d. All of them

15. **Which is not an implementation within storage system?**

    a. Active-Active controller operation

    b. Caching technique

    c. RAID technology

    d. Multipath

16. **Match the following:**

    I.   Throughput   1. LUN

    ii. Storage system   2. IOPS

    iii. Virtual volume   3. Array

    a. (I) - (1), (ii) - (2) and (iii) - (3)

    b. (ii) - (1), (I) - (2) and (iii) - (3)

    c. (iii) - (1), (ii) - (2) and (i) - (3)

    d. (iii) - (1), (I) - (2) and (ii) - (3)

Descriptive questions

1. Describe three primary factors that characterize workload.
2. Describe three storage features that enhance the performance of a storage system.
3. Name caching techniques that influence storage performance and explain how?

Quiz questions

1. An application administrator observed performance degradation due to slow response from storage device and requested storage administrator to implement multipath. Will application performance be improved by implementing multipath?
2. How performance of a storage system is measured for OLTP workload?
3. Typically between small block random read and write, which operation is faster for a storage system and why?

Glossary and key terms

- **Data transfer rate**: Amount of data transferred per unit time. Units are MBps, GB per hour and TB per hour.

- **IOPS**: I/O per second, number of I/O requests completed per unit .Unit is IOPS.

- **Latency**: Time to process a single I/O request. Unit is millisecond (ms).

- **Response time**: Same as latency, time to process a single I/O request.

- **Random I/O**: I/O request patent requested by host server on random block on virtual volume.

- **Sequential I/O**: I/O request pattern requested host server sequentially.

- **XCOPY**: EXTENDED COPY, T10 SCSI standard to copy data within storage without needing to transfer the data between the Storage volume and the server.

- **WSAME**: WRITE SAME, T10 SCSI standard, an initiator to zero a large number of disk blocks without needing to transfer a large number of zeroed buffers.

- **QoS**: Quality of service, allows fair share of resources for optimal storage performance.

Join our Discord space

Join our Discord workspace for latest updates, offers, tech happenings around the world, new releases, and sessions with the authors:

https://discord.bpbonline.com

## CHAPTER 7

Fault Tolerance and Data Protection

Introduction

One of the primary objectives of a storage system is to protect the business critical data from all possible hardware and software failures. In the first three chapters, we learned that the storage solution and storage systems are designed to prevent any disruption of host access to data in the event of hardware failure at every level, starting from multipath, multiple controllers, disk enclosures with dual path cabling, RAID implementation. In addition to these, all storage vendors implement several other features and functionalities, such as snapshot, clone, and data replication to protect data. Organizations also take additional precaution to implement backup solution that helps to recover data, if required.

Structure

Upon successful completion of this chapter, you will learn about:

- Storage features that enhance fault tolerant aspect of the solution
- Local replication
- Remote replication and disaster recovery
- Backup solution
- Continuous data protection
- Copy data management

Objectives

By the end of this chapter, you will learn about various features that enable host application to continue accessing the data in the event of failure within storage solution or storage system. This chapter also explains storage technologies related to data protection, such as snapshot, clone, and replication that allow recovery of data in case of any corruption or accidental loss. This chapter also highlights different type of backup solutions that organizations implement to recover data in case of any loss.

Fault tolerance and data protection

In the context of storage fault tolerance and data protection, two important terminologies, **business continuity (BC)** and **disaster recovery (DR)** are commonly used.

BC is more of proactive planning and strategy that ensures availability of business critical data so that organization's business operates with minimal or no downtime or outage. DR is reactive measure about how quickly data can be recoveredand applications are restored back in operation in an event of a disaster. Features and functionalities of an intelligent storage system, described below,support organizations to implement both business continuity and disaster recovery solution.

Multipath: Multipath is an in-built driver component of any modern operating system running on the host server. This component is considered as part of a storage solution. In case of any link failure between host server and storage system, multipath driver running in operating system redirects all I/O requests to via other surviving paths. Link failure can be caused by any cable fault, switch failure or any other disruption in the environment. Following diagram shows an example, in which path between HBA2 and Switch2 failed, in this situation, all read/write requests will be processed via HBA1 paths. During normal operation, if bandwidth utilization is more than the bandwidth of HBA1 path, then failure of HBA2 paths may impact performance of the read/write requests until failed path is restored.

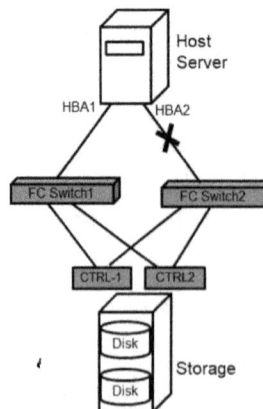

Figure 7.1: Fault tolerance through multipath

Multiple controllers: Every storage system is designed for at least two or more controllers. One of the reasons to have multiple controllers is to continue application access in case of controller failure. Any hardware or software component of a controller can stop functioning, in this situation, application is not even aware about the failure, as other surviving controllers seamlessly take over the read/write operations.

As shown in the following figure, **controller 1 (CTRL1)** failure causes **controller 2 (CTRL2)** to take over the operations

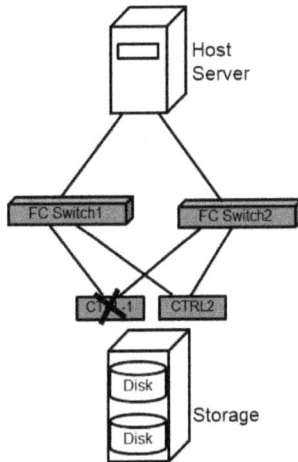

Figure 7.2: Fault tolerance through multiple controllers

Disk enclosures with dual path: In the backend of the storage system, disk enclosures are also designed to have two paths to controllers. This is to ensure, in case of one path failures, communication with physical disks still maintained by the controllers. Each physical disk also has two ports one connected to one path and other to other path.

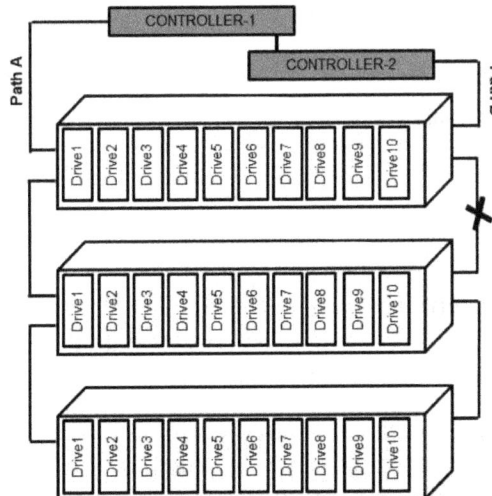

Figure 7.3: Fault tolerance in dual path disk enclosure

RAID implementation: As discussed in *Chapter 3, RAID* is one of the important considerations within storage system to ensure no impact of host accessing data in case of any disk failure. Except RAID level 0, all other RAID levels provide fault tolerance in the storage system. For instance, data on a RAID 6 volume will be accessible even after failure of maximum of two disk failure.

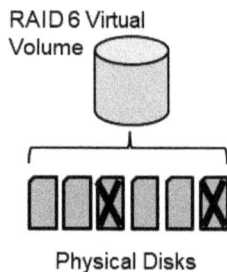

Figure 7.4: Fault tolerance in RAID

An underlying number of physical disks in a virtual volume also determines fault tolerance level. For example, if single RAID 5 volume configured on 10 physical disks, the probability of volume failure is more due to any two disks failure together, compared to having two RAID 5 volumes each having 5 physical disks. Of course, in scenario 2, there would be total two disks space lost due to parity, whereas in scenario 1 one disk space is lost.

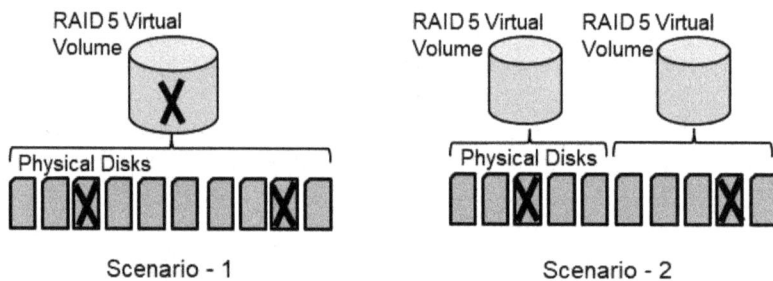

Figure 7.5: Number of disks and fault tolerance

Spare disk

Spare disk configuration within a storage system adds greater value in fault tolerance and data protection. It prevents the system to go in the degraded state. Upon failure of a disk, rebuild process usages the spare disk to generate data that was on the failed disk and make the virtual volume back to a healthy state.

Storage system without spare disk configured goes into a degraded state upon failure of a disk. Depending on RAID level subsequent failure of the disk can result in data loss. Therefore, it is recommended to have multiple spare disks configured to avoid any data loss due to disk failures. Whenever spare disk get consumed by the rebuilding process, it is also important to have the failed disk replaced with working one and have it configured as a spare disk.

Recovery point objective and recovery time objective

In any data protection solution **recovery point objective (RPO)** and **recovery time objective (RTO)** are two important parameters that drive on how to deploy the solutions.

- RPO: The maximum allowable threshold time of the data that is needed to restore in the event of a disaster. For example, if your RPO is 6 hours, you want to be able to restore systems back to the state they were in as of no longer than 6 hours ago.

- RTO: The time needed to recover from a disaster—usually determined by how long you can afford to be without your systems.

Data replication

There are multiple terminologies available for data replication. Replication of data is nothing but making a copy of data. The primary purpose of replication is to recover data in the event of data corruption or data loss. Replication features enhance fault tolerance and data protection aspects of a storage system. Primarily there are two types of replications implemented.

Local replication

Technologies that copies data locally to the same storage system are called **local replication**. Snapshot and clone are the examples of such technologies.

Data on a production virtual volume keep changes, an application constantly accesses it for read or write operations. Therefore, there is a need to have a point in time copy of data on a virtual volume that can be used for taking an offline backup, accessing data to generate report, and so on.

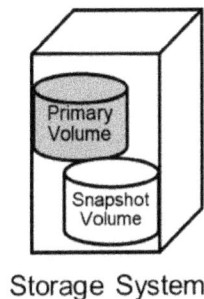

Storage System

Figure 7.6: Local replication: Snapshot

Snapshot is a **point in time** (**PIT**) copy of data on a virtual volume. For example, if a host accesses a snapshot that was created at 9:00 AM, it reflects the data of the primary production volume at that point in time. Some storage system allows restoring snapshot data back to the primary volume. In case of accidental deletion of data on primary volume, data corruption or virus infection, data on latest snapshot can be restored back on to the primary volume to recover the data. Data of snapshot can also be used for other purposes like generating an offline report, analytics, test or development.

Primary volume is also referred as the **parent volume** of a snapshot volume. Immediately after the creation of a snapshot, all blocks of the snapshot points to its parent volume, but as and when data on parent volume changes, old data gets copied to the snapshot and occupancy of snapshot increases. Blocks that are not changed since the creation of snapshot will continue to have the reference to parent volume.

Example:

At the time of snapshot creation, volume had data A, B, and C snapshot would also have the same data but all data is just reference to actual location of data on volume.

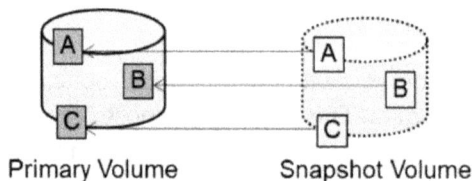

Figure 7.7: Snapshot: After creation

When a block of data is changed, let us say from C to D, data C is first copied to snapshot and then updated in parent volume from C to D. Reference from snapshot to parent volume for this data is also removed. Allocated size of snapshot grows by the size of data C. More writes in parent volume causes more updates and increase of allocated size of snapshot. In this process, snapshot continues to have the data at the time of creation of snapshot. Updated ones are physically located and unchanged ones still maintain reference to corresponding blocks in parent volume.

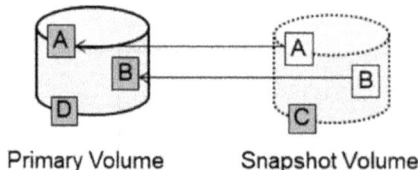

Figure 7.8: Snapshot: After writing or updating data on primary volume

In the above method, before every write operation, data block in parent volume is copied to snapshot, this method of data update commonly used by most vendors and is called **copy on write** (**COW**).

There is another popular method of data update implementation in snapshot technology called **redirect on write (ROW)**.

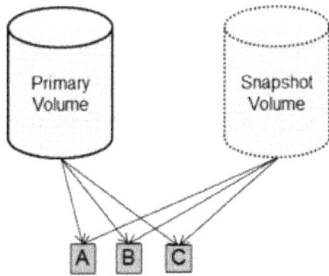

Figure 7.9: ROW After snapshot creation

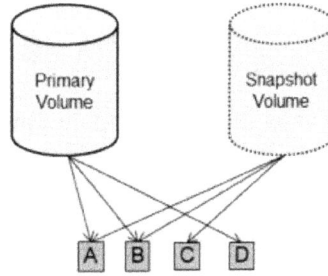

Figure 7.10: After writing or updating data on primary volume

In ROW, after the creation of snapshot all blocks referred by the snapshot are frozen. As shown in above figure, upon any new update for C, the new data D is simply written in a new location in the storage and parent volume refers to it, instead of C. Whereas snapshot continues to refer the C. Therefore, in this method, a copy of operation from parent to snapshot is saved, but data in parent volume may get fragmented.

COW vs. ROW:

Copy on write	Redirect on write
More write overhead	Less write overhead
Makes data contiguous	Makes data noncontiguous
Commonly implemented in storage systems	Few storage vendors implement it

Table 7.1: COW vs. ROW

Snapshot does not provide protection of data against physical media failures of the parent volume. For example, if a storage volume has snapshots and due to multiple underlying disks failure, if data on parent volume is no more accessible, in that case, snapshots associated with it would also not be accessible. However, logical error, such as accidental data deletion or modification from the host server or virus infection, previous data can be recovered from the snapshot.

There are two type of snapshots such as **read/only (RO)** and **read/write (RW)**. RW snapshot allows the host to update data on it. If a copy of production data is required for test or development of an application or some other purposes, a RW snapshot can be created as a copy of original data and then update data further on it.

Snapshot of snapshot:

Before making any change on a RW snapshot, another snapshot of it can be created to keep a copy of it before application writes data on to it. Snapshot of a RO snapshot can also be created to have a second copy of the data.

If application is continuously writing on to a RW snapshot, a snapshot of this snapshot can be scheduled, if the administrator wants to protect data of the snapshot at regular interval.

Snapshot creation of a parent volume at regular interval is called a **vertical tree** and number of a snapshot in the tree is referred to as the **depth** of the tree. In *Figure 7.1*, M is the depth of the vertical tree.

Similarly, snapshot of a snapshot at regular interval creates a horizontal tree and number of snapshots in the tree is referred to as depth the tree. In following diagram, N is the depth of the horizontal tree.

Virtual volume along with all its snapshots is called **virtual volume family**.

Depending on the storage system design, vendors set the maximum limit of the number of the snapshot that can be created for a virtual volume.

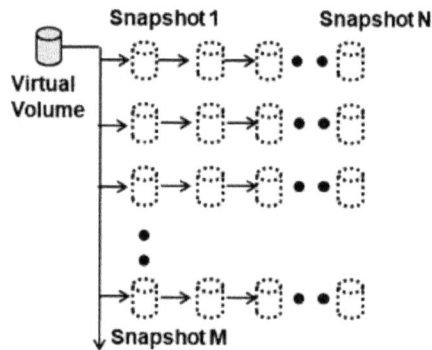

Figure 7.11: Snapshot of snapshot

Clone: The clone is another technology to create a copy of the data on a virtual volume. The clone is the same as a snapshot at the time of creation, but data blocks get copied in the background and eventually, clone becomes a separate and independent volume from the parent volume.

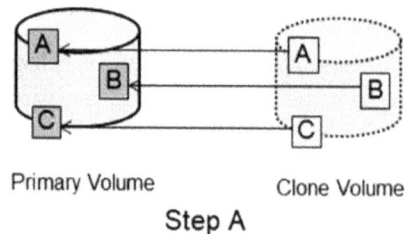

Figure 7.12: Clone creation

Step A:

As a first step of clone creation, all blocks are points to corresponding blocks in parent volume. This is similar to a snapshot.

Some vendors allow host access to the clone at this stage itself.

Step B:

After the creation of clone, blocks starts copying from parent to newly created clone volume in the background. Depending on the size of volume and data in it and system load, this process may take sufficient amount of time.

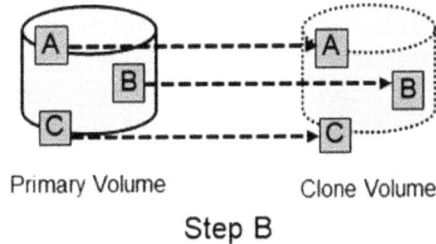

Primary Volume   Clone Volume

Step B

Figure 7.13: Background copy process

Step C:

Once background copy process is completed, clone becomes separate and independent from parent volume, now, clone will have the data same as parent volume at the time of creation of the clone.

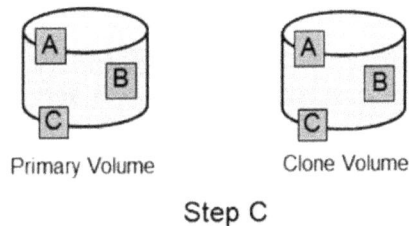

Primary Volume   Clone Volume

Step C

Figure 7.14: Clone separation

Since, clone is independent volume from parent, primary advantage of clone compared to snapshot is, it provides protection of data even in the case of physical failures of the parent volume. but for successful creation of a clone, amount of free space, same as parent volume, needed in the storage system.

Clone sync operation:

Most modern storage systems also allow synchronous operation of clone to its parent volume at regular interval, just to copy the difference in data since, it was last synced. For example, a clone was created on Monday at 10:00 PM, when it is synced with parent on Tuesday at 10:00 PM, instead of copying entire data again, only the blocks that are changed since Monday 10:00 PM to Tuesday 10:00 PM are copied. Clone can be again synced on Wednesday, and so on.

During sync operation application must be stopped and host must discontinue accessing the clone volume. This sync process helps applications that use the clone for analysis or report generation will have access up to data, without creating a new clone every time.

Remote replication

Technologies that copies data from one storage system to other storage system are called **remote replication**. This is typically implemented between two storage systems, which are geographically apart. In case of any disaster strikes, such as flood, earthquake or fire at either site, application can switch over to surviving site and continue its operations. Therefore, remote replication solution is also referred as disaster recovery solution. Large enterprise organizations, which deal with business critical applications, implement this solution to ensure their business continuity in case of any disaster.

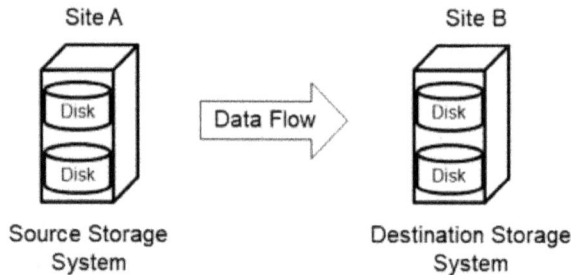

Figure 7.15: Storage remote replication

Different vendor uses different terminologies to name this pair of storage systems such as Source and target, local and remote, primary and secondary storages pairs.

Hosts write data to the virtual volumes in the source array, and the array copies the data to the virtual volumes in the destination array. I/O ordering is important to maintain across the virtual volumes used an application. A replication group is a logical entity that consists of source and target virtual volumes pairs in it. This concept is to configure an application data on all the virtual volumes in a replication group. Replication group ensures I/O consistency on the destination array in the event of a failure of the source array.

In the following example S_Vol1 and T_Vol1 volumes of same size make a replication pair and S_Vol2 and T_Vol2 also make another replication pair, and so on. An application can be configured to use multiple volumes. For example, a database requires minimum of three volumes for data, log and archive. In this case, one replication group needed to be configured, consists of three replication pairs for data, log, and archive.

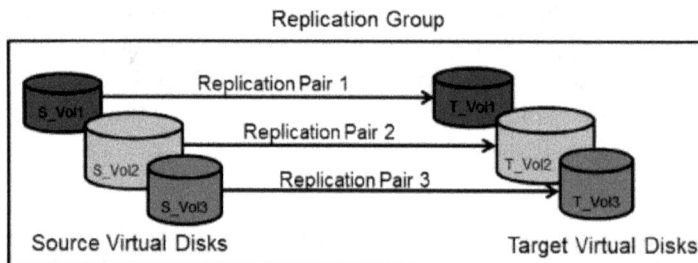

Figure 7.16: Replication group concept

In replication, failover reverses replication direction for a replication group. The destination array assumes the role of the source, and the source array assumes the role of the destination. Similarly, failback sets replication direction back to original. Failover and failback are done as part of planned maintenance or post any unplanned failures.

Storage system can have multiple replication groups to configure different application on each group.

To have load balance and utilize both storage systems effectively, most vendors support bi-directional replication. One or more application can be configured on each storage system and other storage system can be used as destination storage.

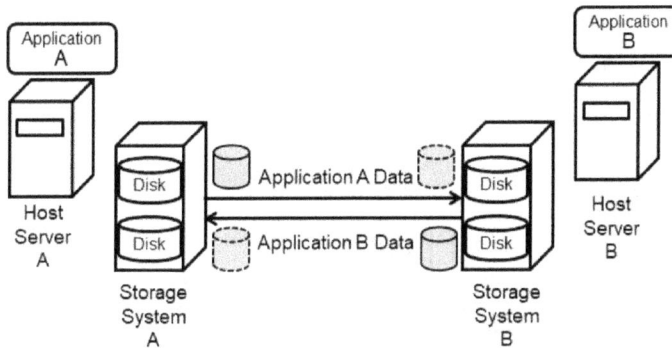

Figure 7.17: *Bi-directional remote replication*

There are typically two different mode of replicating data from source to destination storage systems such as synchronous and asynchronous.

Synchronous replication

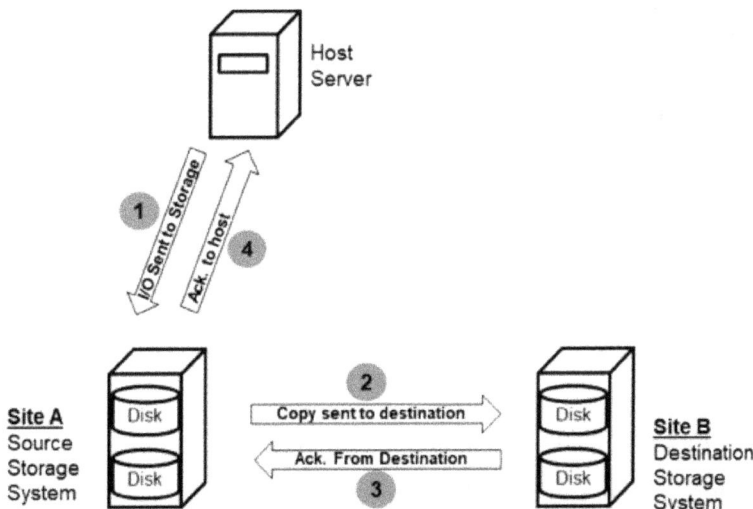

Figure 7.18: *Synchronous replication operations*

Following is the step-by-step process that takes place in synchronous replication:

Step 1: First host writes data to source storage.

Step 2: Source storage writes and then sends data to destination storage.

Step 3: Destination storage sends ACK to source storage.

Step 4: Source storage sends ACK to host server.

In synchronous replication, write I/O completion status not returned to host until both source and destination storage systems write data. Data is mirrored in real-time. Applications for which data consistency is crucial, requires synchronous replication. Since, data is replication real-time, this mode of replication can increase response time to host, if higher bandwidth of link is not used for replication.

Synchronous mode of replication is commonly referred as **sync replication**.

Asynchronous replication

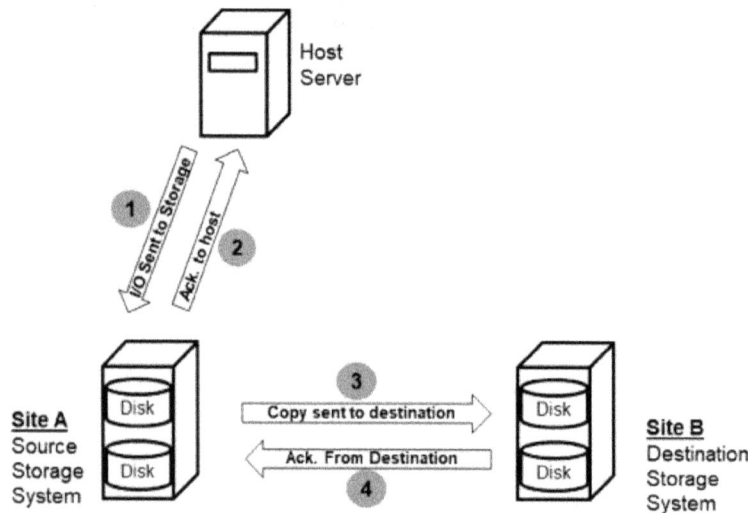

Figure 7.19: *Asynchronous replication operations*

Following is the step-by-step process that takes place in asynchronous replication:

Step 1: First host writes data to source storage.

Step 2: Source storage writes, stores in temporary location and then sends ACK to host server.

Step 3: Source storage sends data to destination storage.

Step 4: Destination storage sends ACKto source storage.

Step 3 and *step 4* are independent of *step 1* and *step 2*.

In asynchronous replication, I/O completion status returned when local write completes. Destination writes are deferred until later. Unwritten datastored temporarily on the source storage system's cache memory or any temporary disk space.

The primary disadvantage of in this mode of replication, unsent data from source to destination at risk if source system fails, but improves host write performance, as ACK sent immediately after writing to the local storage system.

Some storage vendors implement asynchronous replication through snapshot. A snapshot gets created at user to define the time interval and data on it. and get it copied to remote storage system.

In asynchronous replication, frequent updates of the same block of data is replicated only once to the destination within the update period, whereas, in synchronous replication every update, even for the same block, gets replicated every time.

To increase the degree of fault tolerance, replication can also be one to many, multiple hops. Typically, advance storage systems have these implemented.

Asynchronous mode of replication is commonly referred as **async replication**.

Generally replication between two storage systems of same vendor uses their own propriety protocol to copy data at block level. This makes the replication faster and more reliable. Most of the enterprise organizations prefer and implement block level replication in their environment.

Figure 7.20: Block level data replication between same types of storage systems

There are also software solutions available that accesses virtual volumes from both storage systems and copies data from one to other. Copy can be performed at file system level or a volume level. This solution is comparably slower and less reliable, but can be implemented in two different types of storage systems. Software based replication solution is most asynchronous replication.

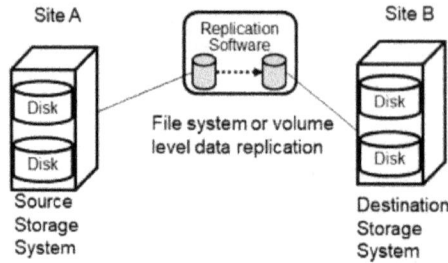

Figure 7.21: Software-based replication solution

Achieving RPO objective through data replication:

Local and remote replication both are data protection solution. For instance, to achieve six hours of RPO objective through local replication, you need to create snapshot at least every six hours. In synchronous remote replication, RPO value is zero. To improve RPO value for asynchronous replication both the storage systems must be have sufficient bandwidth available and unwritten data space at local storage system. In case of snapshot based asynchronous replication, you need to specify replication at least every six hours. Of course, bandwidth must be available to copy the change data within six hours of time to avoid overlap with next replication cycle.

Backup solution

Backup solution is a data backup and recovery solution that ensures critical data is copied on to another system at a regular internal basis. Backup solution is also the part of a storage solution. The system on which data is backed up is called **backup system**; it can have pool of tape drives, disk drives or optical disks. Backup system is also called **secondary storage**, which is typically designed to store more data. Primary storage, such as storage disk arrays are designed for high performance. Applications run on host server, do not perform direct RW operation on to the backup system.

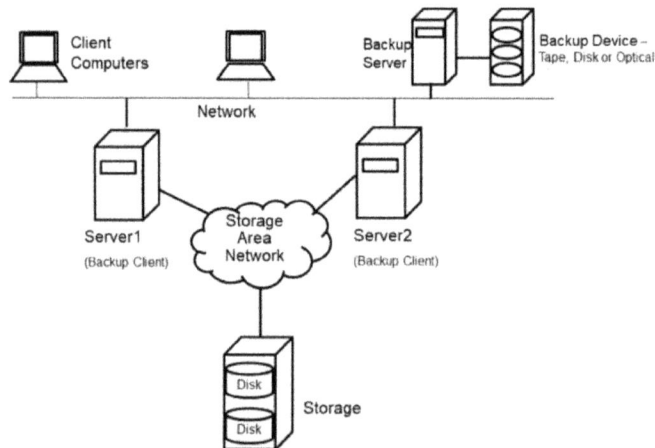

Figure 7.22: Traditional backup solution

Though remote replication technology copies data from storage system to other, it has a disadvantage. In the event of accidental deletion or update of data, data corruption, virus infected data also gets replicated other storage system. Replication solution does not help these scenarios. Therefore every organization must implement backup solution to recover data in case of any loss.

Backup solution typically consists of a backup server that runs backup software, client part of the backup software run on application servers and then backup jobs are configured and scheduled to read data from application server and copy to backup devices. First backup is called **full backup**, subsequent backup of the same set of data is called **incremental backup**, as it copies only the changed data since last full or incremental backup.

Some backup solution also copies the on to cloud storage to ensure double protection of data and easy access from geographical location.

Snapshot based data backup solution:

Recent years storage snapshot based data backup is replacing traditional backup solution. Snapshot is a PIT copy of the data of a primary virtual volume. Instead of reading data from application server, data directly read from snapshot of the virtual volume on which application stores data.

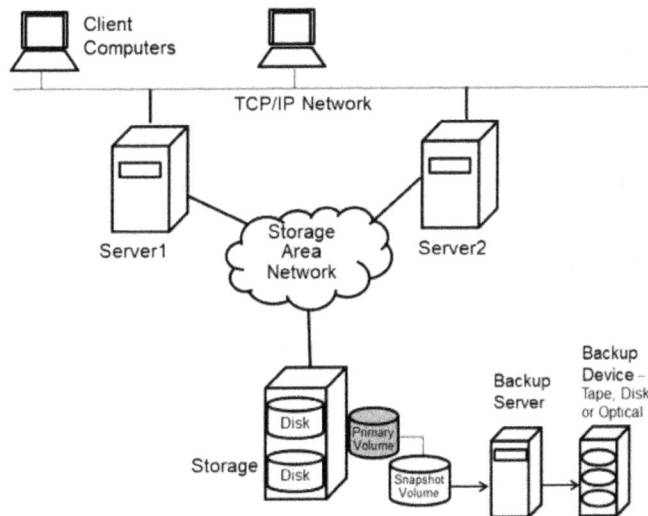

Figure 7.23: Snapshot based backup solution

Every time backup job is run, a snapshot is created and reads the data from the snapshot and copy on to a backup system. This method of backup technology is called **flat backup**.

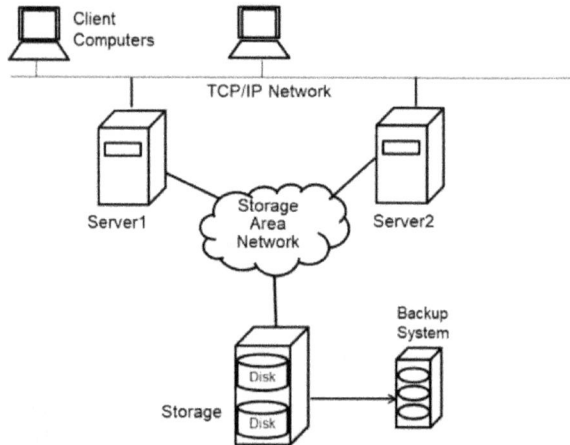

Figure 7.24: *Direct backup solution*

Latest storage systems or backup system have backup software incorporated within it that eliminates the need of a separate backup server in between and copies data directly from storage system to backup system. Thus, it improves efficiency of data copied further.

Some storage systems and backup software are intelligent to understand data blocks on the snapshot that has user data, software backs up only those blocks, thus reduces backup time significantly. However, this impact only first backup.

Subsequent backups are called **incremental backup**. Some intelligent storage system has **changed block tracking** (**CBT**) technology implemented; backup software leverages this technology to backup only the blocks that have changed with respect to previous snapshot and backup.

When application is actively performing RW operations on to the storage volumes, at any given time there may be some part of data in memory, therefore, PIT snapshot may miss in-memory data. Application may find in-consistency upon recovery of the data from this snapshot. To create an application consistent snapshot, backup software sends a command to application to quiesce the I/O operations and flash the data to disk, once completed, snapshot gets created and then I/O is resumed. Quiescing is a technique to pause application I/Os for a while to get it is consistent state.Snapshot created with this method is called **application-consistent snapshots**. Snapshot created without quiescing application is called crash-consistent snapshot.

For instance, to achieve six hours of RPO objective through local replication, you need to schedule backup at least every six hours.

Continuous data protection

Continuous data protection (**CDP**) refers to real-time data backup for every change of data. This technology keeps tracks of all the changes of data and ensures backup is always occurring. Unlike traditional backup, CDP technology does not require any scheduling of backup tasks.

Data on virtual volume can be reverted to any point in time data. For example, suppose the data gets infected or corrupted at 9:41 AM. Data that was at 9:40 AM can be restored back. Therefore, with CDP technology, RPO value is near to zero.

Most vendors offer CDP through implementing frequent snapshots. Some intelligent storage system is capable of keeping track of every change of block in a journal. But these frequent tasks create an overhead in the system and impacts host server I/O performance. Therefore, frequency of CDP backup becomes a tunable parameter and tradeoff for an administrator to decide between performance and granularity of data backup.

Copy data management:

Data on snapshot or backup sets are not only used for recovery, these copies of data can also be used for other purposes, such as report generation, data analytics, test, and development. Recent days need for these is significantly growing because of big data and ecommerce evolutions.

Copy data management is a software solution that manages copies of data more efficiently and meets the demand of several copies at the same time.

Write Once Read Many:

Some storage vendors make backup device or media that allows **Write Once Read Many** (**WORM**) technology, which is used to archive data for long periodof time in terms of years. This way of storing not only prevents accidental deletion or modification of data, but also enhances lifespan of storage device or media. Most organizations look for this feature compliance for their data protection policies for data security and legal reasons.

CD-R or Blu-ray discs are WORM storage, but they cannot store TBs of data, hence special WORM devices or media are used.

Content addressable storage (**CAS**) is a storage technology, in which data is stored based on unique address derived from the data itself. CAS technology primarily is designed for archival solution to store and access of fixed data that does not change over time. Once the data object is stored, it cannot be altered or deleted, thus supports WORM technology.

Modern object stores also rely on **globally unique identifiers** (**GUIDs**) but no longer generate them from the content. Object storage evolved from concept of CAS technology, in which data is used as an object along with the metadata and unique identifier.

Conclusion

Data protection has always been a critical requirement for any storage solution. Fundamentally this has two aspects that is, prevention of disruption due to any hardware of software component failure, that is fault tolerance. and secondly, recovery of data, in case of any disaster or accidental loss of data. There are several features and solutions that are implemented to address both of these aspects. For example, multiple controllers in a storage system, disk enclosure with dual cabling, multipath configuration provides NSPOF. A fully NSPOF solution requires host server with at least two HBAs, two switches and storage system with high availability features like multiple controllers, disclosures, and so on. Any component failure will cause workload to switch to other available active paths.

Snapshot is a PIT copy of primary volume. Initially, all the blocks of a snapshot are referred to the **corresponding blocks** of primary volume, as and when data on primary volume changes, first the old data is copied to snapshot area and then the reference of snapshot block to the primary block is broken.

There is a wide variety of usages of a snapshot. It helps to have a copy of application data at regular interval, data can be recovered to the latest copy or a desired snapshot, if data gets corrupted, and configuration changed accidently, virus infection. Snapshot data can also be used for report generation, analytics, and test and development purposes.

Purpose of snapshot and clone is almost same except, clone becomes an independent volume once all blocks are physically copied and references are unlinked. Snapshot and clone, both are called local replication, as the data gets copied locally within the storage system.

In remote replication, data gets copied to another storage system, called remote and target storage system. Target storage system can be physically located at same place of source storage system or at different geographical location to provide better fault tolerance in the event of any natural calamities, such as flood, fire or earthquake.

There are two primary modes of remote replication. In synchronous mode, every data gets replicated to remote site and acknowledged to host server. If bandwidth between both storage systems are not sufficient, write operations may be slow and copy of each data at both sites are guaranteed, in Asynchronous mode, data first gets written to local site, stored temporarily for replication in later point of time. This mode allows completing the I/O operation faster and replication of data between two, may not be in exact sync always.

Backup solution is also another way to protect data from any accidental loss. In recent days, instead of application server, snapshot technology is used to copy data directly from storage system to backup system. This improves backup performance significantly.

Case studies

Case study 1: An organization has business critical data, ready to compromise with performance

Let us look at the following case study:

Requirement

A financial business organization has business critical data. They are looking for storage solution that can protect from any system failure. They are ready to compromise with performance, but not with data loss situation.

Analysis

Disaster recovery solution makes a copy of data from one storage system to other. Since this organization is concerned protection of data, disaster recovery can be recommended. There are two replication modes available, synchronous, and asynchronous. In synchronous replication node, every bit of data replicates to other system before it acknowledges to host system, thus ensures highly protected solution.

To protect data in the local system itself, RAID 1 or RAID 6 can be suggested, which provides highest level of data protection against any disk failure.

In addition to it, a backup solution can recommended to keep a copy of the data off site.

Solution

Following are the solutions proposed to protect data against any failure:

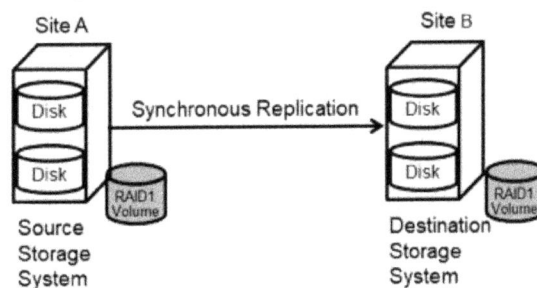

Figure 7.25: Synchronous Replication

RAID level: RAID 1

Replication solution: Yes

Replication mode: Synchronous

Backup solution: Yes

Case study 2: Protect from accidental deletion by end users

Let us look at how to prevent accidental deletion by end users:

Requirement

An origination has deployed a high-end storage solution along with fault protection features. but administrator is still concerned about the data deletion or corruption by the employees of the organization. What solution can be proposed here?

Analysis

Disaster recovery solution replicates data from one storage system to other. but if data is corrupted or deleted at source, same data get replicated at target site. Therefore, disaster recovery does not solve this problem.

Best suitable solution to protect data against accidental deletion is snapshot technology. Administrator can schedule regular interval. In case of any accidental deletion of data, previous data can be retrieved from snapshot.

Frequency of snapshot creation can be decided based on desired RPO value. It can be daily or even five minutes granularity. Let us consider hourly snapshot creation for this case.

Retention of snapshot is also an important decision. Number of days the snapshots can be retained. Let us consider that the retention period of a snapshot is one week.

Solution

A scheduled job can be created to create snapshot of data volume at every hour interval. Also, another scheduled job to delete week old snapshots. Therefore, at any given point in time, the volume will have about 24 x 7 = 168 snapshots. This solution will help administrator to restore data from latest available snapshot, in case of any accidental data deletion or corruption by the employees.

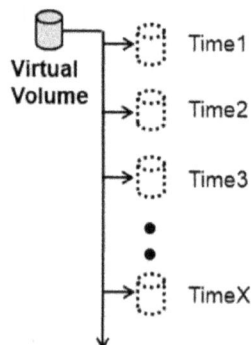

Figure 7.26: Scheduled snapshot

Case study 3: High availability support for a storage solution

Let us look at high availability support for a storage solution:

Requirement

A healthcare institute is planning to deploy a storage solution. Availability is the most critical requirement. They cannot compromise with inaccessibility of data at any cost. What solution can be proposed to this requirement?

Analysis

Most enterprise storage system provides number of features to ensure availability of the data. A fully NSPOF solution needs to be implemented starting from host server:

- At least two host server in cluster configuration
- Each server with two FC HBAs
- Two independent fabric
- Multipath configured
- Storage system with multiple controllers, dual path disk enclosures
- Volumes are configured with RAID 1
- Spare disk configured
- Monitoring any error in the system and take corrective action so on
- Disaster recovery
- A management software to automatic failover application from one site other in event of failure

Implementation of these features enables the solution high available, which allows data availability in the event of any hardware failure or disaster.

Solution

Schematic diagram of the solution shown as follows. All the configurations discussed above are needed to be configured to make solution more robust and protect from all possible failures.

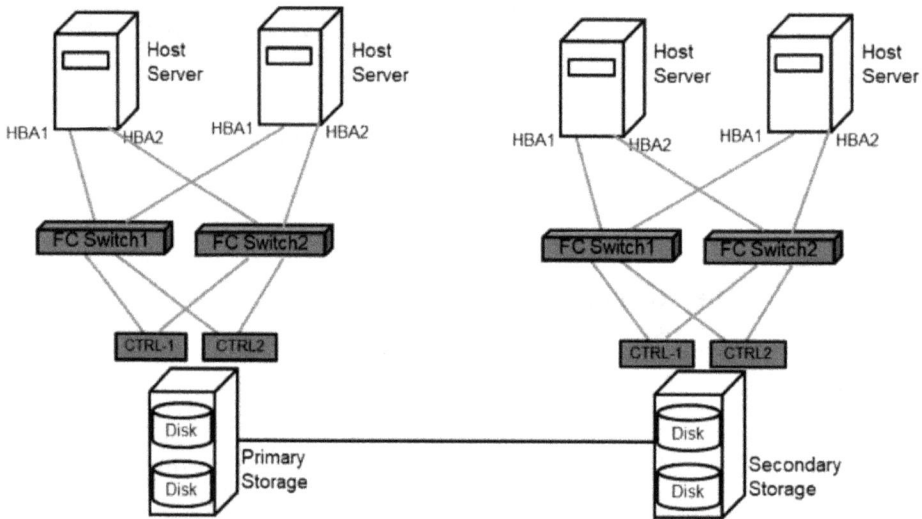

Figure 7.27: High available storage solution

Learning check

Objective questions

1. **Mirroring data of one storage to other is part of:**

    a. Disaster recovery solution

    b. Backup solution

    c. Capacity management solution

    d. Storage management solution

2. **RPO and RTO terminologies are used in the context of:**

    a. Performance enhancement

    b. Data protect and backup solution

    c. Capacity management solution

    d. Storage management solution

3. **In replication solution, failover and failback operations are performed at:**

    a. Storage system level

    b. Replication group level

    c. Virtual volume level

    d. Storage controller level

4. **Snapshot is part of:**

    a. Disaster recovery solution

    b. Backup solution

    c. Remote replication

    d. Local replication

5. **A 100 GB storage has one volume of 80 GB created. Which are the statements true for snapshot and clone creation?**

    a. Clone creation will be successful

    b. Clone creation will fail

    c. Snapshot creation will fail

    d. Snapshot creation will be successful

6. **Local and remote replication solutions are mainly used for:**

    a. Reducing data storage cost

    b. Improvin performance

    c. Protecting data

    d. All of the above

7. **Which two of the following features impact the fault tolerant of storage:**

    a. Dynamic capacity management (LUN shrink/expansion) feature

    b. Thin Provisioning feature

    c. Disk type

    d. RAID implementation

    e. Replication solution

8. **A customer has configured his database on three different storage volumes (500 GB, 2 TB, and 5 TB) from a storage system. He now wants to implement a remote replication solution for better fault tolerance, what he needs to do?**

    a. Buy an additional storage with minimum of usable capacity of 7.2 TB; configure three replication groups, each consisting of one source and one target volume.

    b. No need to buy an additional storage. Configure a replication group on the same storage consisting these three source volumes.

    c. Buy an additional storage with minimum of usable capacity of 7.2 TB, configure a replication group consisting these three source and three target volumes.

    d. Buy an additional storage with any usable capacity; configure three replication groups, each consisting of one source and one target volume.

9. **A snapshot of data object contains:**
   a. An image of data at a particular PIT
   b. An image of data for a period of time
   c. Same data all the time
   d. Incremental data

10. **Which of the following features not only protects data but also prevents disruption of access to the data on primary volume?**
    a. Copy data management
    b. Snapshot technology
    c. Backup solution
    d. RAID 1

11. **Which of the following features provide only fault tolerance in storage solution, but no data protection.**
    a. Backup solution
    b. Snapshot technology
    c. Multipath
    d. RAID 1

12. **Which of the following does not provide data protection in the event of physical failure underlying disks of a virtual volume?**
    a. Snapshot
    b. Clone
    c. Backup
    d. Remote replication

13. **A clone was created at 9:00 AM. It completed background copy at 10:00 AM. Data on the clone volume will same as data on parent virtual volume at:**
    a. 9:00 AM
    b. 10:00 AM
    c. In between of 9:00 AM and 10:00 AM
    d. Cannot be determined

14. **RPO for synchronous replication is:**
    a. 0
    b. 1 hour

    c. 2 hours

    d. 3 hours

15. **Which of the following solution should not be implemented to protect data against any accidental deletion?**

    a. Snapshot

    b. Clone

    c. Backup

    d. Remote replication

Descriptive questions

1. Describe different levels of fault tolerance features that are implemented in a storage solution and as well within a storage system. Starting from host server up to the physical disk behind the storage controller.

2. Explain use case and purpose of snapshot of snapshot.

3. Describe advantage and disadvantage of synchronous and asynchronous mode replication.

4. Describe difference between business continuity BC and DR solutions. Features of a storage system associated to BC and DR.

Quiz questions

1. Difference between COW or ROW, which snapshot technology provides better write performance on to a RW snapshot and why?

2. What is the purpose of bi-directional remote replication?

3. Snapshots are used only for backup purpose. Do you support this statement?

4. What is WORM and name three benefits of it?

Glossary and key terms

- **Business continuity**: Proactive measure to ensure availability of business critical data.

- **Disaster recovery**: Process and procedure of recovering data back in normal operation after a disaster strike.

- **Recovery point objective**: The maximum age of the data you want to restore in the event of a disaster.

- **Recovery time objective**: The time needed to recover from a disaster.

- **Point-in-time**: Refers to Snapshot that holds data at given PIT of parent volume.

- **Snapshot**: A PIT copy of the contents of a virtual volume created without interrupting I/O operations on it. Snapshots are typically used for short-term tasks, such as report generation and backups.

- **Clone**: A copy of parent virtual volume, but separate and intendant virtual volume.

- **Copy on write**: Data first gets written to snapshot and updates data in parent volume.

- **Redirect on write**: Data gets written to a new location and parent volume points to it. Snapshot continues to point to original locations.

- **Continued data protection**: Makes a copy of data for change of data.

- **Sync or synchronous replication**: A mode remote replication, in which data gets replicated before acknowledges write operation to host.

- **Async or asynchronous replication**: A remote replication mode, in which data gets acknowledges first to host and then replicates to destination storage in the background.

- **Application consistent snapshot**: Snapshot that is created after quescing I/O operations on the primary volume and flashing in-memory data by the application.

- **Crash consistent snapshot**: Snapshot that is created without quescing I/O operations.

- **Flat backup**: Backup solution that reads data from snapshot and copies on to a backup system, without reading data from host servers.

- **Changed block tracking**: It is technology using which storage system keeps track of blocks that got updated by the host servers. Backup software refer those blocks to perform incremental backup.

- **Copy data management**: It is a software solution using which number of copies of data is managed efficiently and meets requirement of multiple copies.

- **Write Once Read Many**: A data archival technology to store data in an unalterable way.

Join our Discord space

Join our Discord workspace for latest updates, offers, tech happenings around the world, new releases, and sessions with the authors:

https://discord.bpbonline.com

CHAPTER 8
Space Efficiency

Introduction

For many years of storage technology evolution, primary focus was performance and fault tolerance. Technologies related to efficiently storing data, such as thin provisioning, deduplication, compression, reclamation came into implementation and practice only in recent years. This is because the explosive growth of data in last few years caused demand for more space in the storage system. Today, most modern storage systems have these features implemented to ensure data consumed less amount disk space.

Structure

At the end of this chapter, you will learn about Storage system features that enhance the space efficiency of a storage system:

- Thin provisioning
- Space reclamation
- Dynamic capacity management–volume expansion and shrink
- Deduplication and compression

Objectives

In this chapter, you will learn about the storage features that stores data in the most efficient way. Those features are thin provisioning, expand, shrink, space reclamation (UNMAP), deduplication and compression. Detailed explanation of these features, guides you to understand how each feature works and efficiently stores the data in a storage system.

Thin provisioning

Traditionally, when a volume is created, required storage space gets allocated. When the volume is deleted space gets released.

Again, from a host when you write data on to a file system, free space on the file system reduces and when you delete data, free space increases in the file system.

Now imagine, similarly, at storage level, if space allocation occurs as and when data is written from host, then there would have been many advantages, such as sharing available storage space with more number of hosts. This is called **thin provisioning feature**. Thin provisioning feature is commonly available in almost all modern storage systems today.

With thin provisioning feature, a large volume can be created even with less size of hard drives, and required drives can be procured as and when data grows. Basically pay as you use concept.

For example, you bought four drives of 2 TB, without thin provisioning feature, you can create only one RAID 1 volume of 4 TB. No room left to create any additional volume and provide access to another host.

Whereas, with thin provisioning feature, you can create large size virtual volume as many as you want. Let us say, you created three numbers of virtual volumes of each size 10 TB. After providing access to hosts, operating system would recognize all the volumes as 10 TB. However, if you copy 1TB data to any of those volumes, you would be left with 3 TB worth of space to copy data to any of three volumes.

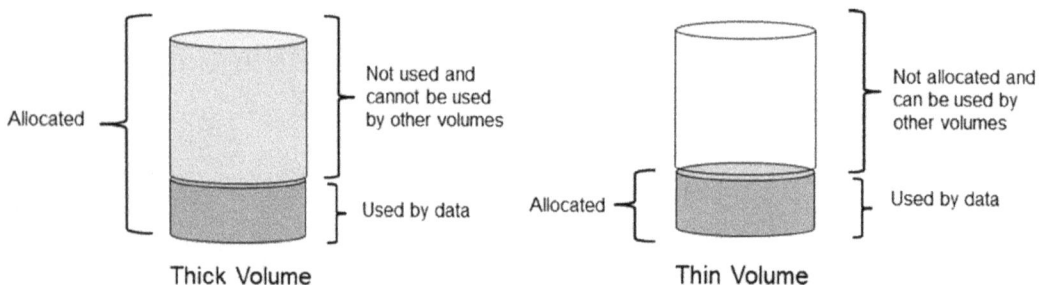

Figure 8.1: Thick and thin volume provisioning

Storage vendors also implement a notification to user when thin provisioning volume about to run out of physical space.

Following is another example to show, without thin provisioning capability, space get allocated during volume creation, no matter how much host data is written. On the other hand, with Thin Provisioning capability, space get allocated as and when host writes data, no matter how big volume is created.

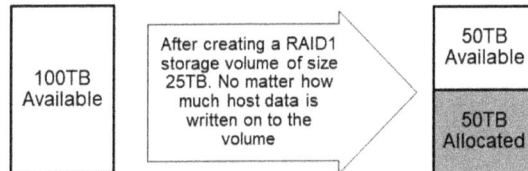

Figure 8.2: Example of a thick volume

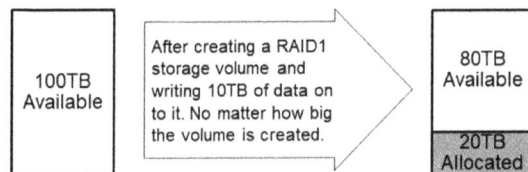

Figure 8.3: Example of a thin volume

Space reclamation

If data is removed from the thin provisioned volume, space is freed up on the file system, but the physical capacity on the storage system remains consumed. Most of the modern storages have space reclamation feature nowadays, which is a space reclamation mechanism used to return blocks of storage back to the array after data which was once occupying those blocks have been moved or deleted. After de-allocation, these blocks can be used by other logical volumes or the same logical volume later.

Space reclamation feature is not applicable for thick volume, as all blocks are always allocated.

This feature is based on T10 SCSI UNMAP standard. Some vendor refer space reclamation feature as UNMAP feature.

Some operating systems, such as Microsoft Windows 2012 or later and VMWare vSphere ESXi, send SCSI UNMAP commands to the Storage system at regular interval to ensure all blocks corresponding to the deleted data are de-allocated at storage system level.

Dynamic capacity management

Storage feature that helps user to expand and shrink virtual volumes is called **dynamic capacity management**. However, different storage vendor may call it with different name.

When you run out of space on the volume, you may like to expand it. Again, to create any additional virtual volume or allow other volume to grow, you may like shrink an existing volume, if you anticipate space will not be used much in future.

Modifying the metadata table pertaining to the virtual volume to allocate more number of blocks on physical disks for expansion and less number of blocks for the shrink.

Though storage system allows you to change the size of a volume, operating file system and application must be intelligent enough to understand this change.

With popularity of thin provisioning feature, expansion and shrink is not much needed, as user can create larger volume than available physical space and share available space more efficiently among all virtual volumes. Expand and shrink mostly used with thick volumes.

Deduplication and compression

Data deduplication and compression are techniques to reduce requirement of storage space. Both are different techniques and solve the different problems. Deduplication removes redundant data, keeping only one, whereas compression keeps all data, just brings them closer so that they consume less space.

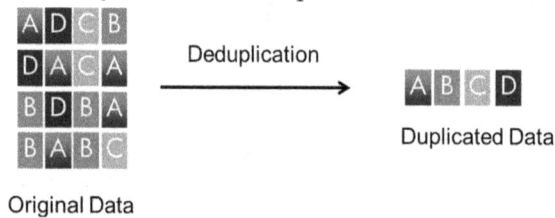

Figure 8.4: Deduplication process

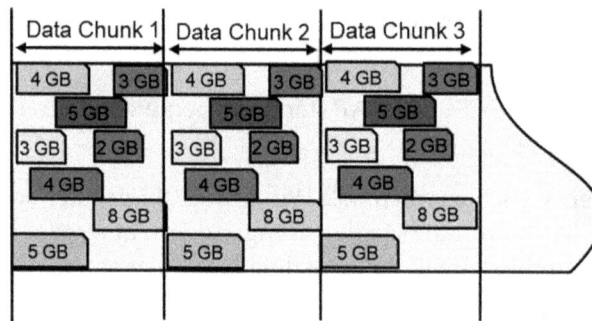

Figure 8.5: Original data

Deduplication keeps only one unique instance of the data on storage media, and redundant data is replaced with a pointer to the unique data copy.

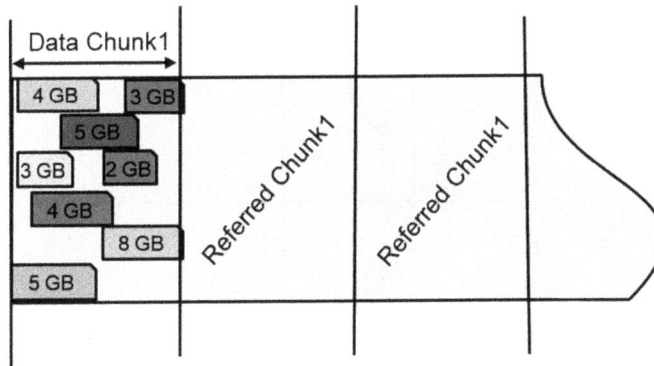

Figure 8.6: After deduplication

Deduplication granularity is referred as amount of data unit at which duplicate data are compared and computed. This is also called **deduplication chunk size**. For simplicity of implementation most vendors design deduplication with internally fixed value of deduplication chunk size, however some vendors allow user to change it as tunable parameter.

A smaller chunk size results in more granular data and results in identifying more duplicates. However, smaller chunks have additional costs of computation overhead and fragmentation. Larger chunk size results in a less deduplication, faster processing, and less fragmentation.

Virtual volume with deduplication enabled is commonly referred as dedup volume.

Compression represents original data with minimum number of bits needed.

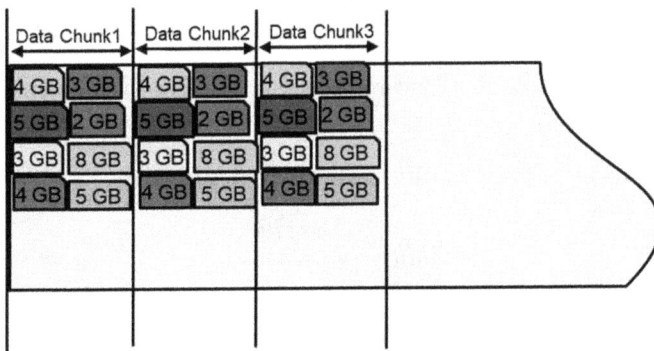

Figure 8.7: After compression

Deduplication achieves better efficiency against smaller data chunks, whereas compression achieves better efficiency against larger chunks.

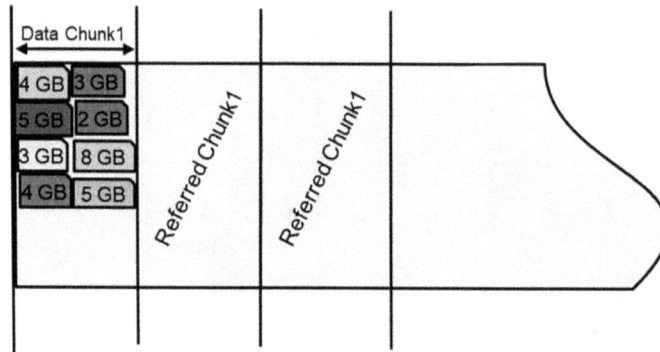

Figure 8.8: After deduplication and compression

Not all data is compressible or deduplicable. Again, degree of compression and deduplication depends on the number of repeating data the data content and a file with common data in it. Depending on data type, deduplication and compression can work together. Upon read request storage controller does un-deduplication of duplicated data. This process is called **rehydration**.

To save time, in most storage systems compression is performed only on unique data chunks after deduplication.

Storage vendors use many different deduplication and compression algorithms. Some are more CPU-intensive and sophisticated than others.

To avoid performance impact, deduplication and compression is generally preferred on cold data, meaning the data that is not being accessed by the host actively. However, some vendor implement inline deduplication and compression with latest hardware and software solutions.

Inline deduplication and compression reduces data while it is being written to the disk, whereas post-process first writes the data on to the disk then reduces it later point in time.

Inline data reduction technologies also reduce the number of I/O operations in storage system.

Space reduction ratios by capacity optimization are depicted as:

$$Ratio = \frac{Data\ in}{Data\ out}$$

Deduplication's effectiveness is expressed as deduplication ratio, meaning the ratio of the amount of data sent by host server to the amount of datastored in storage. For example, if 40 GB of data is deduplicated and requires only 2 GB space to store on disk, the ratio becomes 40:2 = 20:1. A 20:1 ratio means that 20 times data from host server is stored than the actual space required to store it,

Some vendors express this space reduction ratio as multiples or percentage. For above example 20:1 is expressed as 20x or (1 - 1/20) x 100 = 95%

Compression ratio is also calculated using same method as deduplication ratio.

Since most vendors perform compression after deduplication, compression ratio is expressed as ratio of post-deduplication data and post-compression data. In the above example if 2 GB of post-deduplication data further compressed to 1 GB, compression ratio becomes 2:1

Following is an example to illustrate how compression works. In the address table there are some strings which are common; the compression algorithm determines the common strings and stores in a dictionary table along with unique symbols and then the data table is represented by another table which has the symbol of the dictionary.

Address details			
Name	**City**	**State**	**Zipcode**
Ramesh Kumar	Bangalore	Karnataka	56037
Rakesh Kumar	Bangalore	Karnataka	56075

Table 8.1: How compression works

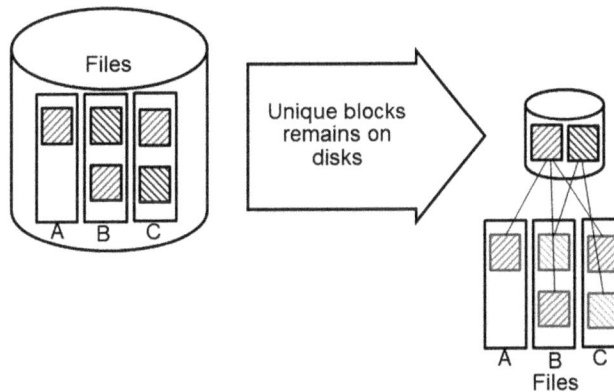

Figure 8.9: how deduplication works

Conclusion

Storing data efficiently is one of the critical considerations while designing a storage system, as this influences cost factor. A storage is said to be good if it is capable to storing more amount of on a less disk space.

There are several features that storage vendors implement to enhance the capability of their storage to store data more efficiently. Among these features, most commonly used feature is thin provisioning, in which blocks of a storage volume get allocated from a free pool of blocks as and when host server writes data on the storage volume. Thus, avoids blocking of space blocks without using them. Space reclamation is another feature in which allocated blocks are released to the free pool when host server deletes data on those blocks. This helps to have more blocks in the free pool for other usages.

Modifying metadata structure a size of virtual volume can be increased or decreased. The function to increase size is called **expand** and decrease is called **shrink**. This is generally done to meet the demand of more space of virtual volume or is shrunk to have more blocks in free pool for other use.

Deduplication and compressions are two technologies to store more amounts of data on less space. As the term deduplication suggests, it removes duplicate information and adds a pointer to it for the future un-deduplication. Un-deduplication process is called rehydration. On the other hand, compression uses a technique to represent the same data with less number of bits.

Case studies
Case study 1: Disk configuration to write intensive application

Let us look at disk configuration to write intensive application:

Requirement

An administrator is looking for a solution to configure volume for an application. Current data for the application is about 3 TB. Data is expected to grow 1 TB yearly. Storage has total 6 disks each of 1 TB size. What solution can be proposed considering requirement for next 5 years?

Analysis

If RAID6 is configured using (6 - 2 parity) x 1 TB disks, usable capacity would be approximately 4 TB, for RAID 5 usable capacity would be (6 - 1 parity) x 1 TB = 5 TB.

Application data would grow after 5 years to 3 TB + 5 x 1 TB = 8TB

Administrator can create a thin provisioned volume now and later add hard disk as and when the space demand increases.

Solution

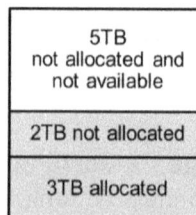

| 5TB
not allocated and
not available |
| 2TB not allocated |
| 3TB allocated |

Figure 8.10: A thin provisioned volume with allocated and unallocated space

Following are the type and size of the volumes recommended:

Type: Thin provisioning

RAID level: 5

Size: 10TB

Next year total allocated space is expected to be 3TB + 1TB = 4TB. New physical disks need to be added into storage to avoid write failure toward the end of second year.

Case study 2: Effective utilization space of a storage solution

Let us look at effective utilization space of a storage solution:

Requirement

An organization is concerned more about cost aspect of storage, meaning how efficiently the storage can store data. The type of data that they have can have approximately 20% of dedup and 10% of compression. They have total 15 TB of data and expected growth rate per year is about 5 TB. How much of physical usable capacity they should plan for next 3 years?

Analysis

Deduplication and compression can work in-dependently on the same data. Deduplication and compression ratios can be applied on to total data after 3 years and calculate actual physical usable capacity required.

Solution

Data after 3 years = 15 TB + 3 x 5 TB = 30 TB

Assuming dedup ratio is D:1; (1- 1/D) x 100 = 20; therefore D:1 = 5:4

After deduplication 14 TB data can be stored on to (4/5) x 30 TB = 24 TB

Assuming compression ratio is C:1; (1- 1/C) x 100 = 10 ; Therefore C:1 = 10:9

After compression 12 TB data can be stored on to (9/10) x 24 TB = 21.6 TB

Administrator needs to plan for 21.6 TB for 3 years

Case study 3: Reclamation of deleted space

Let us look at reclamation of deleted space:

Requirement

An administrator deleted about 7 TB of data from a thin provisioned volume in Windows host. They still do not expected available space in storage system, so that he can create some volume for other application. What solution can be proposed?

Analysis

Upon deletion of data from host server, operating system only removes file system references, does not deleted actual data block in the storage system.

Modern storages have space reclamation feature, which it deallocate the blocks so that other volume can consume.

Solution

After deletion of the data, go to **Server Manager | Tools | Defragment and Optimize Drives**.

Select the drive and click on **Optimize**. This operation sends T10 SCSI UNMAP call to storage to deallocate space.

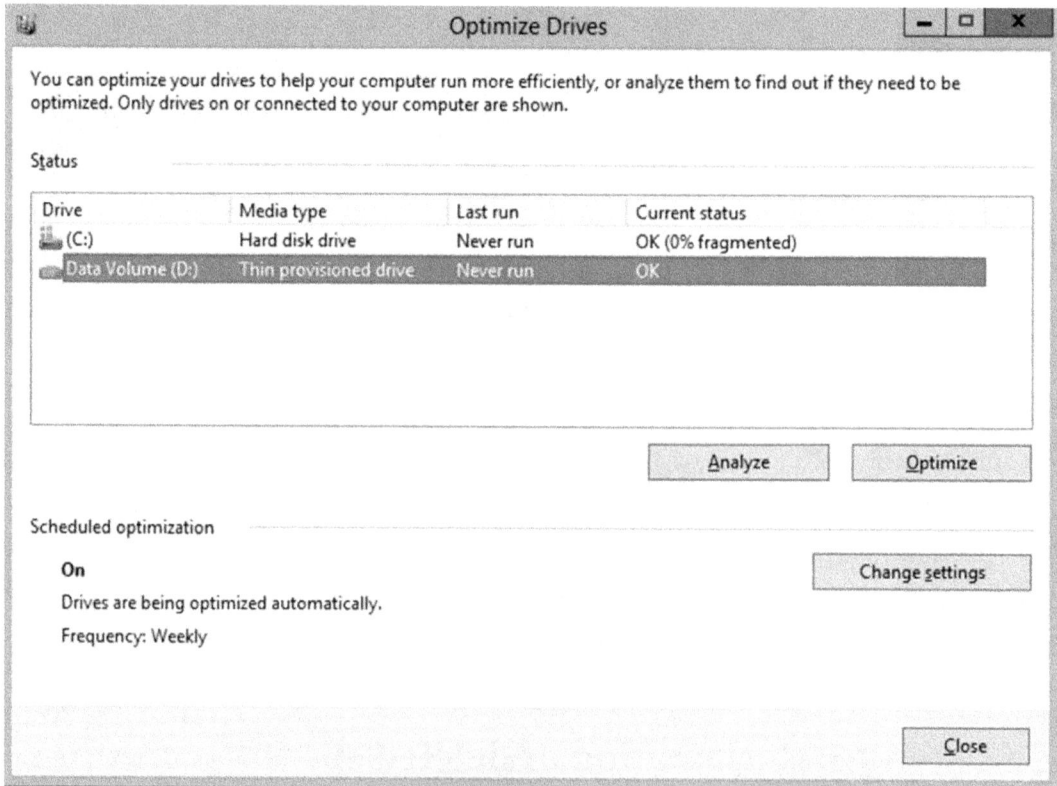

Figure 8.11: Optimize Drive

Power Shell Cmdlet Optimize-Volume also sends UNMAP call to storage device.

```
PS C:\>Optimize-Volume -DriveLetter D -ReTrim
```

Learning check

Objective questions

1. **With thin provisioning feature, space gets allocated as and when you:**

   a. Create virtual volumes

   b. Write data on to virtual volume

   c. Delete virtual volumes

   d. Delete data from virtual volume

2. **Space reclamation feature is based on:**

   a. T10 SCSI XCOPY Specification

   b. T10 SCSI UNMAP specification

   c. T10 SCS I WRITE SAME specification

   d. None of the above

3. **Thin provisioning feature of storage mainly brings benefits in the area of:**

   a. Fault tolerant

   b. Performance

   c. Space efficienct

   d. All of the above

4. **Dynamic capacity management (LUN shrink/expansion) feature of storage mainly brings benefits in the area of:**

   a. Fault tolerant

   b. Performance

   c. Space efficienc

   d. All of the above

5. **Tiered storage management feature of storage mainly brings benefits in the area of:**

   a. Fault tolerant

   b. Performance

   c. Space efficiency

   d. All of the above

6. **Which three of the following features impact the space efficiency of a storage:**
   a. Dynamic capacity management (LUN shrink/expansion) feature
   b. Thin provisioning feature
   c. Disk type
   d. RAID implementation
   e. Replication solution

7. **Shrinking of a virtual volume is mainly done by:**
   a. Reformatting the physically disks with less number of blocks
   b. Modifying the metadata table pertaining to the virtual volume to allocate less number of blocks on physical disks
   c. Restricting host to access only less number of blocks on virtual volumes
   d. Reducing size of each block

8. **Space reclamation (UNMAP) feature available on thick volume (non-thin provisioning) volume:**
   a. Yes
   b. No

9. **Only 24 TB space is utilized when 30 TB datastored on a dedup volume, find space reduction percentage:**
   a. 1.25%
   b. 6%
   c. 80%
   d. 20%

Descriptive questions

1. Describe three storage features that enhance space efficiencies of a storage system.
2. Explain with example, how deduplication and compression ratio are calculated?
3. Explain with example some use cases when expansion and shrink are needed?

Quiz questions

1. Can a storage volume be configured for deduplication and compression both?
2. T10 SCSI UNMAP command deallocates space in a storage system. Which device initiates this command? When does it initiate?

3. An administrator created two storage volumes from same disk pool with same RAID level, but one volume is thick and other one is thin. Which one is expected to perform faster for a write intensive application and why?

Glossary and key terms

- **Thin provisioning**: Type of virtual volume, in which blokes gets allocated as and when host servers write on those. This helps to allocate only required space in the storage system.

- **Dedup**: Deduplication that removes redundant data to reduce requirement of storage space.

- **UNMAP**: T10 SCSI UNMAP standard, space reclamation feature to free up blocks where host data is deleted.

- **Deduplication chunk size**: Unit of data size at which data is compared for duplication.

- **Deduplication ratio**: The ratio between the amount of data received from host server and the actual space required in storing it after duplication.

- **Compression ratio**: The ratio between amount of data received from the host server and actual space required to store it after compression.

- **Rehydration**: Process of un-deduplication of duplicated data.

Join our Discord space

Join our Discord workspace for latest updates, offers, tech happenings around the world, new releases, and sessions with the authors:

https://discord.bpbonline.com

CHAPTER 9
Storage Management

Introduction

Storage management is an important aspect of a storage system. Management software help administrator right from initial deployment of storage solution to monitoring its health and usage on daily basis. Configuration of each feature and functionalities discussed in previous chapters are done through these management software suites.

Every storage vendor provides suite of management applications to manage their storage systems and the overall solution. There are two primary purposes of any storage system management software:

a. **Provisioning storage**: It allows administrator to create storage space, allocates to the host servers.

b. **Monitoring health**: Helps to monitor health of all physical and logical components. Some vendor also allows administrator to monitor current performance of the storage system.

Structure

Upon successful completion of this chapter, you will be able to learn following key areas:

- Storage management software suite
- Steps to implement a storage solution

- SAN storage implementation for host servers in cluster
- iSCSI solution implementation steps
- SMB and NFS client configuration steps

Objectives

Every storage vendor delivers some application software along with storage system to manage it. In this chapter, you will learn different type of management software and their purposes.

This chapter explains basic steps involved to implement a storage solution along with some examples. By end of this chapter, you will have clear idea on how storage solution is designed and implemented.

Storage management software

Different storage vendors have different strategy for designing and implementing storage software suite. Some vendor implement them within storage system itself, some are designed and get installed on separate server. All management software are not just provisioning and monitoring health, there are several type of management software to manage capacity, performance and availability of datastored and the networking devices switches and HBAs.

Some of the examples are:

- **Storage system management software**: The primary software that manages storage system in terms of provisioning and monitoring health. This software offers storage volume creation with different type, such as thin provisioning, de duplication or compression enabled and RAID levels, selection of underlying physical disks, and so on. Capacity management, expansion and shrink all other management of a virtual volume is also performed with this software. Almost all management software now days sends alert notification of any error in the storage system. Some management software are intelligent enough to perform corrective action automatically.

- **Performance tuning and monitoring software**: Monitors and collects performance data read/write operations. User can view historical or real-time storage system performance using charts and graphs. This help to determine trend and pattern of usage of the storage system.

- **Snapshot management software**: Creates deletes and manages the snapshots. Most snapshot manager software also allows creating application consistent snapshot. Application-consistent snapshots are discussed in detail in *Chapter 7, Fault Tolerance and Data Protection*.

- **Replication management software**: The software that manages local or remote replication solution that are discussed in *Chapter 7, Fault Tolerance and Data Protection*. Some replication software ensures high availability of application in remote replication solution and does automatic failover and failback of replication group depending on availability of resources at each site.

- **Data protection and recovery software**: The software that configure and schedules backup jobs to protect data on to a backup system. This also enables user to recover data from previously created backups.

- **Switch management software**: The software that allows configuring and monitoring the switches in the SAN.

- **Adapter management software**: Enables user to change settings of HBA and monitor its health and connectivity.

Though vendors name each of the software differently to highlight their technology and brand value, but fundamental purpose of each software is same as described above. Based on design and implementation, vendors also combine, some of them of these software together into one.

Licensing method of each management software or each storage feature is also different. Depending on availability of license, respective component within the management software or the feature in the storage gets turned on. For example, vendor may design, if thin provisioning license is purchased and installed in storage system, user can create thin provisioned storage volume or thin provisioning can be enabled through availability of license installed within management software itself.

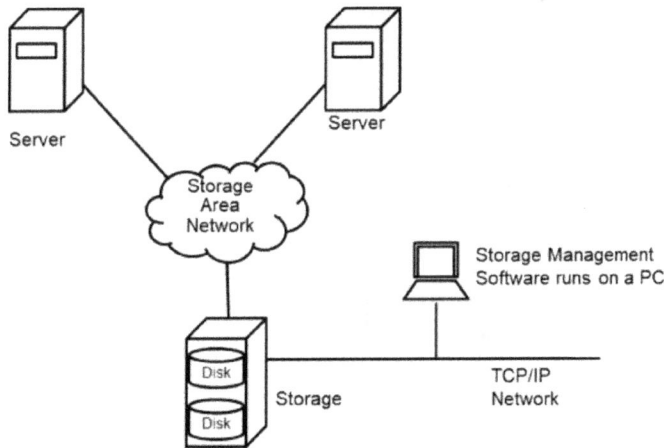

Figure 9.1: *Storage management topology*

Typically the management software is installed on a PC connected to TCP/IP Network. This method of deployment of software is called host-based management software. Some vendor's storage has in-built management inside the storage system itself. Administrator just needs to use a web browser to access it.

All storage systems provide **graphical user interface (GUI)** and **command line interface (CLI)** management interface to create, update and delete logical storage objects, such as storage volume, host, groups etc.

Generally, more than one storage volumes are configured for an application. For ease of management some storage vendors allow to create an additional storage object called **volume collection**, volume set or volume group, which comprises set of virtual volumes in it. A volume set relates to an application.

Similarly, another object called **host collection**, host set or host group for set of hosts in it. A host set maps to host's cluster.

If a volume set is assigned to a host, all the volumes in it gets assigned to the host with a unique LUN ID. Again, when a volume set is assigned to a host set, all the volumes in it get assigned to all the hosts.

Typically each management software can be accessed through multiple interfaces, such as GUI, CLI for performing operations in batch through script and **Representational State Transfer (REST)** API, which is platform independent can initiate **create, read, update, and delete (CRUD)** operations.

Storage management software have several other features such as reporting and alerting capabilities, unified management console that allows the administrator to manage multiple storage systems through a **single pane of glass (SPoG)**, integration with other software solutions, and so on.

Steps to implement storage solution

Typically four are to be followed to implement a storage solution:

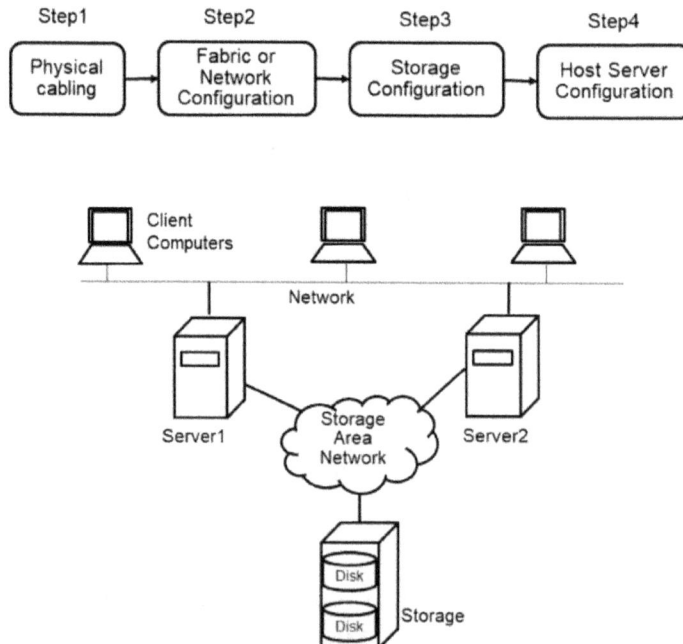

Figure 9.2: Steps to implement a storage solution and storage solution architecture

There are various storage solutions available to meet different purposes. Following three are commonly seen configurations:

- SAN storage connected to multiple hosts in cluster
- Storage connected to host server via iSCSI
- File storage connected to SMB and NFS client systems

SAN storage connected to multiple hosts in cluster

In SAN environment, fabric comprises of one or more FC switches. following is brief description of each step to implement SAN storage solution.

Physical cabling:

- Connect the cable between storage and FC switches.
- Connect cable between host servers and FC switches.
- Label each cable. This is most important for troubleshooting any issue in future.

Configuring switches:

- Identify WWPN of FC HBA

  Refer product document to determine **worldwide port number (WWPN)** of N_ Port device connected to fabric

- Create aliases

  Assign meaningful name to each WWPN

- Create zone

  Follow zoning best practices as per the product documents to provide desired access

- Create configuration or zone set and enable it

Configuring storage:

- Creation of host

  Host is a logical entity in storage that represents the host server, which is going to access the virtual volume. Typically host requires WWPN of FC HBAs or IQN number of iSCSI initiator adapters and operating system name running on it. Some storage vendor may require additional information for creation of host.

  In case of cluster environment multiple hosts may have to be created.

- Creation of virtual volume

  Virtual volume is the logical disk that is created on storage system to provide access to host for storing data and read/write operations.

- Export or presentation or assign the virtual volume to the host

The LUN masking provides access of the virtual volume to the host. In case, cluster, single virtual volume is needed to accessed to multiple hosts in cluster.

Generally more than one storage volumes are configured for an application. For ease of management some storage vendors allow to create an additional storage object called volume collection, volume set or volume group, which comprises set of virtual volumes in it. A volume set relates to an application.

Similarly another object called **host collection**, host set or host group for set of hosts in it. A host set maps to hosts cluster.

If a volume set assigned to a host, all the volumes in it gets assigned to the host with unique LUN ID. Again when a volume set assigned to a host set, all the volumes in it gets assigned to all the hosts.

Configuring host servers:
- Scan for new disk
- Create file system
- Mount file system

Follow the operating system and application documentation to configure your disk and file system.

Storage connected to host server via iSCSI

Physical cabling:
- Connect cable between storage and Ethernet switches.
- Connect cable between host servers and Ethernet switches.
- Label each cable.

Configuring Ethernet switches:
- Create VLAN.
- Follow VLAN best practices as per the product documents to provide desired access.

Configuring storage:
- Identify IQN number of iSCSI initiator adapter. Refer product documentation to determine the IQN number.
- Creation of host.

Specify IQN number to create an iSCSI host in storage:
- Creation of virtual volume.
- Export or presentation or assign the virtual volume to the host.

Configuring host servers:
- Open iSCSI initiator console or CLI interface and login to iSCSI target
- Once login is successful, scan for new disk
- Create file system
- Mount file system

Follow operating system and application documentation to configure your disk and file system.

File storage connected to SMB and NFS client systems

Physical cabling and Ethernet switch configuration is the same as iSCSI described above.

Configuring file server storage:
- Create SMB or NFS share. Refer product documentation for exact steps to create shares.
- Assign permission to share for desired user.

Configuring file share client:
- Mount the SMB or NFS share using this \\Server IP or Hostname\<Share name>
- Supply username and password to access the share.

Conclusion

All storage vendors develop and provide suite of software that manages the storage system as well as the solution.

Primary purpose of any management software of a storage system is to provision and configure the storage system and also monitor health of the storage system. For example, storage administrator uses this software to create a storage volume and monitor connection status of all the ports of the storage controllers.

Apart from storage system management software there is other management software that helps to configure and perform local and remote replications; backups monitor storage live and past performances, and so on.

Typically there are four fundamental steps to configure and access a storage system's virtual volume such as cable, configure switches, create virtual volume and configure host server to access the volume.

Case studies

Case study 1: Provisioning storage space to a Linux host server

Let us provision storage space to a Linux host server:

Requirement

A Linux host is connected to a SAN storage. Network and SAN zoning are already configured. Provide steps to create and configure storage volume in host server via FC and iSCSI.

Analysis

Following steps are followed to provision storage space to a host in the storage system:

Step 1: Creation of a host entry.

Step 2: Creation and presentation of virtual volume to the host in the host server: Although there are several methods available or third party tools available, configure file system on a storage volume, typically these steps are followed using Linux native command and utilities.

Step 3: Scan for new disk: `find /sys/class/scsi_host/host*/scan | while read line; do echo - - - > $line; done`

Step 4: Listing all devices: `fdisk -l`

Step 5: Partitioning disk: `fdisk <device file>`

Step 6: Creating file system: `mkfs <device file>`

Step 7: Mounting file system : `mount <device file> /<mount point>`

Solution

Step 1: Creation of a host entry:

A host entry must be created in storage for the first time configuration for a host server. To create a host entry, couple of information is important:

- WWPNs of FC HBA, IQN name for iSCSI or NQN of NVMe subsystem
- Operating system

The following are some example commands and their output while configuring disk. These example commands are to bring clarity on concept discussed in early part of this chapter. Output may vary depending on the environment, software component versions and configuration.

FC HBA details in Linux host:

```
# lspci | grep -i fibre
0b:00.0 Fibre Channel: Emulex Corporation Lancer-X: Light-
Pulse Fibre Channel Host Adapter
#
```

WWPN of the HBA:

```
# cat /sys/class/fc_host/host?/port_name
0x1000a0b3cc1c2863
#
```

Alternatively, WWPN of FC HBA can also be collected from management software or utilities provided by HBA vendors or from FC switch.

Initiator IQN name:

```
# cat /etc/iscsi/initiatorname.iscsi
InitiatorName=iqn.1994-05.com.redhat:548c8e222b7f
#
```

iSCSI initiator component is needed to be installed in host, if not installed already.

Initiator NQN name:

```
# cat /etc/nvme/hostnqn
nqn.2014-08.org.nvmexpress:uuid:30393137-3436-584d-5137-
333730314a51
#
```

NVMe initiator component (nvme-cli) can be installed in host, if not installed already.

Refer storage system product documentation for steps to create host entry in storage system.

Create a host entry for iSCSI in the storage system with IQN name and operating system details. Similarly create another host entry with WWPN and operating system details.

Step 2: Creation of virtual volume and present the virtual volume to the host:

Refer storage system product document for steps to create a storage volume and present to the host entry.

Host server will use the protocol to access the data on storage device based on type of host used to present the virtual volume is presented. Though both protocols are supported by a host together, but typically either of the protocol is configured and used.

Step 3: Scan for new disk:

In case of iSCSI, an administration utility, iSCSIadm, part of iSCSI initiator component, can be used for discovering the iSCSI target: `iscsiadm -m discovery -t send targets -p <IP of iSCSI Target>`

Eample command:

```
# iscsiadm -m discovery -t sendtargets -p 10.1.1.110.1.1.1:
3260,21iqn.2000-05.com.vendorname:20210002ac008685
#
```

Login all sessions with the node.

Rescan sessions: `iscsiadm -m node -p <IP of iSCSI Target>-rescan`

Example command:

```
# iscsiadm -m node -L all
Logging in to [iface: default, target: iqn.2000-05.com.
vendorname:20210002ac008685, portal: 10.1.1.1,3260]
(multiple)
Login to [iface: default, target: iqn.2000-05.com.
vendorname:20210002ac008685, portal: 10.1.1.1,3260]
successful.
#
```

To list the active iSCSI sessions:

```
# iscsiadm -m session -o show
tcp: [1] 15.213.67.33:3260,21 iqn.2000-05.com.vendorname:
20210002ac008685
#
```

Scanning for the disks:

```
# find /sys/class/scsi_host/host*/scan | while read line; do
echo - - - > $line; done
#
```

```
# iscsiadm -m node -p 10.1.1.1 –rescan
```

Step 4: Listing devices:

Linux native command disk can be used to list all the disks discovered.

```
# fdisk -l
Disk /dev/sda: 299.6 GB, 299573968896 bytes
255 heads, 63 sectors/track, 36421 cylinders
Units = cylinders of 16065 * 512 = 8225280 bytes
Device Boot Start End Blocks Id System
/dev/sda1 * 1 182 1461474 83 Linux
/dev/sda2 183 36421 585741086 8e Linux
LV
Disk /dev/sdb: 299.6 GB, 299573968896 bytes
255 heads, 63 sectors/track, 36421 cylinders
Units = cylinders of 16065 * 512 = 8225280 bytes
Disk /dev/sdb doesn't contain a valid partition table
#
```

Step 5: Creating partition:

Fdisk command can also be used to create partition on the disk. Here is an example to create a partition:

```
# fdisk /dev/sdb
Device contains neither a valid DOS partition table, nor Sun, SGI
or OSF disklabel
Building a new DOS disklabel. Changes will remain in memory only,
until you decide to write them. After that, of course, the previous
content won't be recoverable.
Command (m for help): n
Command action
e extended
p primary partition (1-4)
p
Partition number (1-4): 1
First cylinder (1-36421, default 3):
Using default value 3

Last cylinder, +cylinders or +size{K,M,G} (3-36421, default 36421):
Using default value 36421
Command (m for help): w
The partition table has been altered!
Calling ioctl() to re-read partition table.
Syncing disks.
#
```

Step 6: Creating file system:

```
# mkfs /dev/sdb1
mke2fs 1.41.12 (17-May-2010)
Filesystem label=
OS type: Linux
Block size=4096 (log=2)
Fragment size=4096 (log=2)
Stride=4 blocks, Stripe width=4096 blocks
18284544 inodes, 73133904 blocks
3656695 blocks (5.00%) reserved for the super user
First data block=0
Maximum filesystem blocks=4294967296
2232 block groups
32768 blocks per group, 32768 fragments per group
8192 inodes per group
Superblock backups stored on blocks:
32768, 98304, 163840, 229376, 294912, 819200, 884736,
1605632, 2654208,
4096000, 7962624, 11239424, 20480000, 23887872, 71663616

Writing inode tables: done
Writing superblocks and filesystem accounting information: done
This filesystem will be automatically checked every 39 mounts or
180 days, whichever comes first. Use tune2fs -c or -i to override.
#
```

Step 7: Mounting the file system:

```
# mkdir /data1
# mount /dev/sdb1 /data1
# df -h
Filesystem Size Used Avail Use% Mounted on
/dev/mapper/VolGroup00-LogVol00
15G 2.4G 12G 18% /
/dev/sda1 99M 13M 82M 14% /boot
/dev/sdb1 275G 63M 261G 1% /data1
#
```

If all the disk partitions defined and file systems are to be automatically mounted whenever the system boots, those entries need to be included in /etc/fstab file.

```
# cat /etc/fstab
/dev/VolGroup00/LogVol00 / ext3
defaults 1 1
LABEL=/boot /boot ext3
defaults 1 2
tmpfs /dev/shm
tmpfs defaults 0 0
devpts /dev/pts
devpts gid=5,mode=620 0 0
sysfs /sys
sysfs defaults 0 0
proc /proc
proc defaults 0 0
/dev/VolGroup00/LogVol01 swap swap defaults
0 0
/dev/sdb1 /data1 ext3
#
```

Now, data can be stored in the folder /data1.

Case study 2: Provisioning storage space for a Windows host server

Let us provision storage space for a Windows host server:

Requirement

A Windows host is connected to block storage. Network and SAN zoning are already configured. Provide steps to create and configure storage volume in host server via FC and iSCSI.

Analysis

Procedure to provision storage space to Windows host is same as Linux.

In storage system:

> **Step 1**: Creation of a host entry.

> **Step 2**: Creation and presentation of virtual volume to the host.

In the host server:

> **Step 3**: Scan and list for new disk.

> **Step 4**: Initialize and create volume and file system.

> **Step 5**: Assigning drive letter or mounting file system.

Solution

> **Step 1**: Creation of a host entry in the storage system. Go to **Server Manager | Tools | iSCSI Initiator**.

> iSCSI initiator component is needed to be installed, if not installed already.

> Note: **Initiator IQN name from Configuration tab.**

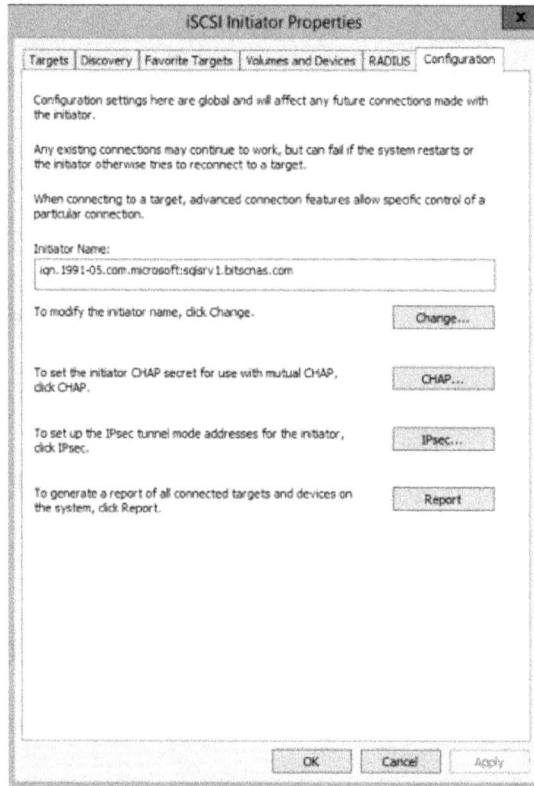

Figure 9.3: iSCSI Initiator properties

On Windows 2012 R2 or later version, PowerShell cmdlets `Get-InitiatorPort` can be used to get:

```
PS C:\> Get-InitiatorPort

InstanceName NodeAddress PortAddress ConnectionType
------------ ----------- ----------- ---------------
PCI\VEN_1077&DEV_
2031&SUBS... 50014380231c70bd 50014380231c70bc Fibre
Channel
PCI\VEN_1077&DEV_
2031&SUBS... 50014380231c70bf 50014380231c70be Fibre
Channel
ROOT\ISCSIPRT\
0000_0 iqn.1991-05.com.microsoft:...ISCSI ANY PORT iSCSI
PS C:\> Get-InitiatorPort | Select-Object -Property NodeAddress
```

```
NodeAddress
-----------
50014380231c70bd
50014380231c70bf
iqn.1991-05.com.microsoft:win-ib813os7csb
PS C:\> Get-InitiatorPort | Select-Object -Property PortAddress
PortAddress
-----------
50014380231c70bc
50014380231c70be
ISCSI ANY PORT
PS C:\>
```

WWPN can also be fetched directly from **Windows Management Instrumentation (WMI)** object:

```
PS C:\> Get-WmiObject -class MSFC_FCAdapterHBAAttributes -namespace
"root
\ WMI" | ForEach-Object {(($_.NodeWWN) | ForEach-Object {"{0:x}"
-f $_}) -
join ":"}
50:1:43:80:23:1c:70:bd
50:1:43:80:23:1c:70:bf
PS C:\>
```

Alternatively WWPN of FC HBA can also be collected from management software or utilities provided by HBA vendors or from FC switch.

Refer storage system product documentation for steps to create host entry in storage system.

Create a host entry for iSCSI in the storage system with IQN name and operating system details. Similarly create another host entry with WWPN and operating system details.

Step 2: Creation of virtual volume and present the virtual volume to the host: Refer storage system product documentation for steps to create a storage volume and present to the host entry.

Step 3: Scan and list for new disk:

Go to **Server Manager** I **Tools** I **Computer management** I **Disk Management**

Click on **Rescan Disks** from **Action** menu to discover new disk that is presented to this host.

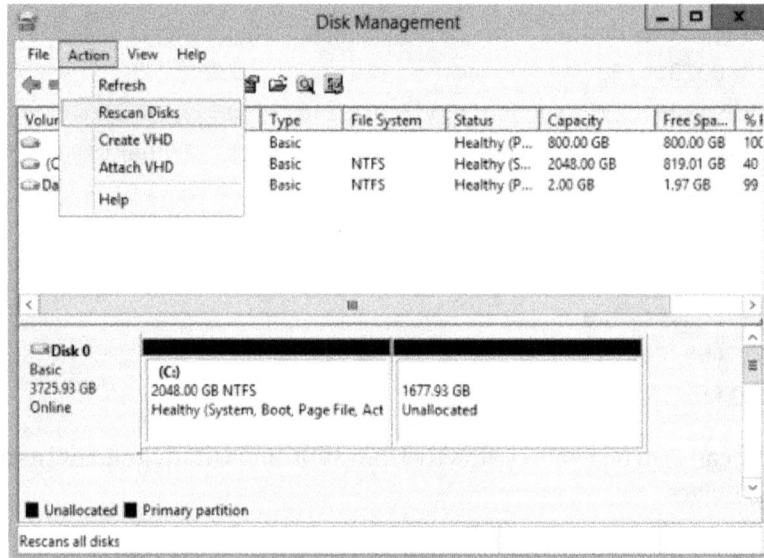

Figure 9.4: *Disk scan*

Step 4: Initialize and create volume and file system:

Right click and initialize the discovered disk. Right click again and create volume and file system.

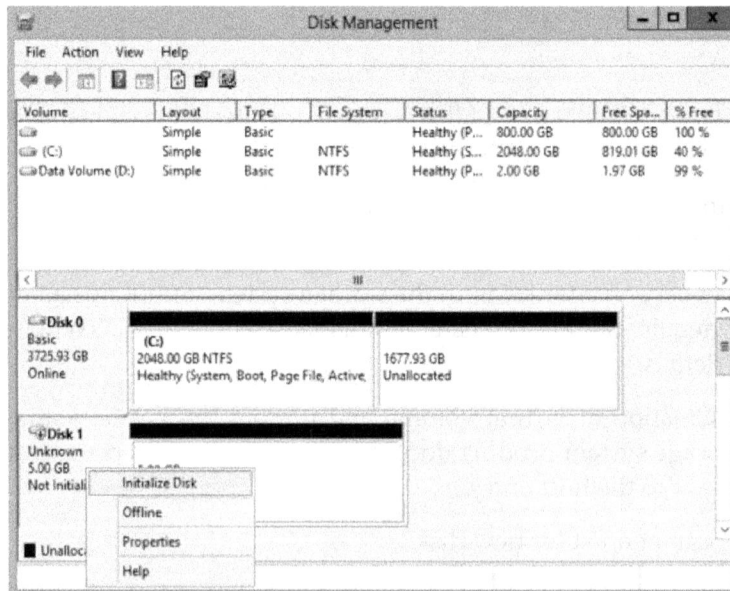

Figure 9.5: *Initialize disk*

Step 5: Assigning drive letter or mounting file system:

At the end of previous step, assigns drive letter so that files and folders can be created or copied.

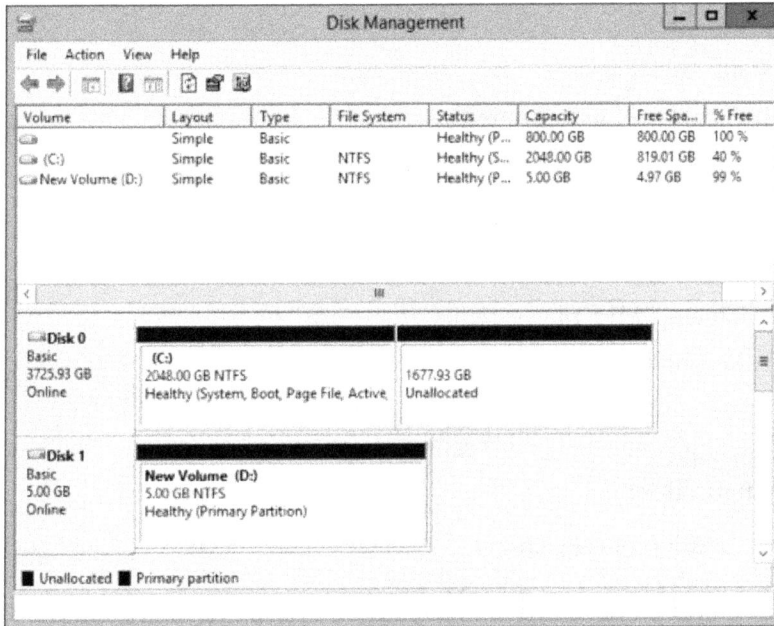

Figure 9.6: Online mounted disk with drive letter

Now, data can be stored in D.

Case study 3: Configure and access a NFS share from an NFS client

Let us configure and access a NFS share from an NFS client:

Requirement

VMWare vSphere ESXi host is connected to a storage system which has both block and file capability. Network and SAN zoning are already configured. Provide steps to create and configure NFS datastore in host server.

Analysis

Following steps are followed to provision storage space for NFS file storage:

Step 1: Create NFS share in the storage system. Refer product documentation for exact steps to create shares.

Step 2: Assign permission to share for desired user.

Step 3: Mount the NFS share.

Procedure to provision block storage space to VMWare vSphere ESXi host is same as other host type.

In storage system:

Step 1: Creation of a host entry.

Step 2: Creation and presentation of virtual volume to the host.

In the host server:

Step 3: Scan and list for new disk.

Step 4: Create VMFS file system.

Step 5: Mount the file system.

Solution

NFS Share configuration:

Step 1: Creation of NFS share:

Refer storage system product document for steps to create a storage volume and present to the host entry.

Step 2: Mount the NFS share:

Although there are several methods available to configure storage space in vSphere ESXi host, here only Center web client referred for configuration share and disks.

Open Center Web Client or ESXi host vSphere Client. Right click on the ESXi host, go to **Storage** menu, then **New Datastore**. Select **NFS** option and provide NFS server details and share name to mount it.

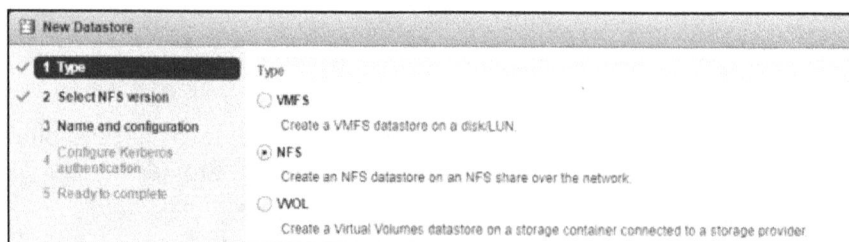

Figure 9.7: NFS datastore

Block storage configuration via FC:

For block storage configuration, as a first step, create host entry in storage system, create storage volume and present it to host.

To gather WWPN of the FC HBA. Select the ESXi host, and go to **Storage** tab and the select **Storage Adapters**.

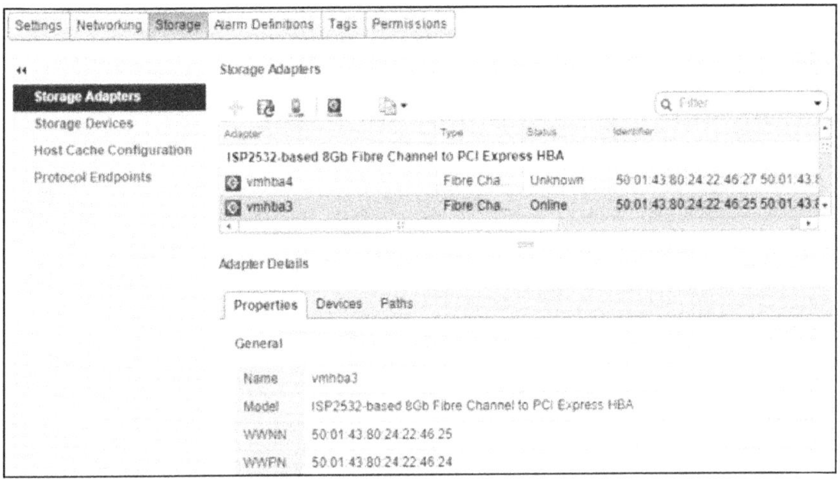

Figure 9.8: WWPN of FC HBA

In the host server:

Step 3: Scan and list for new disk.

Right click on the ESXi host, go to **Storage** menu, then **Rescan Storage**. Wait for completions rescan tasks.

Step 4: Create VMFS file system.

Right click on the ESXi host, go to **Storage** menu, then **New Datastore**. Select **NFS** option and provide NFS server details and share name to mount it.

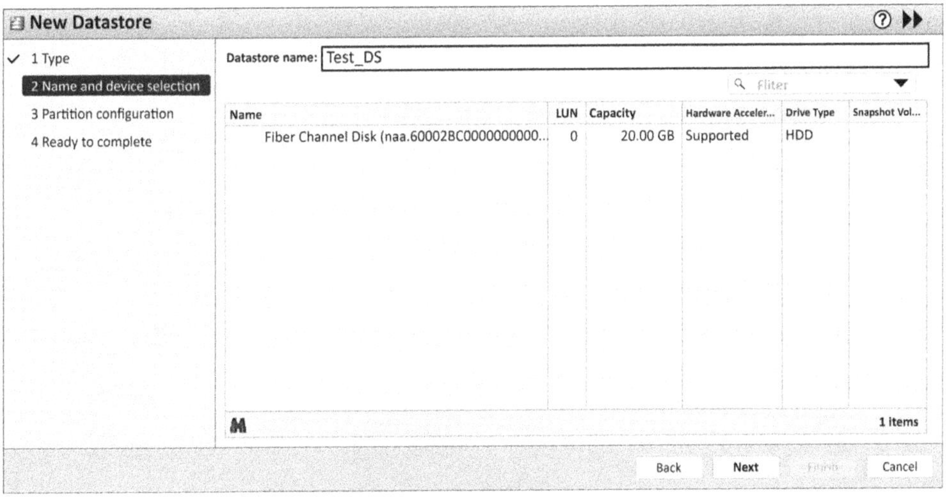

Figure 9.9: File system creation

Step 5: Mount the file system:

Go to **Related Objects** and then **Datastores** to check newly created datastore.

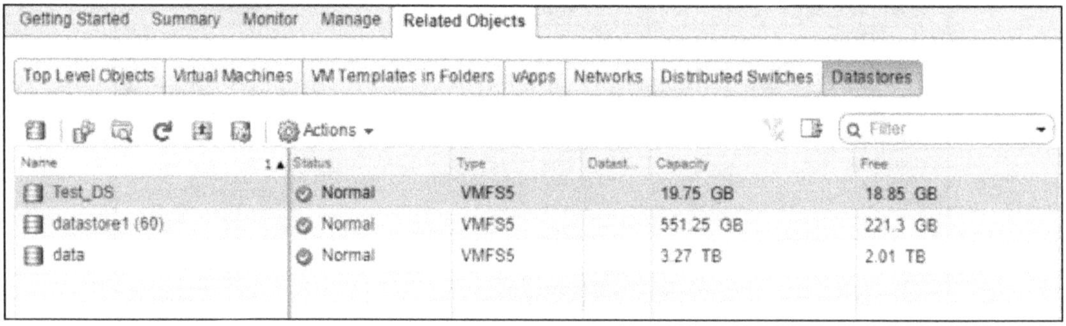

Name	Status	Type	Datast...	Capacity	Free
Test_DS	Normal	VMFS5		19.75 GB	18.85 GB
datastore1 (60)	Normal	VMFS5		551.25 GB	221.3 GB
data	Normal	VMFS5		3.27 TB	2.01 TB

Figure 9.10: Datastore

Now, VMs can be deployed on to this new datastore.

Learning check

Objective questions

1. **A storage management software is mainly used for:**
   a. Managing the storage, such as creation, modifying and deletion of objects
   b. Monitoring performance of a storage system
   c. Applying host I/O load on to the storage system
   d. Monitoring health of storage physical hardware components and the logical objects

2. **Which statement from the following is true, if the system running storage management application is broken:**
   a. Host application cannot do read/write operation to storage system
   b. Further storage space cannot be provisioned to server
   c. Remote replication to other storage would stop
   d. Scheduled backup operation of existing LUNs cannot proceed

3. **What component is a configuration management element of an IP storage solution?**
   a. HBA
   b. VSAN
   c. ISL
   d. VLAN

4. **Configuring a server to boot from an array in the SAN involves:**

   a. Presenting the boot LUN to the server's HBA ports and configuring the OS driver correctly to see the LUN.

   b. Presenting the boot LUN to the server's HBA ports and configuring the HBA card BIOS to boot from the LUN.

   c. Presenting the boot LUN to the server's HBA ports and only modifying the BIOS settings on the server's BIOS.

   d. None of the above

5. **Sequence of management task to provision storage to a server:**

   a. Create virtual volume | assign access of virtual volume to the host | create host | discover LUN at host

   b. Create host | create virtual volume | assign access of virtual volume to the host | discover LUN at host

   c. Assign access of virtual volume to the host | create host | create virtual volume | discover LUN at host

   d. Discover LUN at host | create host | create virtual volume | assign access of virtual volume to the host

6. **What are the main constrains of SCSI in storage networking (Choose two)?**

   a. Implementation complexity

   b. Deployment distance

   c. Number of devices that can be interconnected

   d. Complex fault isolation

7. **Match the following:**

   i.   Volume   1. LUN

   ii. Host   2. A host server

   iii. Volume set   3. Host cluster

   iv. Host set   4. An application

   a. (i) - (1), (iii) - (2), (ii) - (4) and (iv) - (3)

   b. (i) - (1), (ii) - (2) , (iii) - (3) and (iv) - (4)

   c. (ii) - (2), (i) - (1), (iii) - (4) and (iv) - (3)

   d. (iv) - (1), (iii) - (2) , (i) - (4) and (ii) - (3)

Descriptive questions

1. Describe commonly used storage management applications and their purposes.
2. Describe the steps that are followed to configure storage space for a FC host.
3. Describe the steps that are followed to configure storage space for an iSCSI host.

Quiz questions

1. Will an application server lose access to data, if management application crashes?
2. What are the mandatory details required to create an iSCSI host entry in Storage?
3. Which method requires user access credentials a NFS share or a SAN storage volume?

Glossary and key terms

- **Storage system management software**: Software that provisions and monitors storage system.
- **Performance monitoring tool**: Monitors and collects performance data read/write operations.
- **Snapshot management software**: Creates, deletes, and maintains storage snapshots.
- **Replication management software**: The software that manages local or remote replication solution.
- **Data protection and recovery software**: The software that configure and schedules backup jobs to protect data on to a backup system.
- **Switch management software**: The software that allows configuring and monitoring the switches in the storage area network.
- **Adapter management software**: Enables user to change settings of HBA and monitor its health and connectivity.
- **GUI**: Graphical user interface
- **CLI**: Command line interface
- **RESTful API**: An API that uses HTTP requests to GET, PUT, POST, and DELETE data.
- **Single pane of glass (SPOG)**: An integrated management display console that shows all storage solution components.

Concluding remarks

As discussed in the beginning of this book, every feature that is implemented in a storage system has an impact either on fault tolerant, space efficiency or performance. Typically a modern storage system has all these features implemented to provide best performance, fault tolerance and as well as space efficiency to meet an or ganization business demand.

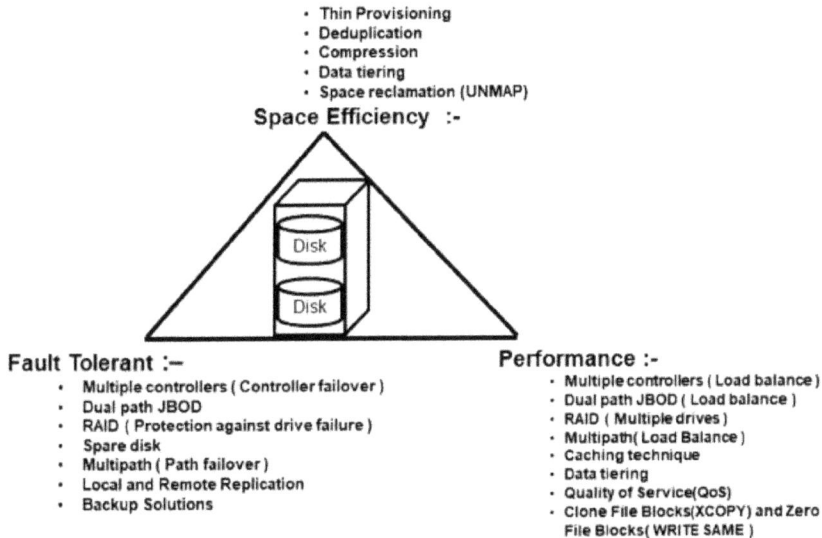

- Thin Provisioning
- Deduplication
- Compression
- Data tiering
- Space reclamation (UNMAP)

Space Efficiency :-

Fault Tolerant :—
- Multiple controllers (Controller failover)
- Dual path JBOD
- RAID (Protection against drive failure)
- Spare disk
- Multipath (Path failover)
- Local and Remote Replication
- Backup Solutions

Performance :-
- Multiple controllers (Load balance)
- Dual path JBOD (Load balance)
- RAID (Multiple drives)
- Multipath(Load Balance)
- Caching technique
- Data tiering
- Quality of Service(QoS)
- Clone File Blocks(XCOPY) and Zero File Blocks(WRITE SAME)

Figure 9.11: *Storage features for performance, fault tolerant and space efficiency*

All storage systems have RAID implemented. Except RAID 0, all other RAID implementation causes loss of storage space at the cost of fault tolerance. But there are other features, such as thin provisioning, deduplication, compression which helps to utilize and share the space more efficiently. On the other hand, multiple controllers, RAID, multipath helps to avoid accessing data on storage in the event of any failure of controller, disk drive or link. Snapshot, clone, and replication help to make copy of the data locally or on a different storage system.

There are also several features and functionalities that help in improving the performance of a storage system through load balancing, temporally copying data in cache area, and so on.

A storage stack comprises of multiple hardware and software components from physical disk up to the applications. The following figure shows all storage stack layers for SAN storage solution:

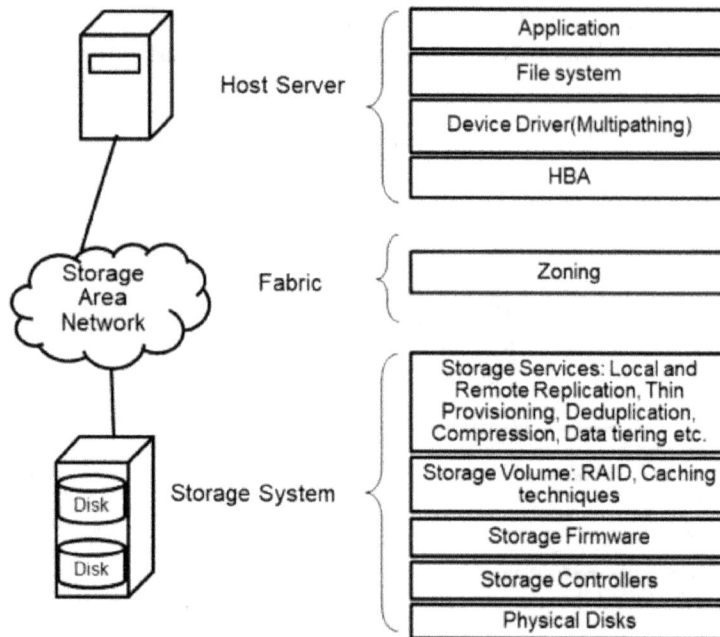

Figure 9.12: Storage stack layers for SAN storage solution

All these hardware and software components are integrated together to build a complete storage solution.

Learning Check Answers

Chapter 1: Storage Systems and Solutions

1. d	2. a, d	3. c	4. a	5. b	6. d	7. d
8. c	9. b					

Chapter 2: Storage Infrastructure

1. a	2. b	3. c, d	4. b	5. b	6. d	7. a
8. b	9. a	10. c	11. a,c,d	12. c	13. d	14. c
15. b	16. a	17. a	18. a	19. d	20. b	

Chapter 3: Storage Disk Array

1. c	2. a	3. b,c	4. b	5. c	6. c	7. d
8. b	9. b	10. c	11. a	12. c,d	13. d	14. b
15. c	16. b	17. b	18. b	19. b	20. b	21. a
22. c	23. c	24. b	25. c	26. b	27. b	28. c
29. d	30. a	31. c	32. c	33. c	34. c	35. a,b
36. b	37. c	38. d	39. b,d	40. b	41. c	42. a
43. a,d	44. d	45. b	46. b	47. a	48. a	49. c, d
50. d	51. b	52. c	53. d	54. c		

Chapter 4: Storage Communications Protocol

1. a	2. c	3. a	4. d	5. b	6. c	7. a
8. b	9. b	10. b	11. b	12. a	13. c	14. d

15. c	16. a	17. d	18. a	19. b	20. a	21. a
22. c	23. a	24. b	25. a	26. a	27. b	28. c
29. c	30. b	31. c	32. b	33. a	34. c	35. d
36. d	37. c	38. d	39. b	40. b	41. d	42. a,c
43. a,b	44. b	45. c	46. d	47. d	48. c	49. a
50. c	51. d	52. c	53. d	54. a	55. d	56. d
57. b	58. a,c	59. a, b, c	60. a,b	61. a,b,d	62. c	63. a
64. a, b	65. d	66. d	67. b	68. d	69. c	70. a
71. a	72. b	73. b	74. d	75. c	76. b,d	77. b,c
78. b	79. a	80. c	81. d	82. b	83. c	84. d
85. d	86. b					

Chapter 5: Storage Networking to Share Storage

1. c	2. d	3. c	4. d	5. b	6. b	7. c
8. a	9. a	10. a,d	11.c	12. a, b	13. b, c	14. b
15. b	16.c	17. a	18. c	19. b		

Chapter 6: Storage Performance

1. c	2. b	3. c	4. d	5. d	6. a	7. b
8. b	9. d	10. a	11. c, d	12. c	13. d	14. a, c
15. d	16. d					

Chapter 7: Fault Tolerance and Data Protection

1. a	2. b	3. b	4. d	5. b,d	6. c	7. d, e
8. c	9. a	10. d	11. c	12. a	13. a	14. a
15. d						

Chapter 8: Space Efficiency

| 1. b | 2. b | 3. c | 4. c | 5. b,c | 6. a, b, d | 7. b |
| 8. b | 9. d | | | | | |

Chapter 9: Storage Management

| 1. a,d | 2. b | 3. d | 4. b | 5. b | 6. b, c | 7. c |

Index